The Gentry

Themes in British Social History

Edited by Dr J. Stevenson

The Gentry

The Rise and Fall of a Ruling Class

G. E. Mingay

Longman
London and New York

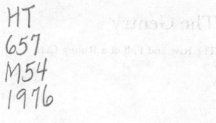

Longman Group Limited London

*Associated companies, branches and representatives
throughout the world*

*Published in the United States of America
by Longman Inc., New York*

© G. E. Mingay 1976

First published 1976

Library of Congress Cataloging in Publication Data

Mingay, G E
    The gentry.

    (Themes in British social history)
    Includes index.
    1. Great Britain – Gentry.   I. Title.
HT657.M54   929.7′2   76–13576
ISBN 0–582–48402–2
ISBN 0–582–48403–0 pbk.

ISBN 0 582 48402 2 cased
ISBN 0 582 48403 0 paper

Set in 'Monotype' Baskerville 9 on 10pt
and printed in Great Britain by
Western Printing Services Ltd, Bristol

To my wife

Contents

O! when degree is shak'd
Which is the ladder to all high designs,
The enterprise is sick. How could communities,
Degrees in schools, and brotherhoods in cities,
Peaceful commerce from dividable shares,
The primogeniture and due of birth,
Prerogative of age, crowns, sceptres, laurels,
But by degree stand in authentic place?
Take but degree away, untune that string,
And, hark! what discord follows.

Troilus and Cressida, Act I, Scene 3.

'Elizabeth's reign . . . was a great age for the gentry. Their numbers, wealth and importance had been increased by the decay of the old nobility that had stood between them and the Crown; by the distribution of the monastic estates; and by the vitality of commerce and land-improvement in the new era. The squire in Tudor and Stuart times led by no means so isolated and bucolic a life as some historians have imagined. He was part of the general movement of an active society. Yeomen, merchants and lawyers who had made their fortunes, were perpetually recruiting the ranks of the landed gentry; while the younger sons of the manor-house were apprenticed into industry and trade. In these ways old families were kept in personal touch with the modern world, and the country was kept in touch with the town.'

(G. M. Trevelyan, *English Social History*, p. 163)

'The character of the English esquire of the seventeenth century was compounded of two elements which we are not accustomed to find united. His ignorance and uncouthness, his low tastes and gross phrases, would, in our time, be considered as indicating a nature and a breeding thoroughly plebeian. Yet he was essentially a patrician, and had, in large measure, both the virtues and the vices which flourish among men set from their birth in high place, and accustomed to authority, to observance, and to self-respect. It is not easy for a generation which is accustomed to find chivalrous sentiments only in company with liberal studies and polished manners to imagine to itself a man with the deportment, the vocabulary, and the accent of a carter, yet punctilious on matters of genealogy and precedence, and ready to risk his life rather than see a stain cast on the honour of his house. It is only, however, by thus joining together things seldom or never found together in experience, that we can form a just idea of that rustic aristocracy which constituted the main strength of the armies of Charles the First, and which long supported, with strange fidelity, the interest of his descendants.'

(Macaulay, *History of England*, I, pp. 251–2)

'In spite of the influx in the interval of Scots, Nabobs, some merchants, a few bankers, and an occasional industrialist, not less than one in every eight of the members sitting for English and Welsh seats in the last unreformed House of Commons, and in five of the House of Lords, belonged to families which, two centuries before, had given representation to the House of Commons in the Long Parliament. Ten English counties had been blessed in 1640 with some sixty-two leading landowners, masters of six or more manors apiece. Of those

in the whole the one-half, of those in five just under two-thirds, had descendants
or kin who owned 3,000 acres or upwards in 1874.'

(R. H. Tawney, 'The Rise of the Gentry', *Economic History Review* XI
(1941), pp. 1–2)

'[In the mid-nineteenth century] with locomotion constantly diminishing the
distance between the village and the city, with the spread of science and
machinery even in the processes of agriculture, in a small island with a dense
urban population that had now lost all tradition of country life, it was only a
question of time before urban ways of thought and action would penetrate and
absorb the old rural world, obliterating its distinctive features and local
variations.'

(G. M. Trevelyan, *English Social History*, p. 535)

1 Who were the gentry?

The gentry, the country squires, the squirearchy, are familiar to us all from the pages of fiction, if not of history. Influenced perhaps by a reading of Fielding or Surtees, by some half-remembered schoolbook, or perhaps by the romantic extravaganzas of the film-makers, these words conjure up a decidedly bucolic picture: most probably of a gentleman finely mounted, proceeding in a lordly manner through his estate, or leaping a fence in excited chase of the hounds. In truth the gentry were typically the proud possessors of mansions and parks, were fond of riding, and delighted in country sports. But they were also much more. Through the years historians as diverse as Macaulay, Tawney and Trevelyan have emphasised the central role in English life played by the gentry. The gentry's rise, their decline; their weight in Parliament and in the balance of political power; their prominence in agricultural, commercial and industrial enterprises from the Middle Ages to the present century; and their not insignificant part in the moulding of English upper-class habits, tastes and recreations – all have attracted attention, whether from admirers, apologists, or critics.

The controversies over the significance of the gentry, the apparently boundless scope for reinterpretation of their role, spring not merely from the preoccupations and prejudices of historians, nor from the new insights provided by research, influential though these may be. Controversy has been fed by an inability to agree on just who the gentry were, and much of the discussion of recent years has been befogged because writers have used 'the gentry' to embrace rather different groups of people. Yet, despite the lack of an agreed definition, 'the gentry' remains an indispensable term; it is one of those vastly convenient portmanteau expressions which historians are obliged to employ in formulating the broad generalisations that make up the main strands of the historical fabric. It is the more indispensable since it was so widely used by statesmen and writers of the past. 'The gentry' was a convenient symbol for them too, and was evidently meaningful to their audiences. Imprecision has its advantages, of course, but it is not a good basis for an extended analysis of so vital an element in our society. In its broadest usage 'the gentry' is a term more vague than helpful, and it has come to comprise so many diverse groups that a closer definition of these is an essential prerequisite to any intelligent discussion. The question, 'Who were the gentry?' is thus the first that we must seek to answer.

The ranks of the gentry

Early writers evidently felt the need for some clarification, though they were primarily concerned with defining gentility – the characteristics which distinguished the gentleman from the mass of common men – and not so much with the gentry as a distinct group in society. But since recognition as a 'gentleman' was the minimal requirement for inclusion in the ranks of the gentry, their views have some considerable interest for us. Sir William Vaughan, of Golden Grove in Carmarthenshire, contended in 1626 that

> the means to discern a gentleman be these. First he must be affable and courteous in speech and behaviour. Secondly, he must have an adventurous heart to fight and that but for very just quarrels. Thirdly, he must be endowed with mercy to forgive the trespasses of his friends and servants. Fourthly, he must stretch his purse to give liberally unto soldiers and unto them that have need; for a niggard is not worthy to be called a gentleman. These be the properties of a gentleman, which whosoever lacketh deserveth but the title of a clown or of a country boor[1].

William Harrison, however, writing in 1577, placed less emphasis on personal qualities and more on attainments. In his view

> Whosoever studieth the laws of the realm, whoso abideth in the university (giving his mind to his book), or professeth physic and the liberal sciences, or beside has service in the room of a captain in the wars, or good counsel given at home, whereby his commonwealth is benefited, can live without manual labour, and thereto is able and will bear the port, charge and countenance of a gentleman, he shall for money have a coat and arms bestowed upon him by the heralds, and thereunto, being made so good cheap, be called master, which is the title that men give to esquires and gentlemen, and reputed for a gentleman ever after.

Harrison's lengthy statement manages to include virtually all the criteria which men at various times held necessary to establish the gentleman: education, profession, military rank, wealth, freedom from manual labour, and the right to wear arms. It is, however, a list of qualifications rather than a definition, and of his qualifications possession of enough wealth to support a gentleman's style of life was the most fundamental. For the gentry were basically a class whose superior incomes made possible a certain kind of education, a standard of comfort, and a degree of leisure and a common interest in ways of spending it, which marked them off from those whose incomes, perhaps as great or greater in money terms, could only be obtained by constant attention to some form of business. The gentleman, in fact, was perhaps most easily recognised as 'a man who spends his money as a gentleman' – a wise and comprehensive tautology, as Professor Tawney noted. For the most part, too, the gentry were countrymen, living on their estates in houses of some note and distinction and deriving much of their means from the rents of farmland: possession of at least a modicum of land was a usual, though not essential, characteristic. Many drew much of their income from town property, investments in the Funds and trading companies, and from commercial and industrial enterprises in which they had a stake. Though the gentry were identified with the countryside and with land, some were distinctly urban in character, residing comfortably in market towns and villages, especially those bordering on the major cities. These 'pseudo' or 'urban' gentry, as they have been called, still had an affinity with the landed gentry through the possession of leisure and a similarity of interests and outlook, and often, moreover, through a direct blood relationship. Typically they included impoverished landowners, the better clergy, retired merchants and maltsters, officers on half-pay, lawyers, doctors, widows of wealthy tradesmen and maiden ladies with private incomes.

Keeping in mind the existence of this fringe of petty urban gentry, let us turn to the main body, the middling country landowners who made up the core of the gentry. Wealth, rank and social status divided them from the yeomen farmers, and equally, at the other end of the scale, from the nobility and great landowners. By the seventeenth century the gentry could be considered as composed of four orders of landowners ranking immediately below the peerage. Analysed in descending order, there were first the baronets, holders of an inheritable title first created in 1611 in order to fill the gap between the small body of peers and the much more numerous knights. Baronets ranked above the ancient orders of knights, which after 1611 constituted the second stratum of the gentry. The dubbing of knights goes back beyond the Norman Conquest, and traditionally a knight (derived from the Old English *cnicht*, a boy or attendant) was an armed horseman who accompanied the king and his barons to the battlefield. The military obligations of knighthood were gradually made dispensable during the Middle Ages, but in later periods the title still had associations with distinction in war and new knights might still be dubbed on the field of battle. The third rank of 'esquire' also had medieval and military origins. The esquire was an attendant who followed a knight to war and rendered him personal services. By the latter part of the fourteenth century he was rewarded by a grant of arms, and the title 'esquire' came to denote the first degree of gentility. Use of the term gradually widened to include the sons of peers and the firstborn sons of baronets and knights, and in the course of time the esquire, or squire, came to rank above the 'gentlemen', our fourth category. This lowest level of the gentry was distinguishable from the yeomen or landowning farmers by the elusive quality of gentility, a distinction acquired principally by birth, education, and the wealth and leisure to follow gentlemen's pursuits, as we have already seen. The modern devaluation of the titles of 'esquire' and 'gentleman' in our more equalitarian society has obscured the distinctions which originally attached to them, but in the fairly recent past, certainly up to the later nineteenth century, the descriptions in documents of a person as 'Esq.' or 'Gent.' still conveyed an indication of a particular status. It is interesting that in Mrs Gaskell's celebrated novel, *Cranford*, first published in 1853, she has a character, Mr Holbrook, a kind of superior gentleman farmer living on his own estate, but whose property

was not large enough to entitle him to rank higher than a yeoman; or rather, with something of the 'pride which apes humility', he had refused to push himself on, as so many of his class had done, into the ranks of the squires. He would not allow himself to be called Thomas

Holbrook, *Esq.*; he even sent back letters with this address, telling the postmistress at Cranford that his name was *Mr* Thomas Holbrook, yeoman.

The division between the gentry and the peerage was in part a legal one. Since the emergence of the parliamentary peerage in the fifteenth century the peers formed a distinct section of the aristocracy, a hereditary nobility recognised by law, holding privileges (such as the right to sit in the House of Lords) denied to the gentry. But more important perhaps were the differences in wealth and influence. It is true, as some writers have emphasised, that both nobility and gentry formed part of a homogeneous political and social elite, bound together by a common interest in land and a common way of life, but the significance of this can be exaggerated. The line between the more wealthy baronets and the less successful of the barons, earls, or even dukes, may indeed be difficult to draw, but this does not diminish the fact that between the main body of the peerage and the great majority of the gentry there yawned always a measurable social gulf.

The inflation of honours

Among the gentry, as detailed analyses show, wealth generally went with rank, most baronets being richer than most knights, and most knights richer than most esquires and gentlemen. The situation was confused, however, by the continual fluctuations in family fortunes, with some families rising in wealth above the level normal in their rank, and others falling below it. Certain periods saw very marked changes of this kind, particularly the middle decades of the sixteenth century, when the alienation of the lands of the monasteries and sales of royal estates provided the enterprising or fortunate with new opportunities for advancement, and the middle years of the following century when the shifting fortunes of the Civil Wars, the Protectorate and the Restoration meant rapid progress for some families and disaster for others. In consequence, formerly obscure families made a sudden rise to social eminence, while in the early decades of the seventeenth century the inflation of honours under the early Stuarts brought about a considerable expansion in the upper ranks of the gentry.

At the end of the fifteenth century, it is estimated, there were some 60 lay peers, 500 knights, 800 esquires and 5,000 gentry entitled to coats of arms. The order of knighthood was intended to be assumed by all landowners with an annual income of at least £20 (subsequently raised to £40); but in practice many of those so qualified were permitted to evade the honour with its possibly onerous and expensive obligations. In the closing years of Elizabeth's reign there began a depreciation of the rank and social status attached to knighthood, part of a more general process aptly called by Lawrence Stone 'the inflation of honours'. At this time the very limited number of knights came to be supplemented by the numerous poor adventurers dubbed by their commanders in the Irish wars and other expeditions. Those created by the Earl of Essex in his campaigns in Ireland and France were especially notorious for their unsuitability, being 'many of them hardly good gentlemen', and 'scornfully called Cales (Calais), Roan (Rouen) or Irish knights'.

The Crown had formed one of the main bulwarks against this kind of social devaluation, and Elizabeth had been sparing in the extreme in her distribution of honours. The arrival of the Stuarts was the occasion of a reversal of royal policy. Both James I and his successor, Charles, showered honours almost indiscriminately, first at their respective coronations as an indication of goodwill towards their subjects, and subsequently by the deliberate sale of titles in order to raise much-needed revenue. The peerage, only 55 strong at the death of Elizabeth, grew from 81 to 126 between 1615 and 1628. The gentry were affected even more. Charles went so far as to fine all those duly qualified who had not appeared to be knighted at his coronation, reviving, as had James, the old minimum of £40 a year income from land. The consequence was not only that the number of knights was greatly expanded (James trebled their ranks within eighteen months of his accession), but also that the title found its way into many unworthy hands, including, we are told, those of a barber, a former innkeeper and an ex-convict. The new title of baronet, at first jealously restricted, also declined in status as financial needs led to many sales of the title after 1617. The price of a baronetcy fell with the loss of its scarcity value from £700 in 1619 to £220 in 1622. Charles, in his turn, succumbed to financial and political pressures, and created numerous new baronets for cash in the later 1620s, and again just before the outbreak of the Civil War [2].

With, first, the rise of new landed families out of the sales and grants of Church and Crown lands, and second the ready grants of titles by the early Stuarts, there was a heavy demand for the recognition and respectability conferred by grants of coats of arms and pedigrees. The reorganisation of the College of Heralds in the fifteenth century provided a kind of official register of gentility, and while the heralds undoubtedly allowed many doubtful claims and ignored some good ones, they at least rejected a proportion of the more blatantly spurious, and so provided some check on the growing demand for the recognised symbols of high social status. However, the heralds could register any person ('not vile born') who had at least £10 a year in land or £300 in movable goods, and nearly 4,000 grants of arms were made between 1560 and 1640, many of them to the newly swollen ranks of the esquires and gentlemen. With the influx of new families of some wealth the title 'esquire' came to be assumed by all those 'of some competent quantity of revenue fit to be called to office and authority', as Thomas Wilson vaguely put it, and who were prepared to risk an investigation into their claims by the heralds. The lowest honorific description of 'gentleman' became even wider in its usage. Originally supposed to be limited to the younger sons and brothers of esquires and their heirs, it was adopted by a very broad stratum of minor landowners and professional men who evidently thought of themselves as members of the gentry by reason of their birth, their education, or merely their social aspirations.

Social mobility

According to Lord Burghley gentility was 'nothing but ancient riches' (and, as Tawney noted in an aside, need not be so ancient) [3]. The gentry, in fact, were constantly being replenished and revitalised by the arrival of new families from office, trade, finance, farming and the professions (especially the law). Of these newcomers many were already related to existing landed families by marriage or by birth, being younger sons, sons-in-law or nephews. They might not have to possess a landed estate in order to assume a title, and some of the leading London businessmen were knights or called themselves esquire or gent. But others preferred to enter into true gentry status by buying an estate, as did for example Sir William Herrick and Samuel Ongley. Sir William, a leading London merchant and goldsmith, acquired a country residence at Beaumanor in his native Leicestershire, and received large grants of crown lands in return for his loans to James I. Ongley, a Cornhill linen-draper and director of the East India Company, about 1696 bought an estate in Bedfordshire and founded a new county family.

In his definition of the gentry Tawney included not only landowners above the yeomanry and below the peerage, but also the better-off tenant farmers, professional men and leading merchants. They were all bound together, he held, not by the possession of land but by their common education, by their freely mixing together in society, and not least by a similar 'bourgeois' attitude towards the exploitation of their assets and the making of money. Yet it is clear that contemporaries interposed a certain barrier between business and land, a certain hostility towards the presumption that wealth derived from trade by itself entitled its owner to gentility. Landed gentry, it is true, freely intermarried with the wealthier merchants and professional families, the superior parsons and prosperous gentleman farmers. In the seventeenth century the Walpoles of Houghton, for instance, married into the Turners of Lynn, attornies become leading merchants and mayors of that city, as well as into families of gentleman farmers and minor gentry of the region [4]. Alliances between gentry and yeomen freeholders were also fairly commonplace, though not always concluded without some doubts about the suitability of the match. A gentleman of Kent, whose bride was a yeoman's daughter, felt it necessary to point out that there were indeed yeomen and yeomen: for 'true it is her father was a Yeoman, but such a Yeoman as lived in his house, in his company, and in his sports and pleasures like a gentleman', keeping his daughter 'four years at school, amongst other gentlemen's daughters, at the same costs and charges'. The dividing line was somewhat indistinct. Younger sons of gentry families were frequently described as yeomen, while Thomas Fuller wrote that many a yeoman was 'a Gentleman in Ore, whom the next age may see refined'. Numbers of yeomen bordered on gentleman status, like 'old Woodcock, a man of Kent, "half farmer and half gentleman", whose horses pulled the plough all week and were "put into the coach o'Sunday". In 1664 the son of a well-to-do Lancashire yeoman presented a valuable silver dish to the London Weavers Company when he was made a freeman' [5]. A further illustration of the refinement of yeoman stock was provided by the career of John Smyth of Nibley. In the 1580s he entered Magdalen as companion to the young Lord Berkeley, and later completed his legal education at the Middle Temple at the expense of the Berkeleys. He became their steward, and in due course wrote their family history. His career laid the foundation of a new county family, and his son was sufficiently prominent to be named a justice of the peace [6].

Sixteenth-century writers allowed the gentleman to take up law, medicine or the Church, but they drew the line at trade: 'the exercise of merchandise is accounted base and most derogating from nobility.' And there were always those of a conservative cast of mind who found the influx of upstart families from any source distasteful. Sir William Vaughan complained bitterly that 'Joane is as good as my Lady, Citizens' wives of late grown Gallants. The Yeoman doth gentilize it. The Gentleman scornes to be behind the Nobleman.' But the Welsh gentry, with their 'parchment squires', were notoriously proud of their ancient origins. 'As long as a Welsh pedigree' was a not unmeaningful hyperbole. In Wales, as in some counties of England, intermarriage, a common culture and common interests, made for closeness, the presentation of a united front to the outside world and a mutual exclusiveness [7].

Hostility to the pretensions of merchants and such upstarts persisted into later periods. Locke held that trade was 'wholly inconsistent with a gentleman's calling', while Addison and Steele, the essayists, remarked that poorly provided younger sons would rather 'be starved like Gentlemen, than thrive in a trade or profession that is beneath their quality'. In fact, it was very common for younger sons to enter trade as one of the best means of improving a modest fortune. Trade was expanding, and in Defoe's words, had become 'so vastly great . . . no wonder that the gentlemen of the best families marry tradesmen's daughters, and put their younger sons apprentices to tradesmen'. Yet despite his partiality for trade, Defoe fell in line with traditional views when he argued that a gentleman must be born of a family which has 'at least for some time been rais'd above the Class of Mechanicks'. But to enquire how long 'some time' must be was, he admitted, a dangerous question, for then

> we dive too deep, and may indeed strike at the root of both the Gentry and Nobility: for all must begin somewhere, and would be traced to some less degree in their Original than will suit with the Vanity of the Day: It is enough therefore that we can derive for a Line of two or three Generations, or perhaps less.

The persistence of the social distinction between trade and land kept in being an active market in small estates and country houses, particularly noticeable in the home counties where, as Defoe noted, many of the older gentry had been displaced by *nouveaux-riches* who aspired to leave the plebeian purlieus of Cheapside and Billingsgate for the more refined air of a not-too-distant countryside. The growth of London as a commercial metropolis considerably affected the gentry of a county such as Hertfordshire or Essex. The western borders of Kent were similarly subject to its influence, as William Lambarde remarked as early as 1576:

> The Gentlemen be not here of so ancient stock as elsewhere, especially in the parts nearer to London, from which city (as it were from a certain rich and wealthy seed plot) Courtiers, Lawyers, and Merchants be continually translated, and become new plants amongst them. Yet be their revenues greater than anywhere else: which thing groweth not so much by the quantity of their possessions, or by the fertility of their soil, as by the benefit of the situation of the country itself, which hath all that good neighbourhood, that Marc Cato and other old writers require to a well planted grange, that is to say, the Sea, the River, a populous city, and a well-traded highway, by the commodities whereof, the superfluous fruits of the ground be dearly sold, and consequently the land yield a greater rent [8].

Many examples might be given of these 'new plants' of not 'so ancient stock', as Lambarde described them. There were merchants, for instance, like the Wottons and the Boleyns, who joined the company of those who prospered in the service of the Crown, the Oldhalls, Hungerfords and Stanleys. About a dozen of the seventy-eight outstandingly successful families in sixteenth-century Worcester established themselves as gentry in the county by the middle of the following century. There was William Mucklowe, cloth exporter and mercer, whose father was a yeoman farmer from Halesowen and whose son settled as a country gentleman near Areley. There were also the three sons of Ronald Barkley who all founded families of minor gentry: their father had begun as a clothier's apprentice in the city. And there was Robert Wilde, son of a distinguished Worcester clothier, who converted a one-time hospital at the edge of the city into a mansion, and gave up cloth to live on his rents and a little farming. More spectacular and more unusual was the dramatic rise of Sir Horatio Palavicino, of Genoese extraction, money-lender, and financial adviser to the Crown. He was knighted through the favour of Elizabeth and accumulated property in three counties, with a stately home at Babraham, and became a sheepmaster on a big scale[9]. In eighteenth-century Hull a small number of the port's merchants, men such as Charles Healey and Francis De la Pryme, came of minor gentry stock, while a few of the successful merchants – the Maisters, the Sykeses of Sledmere and the Broadleys – invested in country property and built up estates[10]. About the same time Samuel Whitbread, the famous London brewer, retired to Bedfordshire, where his family had long been farmers and landowners, and proceeded to build up a new estate in the family's home parish of Cardington.

However, it has been argued that rather few of the successful businessmen of the Jacobean period originated among the substantial landowners, and that there were not many wealthy London merchants who sought to acquire a stake in the country and dissociate themselves from city affairs[11]. Some families rose to gentry status within a generation, as did the Ishams and the Spencers in sixteenth-century Northamptonshire. Law hoisted some of these, farming others. The law was a prolific source of new gentry. According to Thomas Wilson, who had some apparent antipathy towards lawyers, there was 'no province, city, town nor scarce village free from them, unless the Isle of Anglesey, which boasts they never had lawyers nor foxes'. Their rise, he darkly suggested, was based on an ability to

> buy up all the lands that are to be sold, so that young gentlemen or others newly coming to their livings, some of them prying into his evidence will find the means to set him at variance with some other, or some other with him, by some pretence or quiddity, and when they have half consumed themselves in suit they are fain to sell their land to follow the process and pay their debts, and then that becomes a prey to lawyers.

Successful yeomen, patiently acquiring field upon field, or capitalist graziers running their thousands of sheep on extensive sheepwalks, could also rise to gentility. There were the Gostwicks, who in 1529 acquired the Bedfordshire manor of Potton from the Mowbrays, and the Francklins who in 1493 obtained a lease of Glyntils manor from the Canons of Canons Ashby[12]. Then there were soldiers, like Sir Anthony Denny, knighted for his services at the siege of Boulogne in 1544, who amassed considerable estates in Hertfordshire through the personal favour of Henry VIII. Even a writer like Sir John Hawkins, youngest son of a carpenter, could rise to social eminence through a combination of ability with his pen and fortune in the marriage stakes, a combination which enabled him to make his residence in countrified Twickenham and take a seat on the Middlesex Bench.

A judicious choice between the factions which contested political and religious issues of the day could also be important. Opposition to royal policy on the dissolution of the monasteries was fatal to some families, just as a more circumspect acquiescence was vital in the rise of others. In Lincolnshire, for instance, the fortunes of the Ayscoughs, the Lascelles, Markhams, Babingtons and Tyrrwhits were closely bound up with the consequences of the Reformation [13]. Numbers of families were thus affected in every county. To take just one example, the Levesons of Staffordshire used their profits made in the wool trade to invest to good effect in the booming land market of the sixteenth century, and established their main seat at Trentham, a former Augustinian priory. Subsequently, by marriage with the old-established Yorkshire Gowers, they founded a family which was destined to become one of the most fabulously wealthy in the country, the Leveson-Gowers, Dukes of Sutherland. Similarly, in the succeeding century, the Great Rebellion was productive of many pitfalls as well as opportunities. Again, a judicious choice of sides, and perhaps a little luck, went far to advance many families, witness the Ashburnhams of Sussex and the Pierreponts of Nottinghamshire.

Through these and other influences, prudence in financial as well as political affairs, the fortunes of marriage, and such imponderables as the number and sex of heirs, the composition of the gentry was always changing. The extent of change varied greatly, however, from one area to another. The home counties, especially, were marked by the rise of new families and the disappearance of old ones. In Hertfordshire, for example, of those leading gentry families who took sides at the outbreak of war in 1642 less than one in ten had been settled in the county before 1485; the comparable figure for Essex was 18 per cent, for Suffolk 13 per cent, and for Norfolk 42 per cent. In Hertfordshire a correspondingly high proportion of leading gentry, 43 per cent, had settled in the county as recently as since 1603; the comparable figures were 26 per cent for Essex, 18 per cent for Suffolk, 14 per cent for Norfolk, and only 12 per cent for Kent [14]. The western borders of Kent nearest London were affected, it is true, by the exodus of commercial families from the capital; but the central and eastern parts of the county held many ancient families of gentry, long established and much intermarried.

As the figures indicate, the stability of the gentry varied greatly from county to county, and also within counties. While some parts of the home counties were characterised by a rapid turnover of families, elsewhere could be found substantial numbers of gentry who had been established in a particular district for many generations, and through centuries of occupation had become closely identified with a certain house or parish. Such were the Gowers of Stittenham in Yorkshire, who had been settled there since the time of the Conquest, as had the Cholmondeleys of Cholmondeley in Cheshire, and the Pierreponts of Holme Pierrepont, near Nottingham. Equally ancient were the Okeovers of Okeover in Staffordshire, who had provided high sheriffs for the county since the thirteenth century. Not much more recent were the Walpoles of Houghton, said to have derived their name from the village of Walpole in west Norfolk, and another Norfolk family, the Wyndhams of Felbrigg. Elsewhere one might note among many the Chetwynds of Ingestre in Shropshire, the Grosvenors of Eaton Hall near Chester, the Monsons of South Carlton, Lincolnshire, and the Heskeths, who had made their home at Rufford in Lancashire since before the reign of Edward I.

The long continuity of many gentry, and of some yeomen too, gave to their districts a degree of permanence and a stable base to society and so helped to create the sense of a real county community, as Professor Everitt has noted. This sense of community had no small influence on the independence of provincial opinion and local freedom of action, and played a major part in the varying reaction of the counties to the series of crises stemming from the Great Rebellion. In addition, the continuity of so many gentry estates had the effect of restricting the intrusion of newcomers. In some areas of old-established gentry there was frequently not an estate to be had, and a newcomer might have to build up his stake in the county by gradual piecemeal acquisitions. Even then such acquisitions had to be made against the competition of existing families who were always on the lookout for small properties which might round off their estates or extend their local influence. The social and political importance of land, added to its security as an investment, kept up its price and so made it difficult for all but the wealthier outsiders to become full-blown country gentry, except perhaps over a period of several generations. Merchants and other newcomers could more easily ally themselves with county society through marriage, and there were always some down-at-heel nobility, and more gentry, willing to improve their fortunes by the judicious infusion of a handsome dowry, even though it might be somewhat tainted by contact with trade. Ambitious outsiders, successful merchants, financiers, lawyers and office-holders, might prefer to found new landed families themselves, but the cost of purchasing an estate was such that they generally had to start in a modest way with perhaps a farmhouse and a few hundred acres, and build up a more impressive domain by patiently gathering in neighbouring properties as opportunity offered.

A substantial proportion of English landed families, therefore, was always of quite recent origin, though locally the proportion varied according to proximity to centres of trade and the availability of land for acquisition. The consequence of this flexibility in gentle society, the decline and disappearance of some old-established families through political misfortune, extravagance, ineptitude, or mere failure of male heirs, and their replacement by newcomers from among the merchants, yeomen, businessmen and the professions, was to make society less caste-conscious than was the case with the continental aristocracies. At the same time, flexibility meant a continuous inflow of new energy and talent, a breadth of vision and wider range of interests, a down-to-earth realism, not to say vulgar materialism, that made for considered moderation, ready adjustment to circumstances and willingness to seize the economic opportunities of each age as it advanced. This goes far to explain the continued importance of the gentry as a major political influence, and why their local leadership and control continued to be accepted down to a time that, in view of the early industrialisation of the country and the spread of democratic institutions, is remarkably recent.

Incomes of the gentry

How far can we analyse the gentry by looking at their incomes? Estimates of average incomes have been made by a number of scholars, who have followed in the path of the late seventeenth-century statisticians, Chamberlayne and King, and the Table 1.1 is an attempt at summarising and condensing their findings. A number of features of this table call for comment. First, it should be

Table 1.1 Average income levels of the gentry

	Early Tudor	1640	1669 (according to Chamberlayne)	1690 (according to King)	1790	1815
	£	£	£	£	£	£
Baronets	—	1,000–1,500	1,200	880	2,000	4,000
Knights	200	500–1,000	800	650	1,000	2,000
Esquires	80	100–300	} 400	400	} 400	} 600
Gentlemen	17	Under 100		240		

emphasised that the figures are for *average* incomes, and that there were very wide variations from the average. For example, of forty-four Derbyshire gentry listed in 1662, ten had an income of £5,000 a year or more, and four had over £10,000 [15]. There were also wide regional variations. The average figures, therefore, even if reasonably accurate, cannot at best do more than suggest the kind of middling size of income that pertained over much of the country among a particular status group of the gentry. Secondly, it should be noted that the table is a collection of extracts from disparate sources, and the individual figures cannot be regarded as more than intelligent guesses: the reader should not be surprised, therefore, by the existence of discrepancies.

Among the changes indicated by Table 1.1 is a noticeable jump in average incomes between the early Tudor period and 1640. This is to be explained, principally, by the effects of the great increase in prices which occurred during the sixteenth and early seventeenth centuries and by the tendency for incomes from land to rise much faster towards the end of this period than did incomes in general. The indication of a large rise of landed incomes at this time is supported by information from landlords' accounts and rentals, and also by some figures relating to amounts bequeathed to their daughters by justices of the peace in selected counties [16]. A summary of these bequests is shown in Table 1.2. In the same period the average income of peers more than

Table 1.2 Bequests by justices of the peace to their daughters

County	Average 1558–79	Average 1620–40
	£	£
Kent	1,214	3,380
Norfolk	854	2,250
Northants	743	2,128
Somerset	373	2,239

doubled [17]. It appears that the incomes of the upper gentry were stable or falling somewhat between 1640 and the later seventeenth century, although there are grounds for thinking that Gregory King's figures are pitched on the low side. The incomes of the lower gentry, on the other hand, seem to have risen substantially in the same period, unless both Chamberlayne and King here erred on the high side. It seems rather more likely that here the 1640 figures are too low. Certainly, from what we know of movements of prices and rents in the second half of the seventeenth century, there seems little reason to expect any considerable improvement in the incomes of the lower gentry at this time.

A further jump in incomes evidently occurred between the middle seventeenth century and the early nineteenth, though the extent of this change may well be exaggerated by the probable underestimates of Chamberlayne and King. The major part of this improvement occurred towards the end of the period, and, as in the later sixteenth and early seventeenth centuries, was associated with expansion of the economy in general and with rising agricultural prices and rents in particular. After being stationary, or even falling, until about 1750, rents rose by some 40 or 50 per cent between 1750 and 1790. After 1790 the acute shortages of the Napoleonic Wars saw rents double within twenty-five years, and although there was a subsequent fall it was followed by a recovery in the middle nineteenth century, and the level reached in 1815 proved to be broadly that which ruled over much of the nineteenth century.

Professor F. M. L. Thompson has estimated that the wealthier gentry of the nineteenth century had incomes stretching from £3,000 a year up to £10,000, while there were many country gentlemen living comfortably on incomes rising from a few hundred pounds. If we can trust the earlier figures it seems that the average baronet or knight (and also the average member of the lesser gentry) of the nineteenth century were enjoying incomes at least three times as high as in 1640, and well over ten times as high as in the earlier sixteenth century. Of course, a substantial part of this great increase in money incomes represented changes in the value of money, and the rise in the real incomes of the gentry over the three hundred years from the sixteenth century was not so great as the change in monetary levels suggests. It is impossible to compare the levels of living standards over such a lengthy period, in which tastes, fashions, patterns of expenditure and the commodities available for consumption all changed considerably; but undoubtedly the typical squire of the later nineteenth century enjoyed standards of housing, comfort and diet, a range of leisure activities and ease of travel, all much superior to those available to his predecessor of three centuries earlier.

Detailed studies of the whole of the gentry families of individual counties have produced income figures for about 1640 which are the most accurate we are ever likely to have. In Kent the thirty-one baronets averaged £1,405, fifty knights had £873 apiece, and the 750 squires and gentlemen £270. The figures for Yorkshire are quite similar if somewhat higher: twenty-eight baronets averaged £1,536, sixty-two knights £1,097, and 589 squires and gentlemen £270. The incomes of peers made up only 12 per cent in Kent, and 15 per cent in Yorkshire, of the total incomes of peers and gentry together [18]. It is dangerous to generalise from only two counties, but it seems from these figures that the gentry in Kent and Yorkshire enjoyed incomes possibly rather above the national average, and it would also seem that the supposed inferior wealth of the northern counties as compared with the south was less general than contemporaries, and many historians, believed.

There are numerous references to the existence of regional variations in income. Celia Fiennes tells us that at the end of the seventeenth century the lesser gentry of Kent were worth 'about 2 or 3 or £400 a year, and eate and drink well and live comfortably and hospitably; the old proverb was a Yeoman of Kent with one year's Rent could buy out the Gentleman of Wales and Knight of Scales [19] and a Lord of the North Country, his Estate was so much better'. And a few decades earlier, Major General Berry reported to Oliver Cromwell from his command in Wales that in that part of the country 'you can sooner find fifty gentlemen of £100 a year than five of £500'. Earlier still, in about 1600, Thomas Wilson remarked that in the home counties a gentleman 'is not counted any great reckoning unless he be betwixt 1,000 marks or £1,000, but Northward and farr off a gentleman of good reputacion may be content with £300 and £400 yearly'. While these contemporary views suffered no doubt from some degree of exaggeration, differences in wealth between the south and east of the country on the one hand, and the north and west on the other, were probably significant; and especially so when the whole regional society, and not merely gentry incomes, are considered. Generally, regions with more diversified economies, with more commercial and industrial activity and less dependence on agriculture, were the more prosperous. Certainly national taxation was adjusted so as to bear less heavily on northern and western counties – for instance, the quotas given to Herefordshire of taxes imposed in the seventeenth century were always under 2 per cent of the whole. Furthermore, perhaps in consequence, greater political weight was attached to the gentry of the southeast as compared with those of the north, a point of some importance in the Great Rebellion.

A further problem is posed by the considerable overlap which existed in the incomes of the various strata of gentry. While it is true that income rose with title, there were no clear dividing lines. Some of the wealthy gentry had substantially higher incomes than some members of the peerage, while knights overlapped with baronets, and esquires with knights, gentlemen with esquires. Thomas Wilson observed that many of the knights of his day, at the beginning of the sixteenth century, possessed incomes equal to 'the best barons and come not much behind many earls as I have divers, viz. Sir John Peeter, Sir John Harington, Sir Nicholas Bacon, and others, who are thought to be able to dispend yearly betwixt £5,000 and £7,000 of good land'. Dr Cliffe, in his recent study of the Yorkshire gentry, noted some wide disparities in incomes. Twenty-three of his county's baronets had over £1,000 a year in 1640, while on the other hand two baronets and twenty of the knights had less than £500. He also found that in Yorkshire all the untitled families with £250 a year or more adopted the title 'esquire', and all those with less than £100 used the humbler 'gentleman' [20].

This overlapping of incomes makes it simpler, and more realistic, to distinguish three income groups among the gentry: the wealthy or greater gentry (including most baronets and some of the knights); the lesser gentry (most of the knights, some esquires, and a few gentlemen); and the country gentlemen (including, probably, some of the esquires). The wealthy gentry had incomes rising from a minimum of £1,000 a year in the seventeenth and early eighteenth centuries, and from at least £3,000 a year in the nineteenth century. They probably numbered about a thousand families, and owned about 15 per cent of the land of England. The figure from the New Domesday returns of 1873 is 17 per cent. The lesser gentry, with incomes of between £250 and £1,000 a year in the seventeenth century and between £1,000 and £3,000 in the nineteenth, included some 2,000 families and had 12.5 per cent of the land in 1873. The country gentlemen (a term which would include many small squires, clergymen, professional men and retired officers and merchants) had incomes of perhaps about £250 in the seventeenth century, and from £200 or £300 to £1,000 in the nineteenth; they were perhaps as many as 10,000 families. Individually their estates were small, often no larger than a good-sized house and paddock with perhaps one or two farms, but they frequently had other sources of income from investments in stocks and shares or urban property, for example, and collectively they owned as much land as did the great proprietors – about a quarter of the land of England in 1873.

Within the gentry, it is clear, the uppermost stratum of wealthy families formed always a small proportion of the whole (as indeed did the ranks of baronets and knights which largely made up this wealthy element: King estimated them as forming under 9 per cent of the total in his day). Numerically, the gentry were heavily weighted towards the lower end of the income range. But a family's influence was not determined solely by income: other factors, lineage, reputation, the holding of public offices, were also important. However, the families filling the county seats in the Commons, and holding office as justices or Crown commissioners of various kinds, were usually the wealthiest in the county; although there were other families just as wealthy who were not represented among the officeholders, either because they lacked influence with the great lords and county magnates who had the say in the matter of appointments, or because these families lacked men of suitable age, health, and ambition.

Among the lesser gentry the more prominent families might hold some lesser county office – they might be high constable of the hundred – and they were certainly men of influence in their own neighbourhood. The country gentlemen, for the most part, were too lacking in property and standing to be selected for county office, other perhaps than that of grand juror. Many of them depended on farming for their main source of income, others lived modestly on a combination of rents, mortgages, annuities and dividends, while considerable numbers drew their main income from a profession or business. They might well be connected by marriage with the lesser gentry, and rather less probably with the greater gentry. For the more modest however, a social gap of large proportions loomed between them and the wealthy knight or baronet whose home rivalled the mansion of the great landlord, and whose name carried more than a little weight in the affairs of the county, and even in those of the nation.

In the later nineteenth century, as land began to lose its old pre-eminence and the business world greatly expanded, there was among the gentry some closing of the ranks. Younger sons more readily found their occupations in the expanding professions and in the rapidly growing civil service and colonial service, where a similarity of background and common career interests encouraged a feeling of greater solidarity and a new sense of élitism. The character of the gentry was slowly and subtly changed by these new influences. There was a new sense of mission, the mission to govern, administrate, civilise. As the possession of land became more of a social responsibility and less of a profitable asset, and as political forces gradually thrust the gentry further from the old centres of power, so new sources of income and influence were increasingly exploited. Lady Bracknell remarked that land gave one position and prevented one from keeping it up. The solution of many of Lady Bracknell's contemporaries was to seek new sources of status and income in the expansion of government, the Empire and the growing demands of the middle classes for professional expertise and enterprise.

The geographical distribution of the gentry is of some interest. The figures taken by F. M. L. Thompson from Bateman's *Great Landowners of Great Britain and Ireland* show that in the later nineteenth century gentry estates of between 1,000 and 10,000 acres occupied 29.5 per cent of the total area of England, excluding waste[21]. (Wales, of course, was very much a stronghold of old-established gentry, with 35 per cent of its area occupied by estates of 1,000 to 10,000 acres.) In England some areas were substantially stronger in gentry than others. The highest proportion of gentry land was found in Shropshire with 44 per cent, the lowest (excepting Middlesex) in Westmorland, with only 20 per cent. The most gentrified counties fell into three main areas: the home counties; the west country from Hereford and Somerset eastwards through Gloucestershire, Wiltshire and Oxfordshire; and a belt of three southern counties, Dorset, Hampshire and Sussex. Norfolk and Northumberland were isolated gentry bastions in the east and north. The counties with less than a quarter of their area occupied by gentry estates were mainly in the north: Cumberland, Westmorland and Durham, and in the east Midlands, Cambridgeshire, Nottinghamshire and Lincolnshire. There may be something in the view that the estates of the great owners tended to lie in areas where the land was generally of lower value, although the pattern is not entirely consistent with this. At all events, the differences between the majority of the counties were not very marked: in twenty-five out of thirty-nine counties the proportion of land occupied by gentry varied only between 26 and 35 per cent. It seems clear, however, that the concentration of gentry in the home counties reflected in part the more commercial character of the farming and the influence of London. Many of these home-county gentry had spawned in London itself, and when they sought a more salubrious residence they took care that it was still within easy reach of the capital. As Defoe noted, Essex was popular with London merchants and tradesmen who had purchased

> very considerable estates, as Mr Western an iron merchant, near Kelvedon, Mr Cresnor, a wholesale grocer, who was, a little before he died, nam'd for sheriff at Earls Coln, Mr Olemus, a merchant at Braintree, Mr Westcomb, near Malden, Sir Thomas Webster at Copthall, near Waltham, and several others. I mention this to observe how the present encrease of wealth in the city of London, spreads itself into the country, and plants families and fortunes, who in another age will equal the families of the antient gentry, who perhaps were bought out[22].

As a proportion of the total population of the country, of course, the gentry were almost insignificant – only about 3 per cent according to King's figures, or between 1 and 2 per cent according to an estimate for the early sixteenth century. But the political, economic and social weight of the gentry was not determined by their numbers but by their stake in the country: this was what gave them their influence both in the counties and at Westminster. In the age of their political dominance they probably owned a half, or nearly as much, of all the land, leaving the other half to be shared among the great lords, the yeomen freeholders, the Crown and the Church; and land was more than income, it was power.

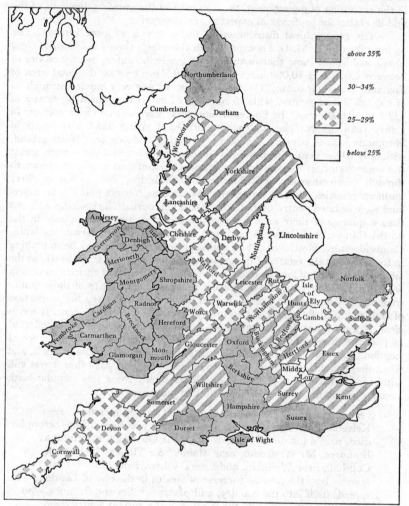

	above 35%
	30–34%
	25–29%
	below 25%

The forces of social cohesion

To sum up, the gentry consisted of all the landowners below the peerage and above the yeomanry, owning after 1550 somewhere between 40 and 55 per cent of the land. Analysed by income, they took the shape of a pyramid broad at the base but very narrow and steeply raked towards the top. The proportion of the gentry who bore the title of baronet or knight was always small, only 8 or 9 per cent, if we accept seventeenth-century estimates. Social divisions were accentuated by the great disparity of incomes, stretching in 1640 from under £100 a year to several thousands, and in the nineteenth century from a few hundreds to £10,000 or more. Clearly, this not only made for enormous differences in living standards, interests, outlook and social standing, but also for differences in influence and power within the community. Important county offices, and the county seats in Parliament, tended to be held for long periods within a small circle of the wealthiest families, from which some families of equal wealth were excluded by lack of influence or other circumstances. While many of the leading families retained their influence over a long series of generations, others which perhaps at first had come as rapidly to the fore, soon lost their momentum and fell into the background. In this the fortunes of marriage and a sufficiency of male heirs, and the continued ability of a family to produce men of talent and energy, and to restrain extravagance, litigiousness and other forms of imprudence, all played a part. Declining families were replaced by newcomers, often from outside the county, and some from outside the ranks of landowners. Estimates suggest that at any one time one of every twenty gentry families was a new arrival, and that under half of all the families had been established in their county for much over a century.

In view of these wide differences in income, status and influence, and the marked fluidity of membership, what gave to the gentry their cohesiveness and permanence as a social force? Most important, undoubtedly, was the common interest in land and the income to be derived from it. Before the nineteenth century land was the greatest source of income, the most secure type of investment, the most permanent form of asset and the principal fount of influence and power. The common interest of the gentry was their concern with the same kind of property: land. But there were other forces that brought and kept the gentry together. To a remarkable extent the baronet, squire, parson and lawyer shared the same education and culture, and thereby enjoyed the same tastes and held the same ideas (although the wealthier gentry were undoubtedly much more travelled and more sophisticated men of the world). Marriage and kinship tied these cultural bonds more closely together, while the social gatherings on the occasions of county and parish business, at fairs and markets, on feast days and celebrations, at field sports and local entertainments, helped to maintain a sense of community and familiarity. They shared a similar style of life, with the humbler aping the greater so far as his lesser resources would allow; and although each understood his proper place in the hierarchy, and in general kept to it, the binding forces of common interest and a common viewpoint were stronger than the divisive influences of rank and wealth.

2 The emergence of the gentry

Feudalism

The origins of the gentry must be looked for in the growth of feudal institutions in western Europe in a period of insecurity and weak central control. The practice whereby a warrior bound himself to follow a chief in return for maintenance and a share of the booty was well established among German warlords by the time of Tacitus. The Germanic chieftain called his band of warriors his *comitatus*, and the Frankish kings, similarly, had their *truste*, while the Saxon kings of England surrounded themselves with groups of *thanes*. Over the long period between the eighth and thirteenth centuries the gradual evolution of the feudal rights and obligations of lords and their vassals resulted in a complex hierarchy. At the apex stood the king with his close circle of great nobles, lay barons and princes of the Church, as direct vassals of the Crown; in turn these great nobles held numbers of lesser lords in thrall; and they in their turn had their own vassals down to the lowliest knight who held just enough land to support his family, his horses, and his weapons of war. Below him, and subject in some degree to his authority, stood freemen farmers, and the large numbers of unfree peasants, who sought the protection and security of a lord, and whose function it was to cultivate the land set aside for the support of the military, administrative and ecclesiastical classes. For although the fundamental purpose of the feudal system was that of establishing a military organisation, and the basic tie between a lord and his vassal remained a military one, provision had also to be made for the support of the churches, monasteries and nunneries, as well as a numerous body of lay administrators engaged in serving the Crown and the greater lords.

In England the Norman conquest resulted in the establishment of a new military aristocracy, one which displaced the Saxon thanes and introduced a more thoroughgoing form of feudalism, where service in war was strictly bound to the tenure of land. The conquest further entailed the legal principle that all land must have a lord, who granted it upon terms of suit and service. Thus the peasantry were thrust into a state of deeper dependence on the more powerful, and the term 'villein', originally villager, came to imply servitude – the servitude of a serf tied to the lord's soil. However, as time went by the strong military basis of the feudalism introduced by the Normans tended to wane, as did also the servile status of the bulk of the peasantry.

In theory a knight served his lord by making a personal appearance with his horse and arms when required, and his portion of land made up what was known as a knight's fee or fief. In practice the payment of a money composition, 'scutage' or shield money, came to replace personal service in the lord's castle or on the battlefield. Scutage proved a convenient way both of discharging the vassal's irksome and possibly dangerous obligations, and of providing the lord with the means of hiring a competent body of professional soldiers. After all, it was unlikely that all or even the majority of a lord's vassals would be of a suitable age, temperament or state of health for immediate and arduous service in the field.

With the development of castles as permanent fortresses, knights often owed their lords regular garrison service as well as more occasional escort duty and appearance on the field of battle. The knights of the barony of Richmond, for example, each helped garrison Richmond castle for three months in every year. To ensure a sufficient supply of trained men for their garrisons and retinues the great lords maintained household knights, who lived with them free of charge in return for their military duties. The needs of this armed establishment had a powerful influence on the education of the sons of both great lords and lesser vassals. At an early age a boy was prepared for his adult function by being placed away from home, in the household of a wealthy relation or in the home of his parents' lord. He was trained in the use of arms and spent a good deal of time in hunting, an occupation which helped him become a proficient horseman, and one inured to hardship and danger.

His prowess in arms was tested at tournaments, which enjoyed a great vogue from the twelfth century. In the course of time tournament rules were introduced, and these together with developments in armour and the influence of the ideas of chivalry, changed the character of the tournament. From a violent, confused mêlée of opposing sides ranging over an open plain, it became an orderly spectacle based on jousts or charges between pairs of combatants in enclosed spaces or 'lists'. Jousting, or a 'round table' as it was called from Arthurian associations, was carried out in accordance with a strict code of ceremonies, accompanied by a magnificent display of pageantry. Henceforth the tournament became a great social occasion, attended by lords and their ladies as well as throngs of the common people, and was followed by feasting and dancing. At these staged combats the need of the heralds and spectators to distinguish individual contestants led to the practice of knights carrying personal marks on their armour, and so to the science of heraldry. When he was considered of full strength and sufficiently skilled, usually at the age of twenty-one, the young man was given his arms in an elaborate and costly ceremony and was dubbed a knight by the customary stroke of a sword on the shoulder. Younger sons who had no land of their own received a similar military training and made a career as professional soldiers, household knights or 'knights bachelor', and meanwhile looked for a powerful patron or a wealthy heiress as a step towards establishing themselves among the feudal landowners.

Knighthood did not come to confer social distinction, as against military standing, until the middle of the twelfth century. The improved social status of knights owed a good deal to their role in the crusades, the fact that knighthood was adopted by the aristocracy, and that knights became increasingly used by the crown for performing legal, administrative and political services. The wealthiest knights were not very far from baronial status, holding perhaps as many as six manors, though the majority had fewer [1]. In time of peace the lord's following of knights and other retainers might be called to his principal residence to give advice in council or to ride in their lord's train on some great occasion. They were expected to appear, for example, when the lord's son was knighted or his daughter married, or when some great personage such as the king was expected. A nobleman's standing depended in large part on his 'power', the military force he could command, and when he wished to display his strength he would summon his barons, knights and other supporters to make up a magnificent assembly. On such occasions the number, distinction and dazzling appearance of his followers were matters of no little importance. At the beginning of the fourteenth century Thomas of Berkeley had a household of over two hundred – knights, esquires, serving men and pages. The lord's followers bore his emblem or livery, the rising sun of York, the bear and ragged staff of Neville, the portcullis of Beaufort[2].

Vassals owed numerous financial obligations to their lord, which he used in part for meeting the expenses of his swollen household and paying his fighting men. His tenants paid 'reliefs' or fees when a fief was passed to an heir, and from the twelfth century they might be asked for additional aids when a lord was faced with extraordinary expenses in mounting a military campaign or when going on a pilgrimage. The rule of primogeniture, which had become fully established by the later thirteenth century, was associated with the need of the lord to ensure that the obligations of his tenants were duly fulfilled when their land changed hands. Under strict feudal tenure the lands so held had to go to the eldest son; except in Kent, where the practice of gavelkind or division among heirs ruled, a tenant could not bequeath his land to younger sons or daughters. In due course, however, 'uses' developed by which these restrictions were overcome, and by 1327 all feudal tenants had achieved a degree of freedom of alienation over their lands. So, if there were no son to succeed, the inheritance was shared between the daughters. Exceptions to the rule, inheritance by the youngest son, for example, or equal division among all the sons, were regarded as anomalous customs.

The passing of land to daughters and widows made marriage the simplest and quickest way of acquiring additional wealth, and lords were careful to maintain rights of consent over the marriage of a tenant's daughter and the re-marriage of his widow. Particularly valuable was his power of controlling the fiefs of those vassals who died leaving an unmarried daughter as heiress or a son who was still a minor. Such rights over 'wardships', established from the twelfth century, enabled many lords to augment their incomes by exploiting the estates of their wards and by arranging profitable matches for them in return for a fee. Right of wardship persisted over a male heir until he reached the age of twenty-one, and in the case of an heiress until she was sixteen, unless she was already married or betrothed, when it was only fourteen. Heiresses were so much in demand that ambitious men married them off in childhood, though the 1275 Statute of Westminster laid down that the eldest daughter could not be married until she was at least seven years old.

The vassal's fief or grant of land was usually his principal or only means of income, though he might hold land of several lords. The unfree peasants who worked the lord's land for him needed land for their own support, and so they had a share, usually the major share, set aside for them. In return for their holdings the peasants were under obligation to work on the lord's demesne for a number of days each week, and to perform additional 'boon' tasks at harvest. In addition to these labour services, the lord demanded the best beast or other fee for permission for the farmer's son to succeed to the holding or for the marriage of the farmer's daughter. Other payments in kind included 'larder silver' at Christmas, eggs and capons at Easter, and payments for grazing swine and gathering timber. The lord's privileges included not merely overlordship of the waste, but also authority over forests and game, powers over the use of rivers for transport and water mills, demands on the peasants' teams and carts for carriage services, and sometimes the prerogative of putting hunting dogs out to board with the farmers. Extensive though these rights were, they were often less oppressive than on the continent: only rarely in England, for example, did the lord attempt to maintain an exclusive monopoly of the local flour mill, bread ovens, or dovecotes.

After the Conquest William distributed the lands of his chief barons across the country so that none of them owned a predominance of territory in any area which might form the base of a rival power and become a potential source of insurrections. An 'honor' or group of estates seldom lay within the bounds of one shire. The lands of Henry de Ferrers, one of William's commissioners for the Domesday inquest, lay in no less than fourteen counties, though with a certain emphasis on Derbyshire, Staffordshire and Leicestershire. The lands of his tenants were equally scattered, the three knight's fees held of him by Hubert de Curzun, for instance, lying in Staffordshire, Berkshire, Leicestershire and Oxfordshire [3]. Indeed, it was even uncommon outside the Midlands for the consolidated estate or 'manor' held by a lord to coincide with the village: many villages, especially in East Anglia, were divided among the manors of two, three, or even more lords, producing a fertile source of disputes over boundaries and jurisdictions through the centuries, while large numbers of villages had no resident lord. Only in the wild and remote borderlands nearest Wales and Scotland did the local magnates or marcher lords assume a large degree of independent power, and this owed much to the security their castles provided against the incursions of marauders, and to the prevailing sense of danger and insecurity. However, through marriage and exchanges of lands, many nobles managed to build up a significant if still scattered holding in a particular district with which they became closely associated, as the Percies, for example, were associated with Northumberland, the Nevilles with Westmorland, and the Stanleys with southwest Lancashire.

The Norman kings had sufficient grip on the country to prohibit resort to arms in settlement of private disputes, and they succeeded in securing the more important powers of justice firmly in their own hands. The royal justices moved their courts from place to place in circuits round the kingdom and there dispensed the king's justice, leaving only local police powers in the hands of the lords. Similarly, in each county the sheriff, as the king's direct representative, mobilised men in times of danger and collected taxes and levied fines, while from the end of the twelfth century another official, the coroner, had the power of enquiring into the causes of sudden death.

The lords punished such offences as minor assaults and petty nuisances in their own manorial courts. They even had power to hang a thief if he were caught with stolen goods on him, and in the west Midlands there were plenty of private gallows at the end of the thirteenth century, as Professor Hilton tells us [4].

Local courts of barons and upper gentry exercised powers over weights and measures, particularly those relating to the sale of bread and ale, where fraudulent measures were a frequent cause of public protest. In addition, markets and fairs and the activities of pedlars and chapmen were duly regulated, while the courts of some more powerful lordships took the 'view of frankpledge', the presentation of tithings or groups of ten into which adult males were collected for purposes of 'telling tales' or reporting crimes. Through his manorial court every lord exercised some powers of justice and administration, and the fines and dues levied in the exercise of these powers might form a significant source of income. The courts were valuable, too, as a means of keeping a check on the tenants of scattered properties, to ensure that labour services were performed, and customary dues were paid. Inevitably disputes arose over titles to land, boundaries of holdings, use of commons and the performance of labour services; these and similar disputes were heard by the lord or his representative and a judgment handed down in accordance with the custom of that particular manor. From Henry II's time, however, freeholders in the manor, unlike the unfree farmers and labourers, could take their grievances to the king's court, and this valuable right was in fact the distinguishing mark of the freeman.

The waning of feudalism

From the earliest days of the feudal period there were important distinctions between the great lords – the hundred or more magnates such as the abbots, bishops, princes, dukes and earls – and the more numerous ranks of lesser lords, lower vassals such as the several thousand knights, the esquires and country gentlemen. The latter group, made up of the middle ranks of landowners interposed between the great lords on the one hand and the freemen farmers and servile peasantry on the other, emerged as the gentry. Unlike the magnates, who were concerned primarily with politics and great offices of state, and whose estates were managed for them by a small army of private officials, the gentry were more directly engrossed, at least in the early Middle Ages, in the administration and farming of their own little handful of manors. They formed, as Georges Duby has put it, 'an entrepreneurial class which was at that time the principal dynamic element in the economic life of the countryside' [5]. Already at this early period important differences of wealth, function, power and influence distinguished the great lords from the more humdrum life of the typical member of the gentry. But in his turn the petty lord was far removed from the common mass of the peasantry, not so much in his way of life or standard of living as in his status, which affected the extent of his freedom and privileges. The gentry, together with the substantial freemen farmers, were free of the constraints and obligations imposed on the ordinary countrymen, and indeed the lords not only drew on unfree tenants for the labour to work their demesnes but also obtained a significant part of their income from their rights over the peasant's holding, his daughter's marriage, and the movement of members of his family away from the manor.

The military ties that originally bound the vassal to his overlord weakened as the Middle Ages advanced. By the thirteenth century, if not earlier, the knight usually discharged his obligation by paying his lord a sum of money rather than by personal military service. Many holders of knight's fees had no intention of incurring a heavy outlay on armour and horses, and they even avoided being knighted in order to escape the expenses of the ceremony and the unpaid administrative duties which knights were expected to perform in their shires. The magnates themselves came to pay the king in money or met their obligations by producing a band of hired knights. English barons fell into the practice of giving out fiefs that were far too small to support a knight, and the holders of these petty fiefs could only respond with money when a call to arms was made. There was also a growth of new pseudo-manors. For example, at Wootton in Bedfordshire Thomas de Stodley began by marrying an heiress and in some thirty transactions between 1318 and 1340 'he steadily added to his holding anything from a rood to a virgate, and began to hold a court; hence, Stodley's manor' [6].

Considerations of private profit took precedence over military obligations. From an early period many lords concentrated on managing their lands to the best advantage. Demesnes were run in a commercial way as agricultural production became highly specialised in response to the growth of markets and in accordance with local circumstances of climate, soil, situation and transport. Natural conditions necessarily made for a wide variety of land use. Extensive woodlands covered large areas in which farming was small-scale and subsidiary to other occupations. In upland areas, as in sparsely populated northern England and Wales, and in marshy districts like the Fens, the production of wool and the rearing of cattle formed the basis of the farming, and in the later Middle Ages pasture tended to gain at the expense of arable on some marginal lands. Partly as a result of these developments, some lords found it convenient to commute the labour services of their unfree tenants into money rents, and resorted to hired labour for the working of their demesnes. Others found it more profitable to abandon altogether direct management of their lands and instead leased them out to tenant farmers. Whether commutation was the rule, or demesnes were cultivated by labour services, depended on prices and market conditions. In the thirteenth century commutation of labour services was often stopped, and on some estates reversed, when conditions favoured demesne production of grain. Already by 1300, however, a large proportion of the lords were *rentiers* rather than agricultural producers. In Leicestershire, for example, Professor Hilton found that at the beginning of the fourteenth century, a considerable amount of wage labour was being used to cultivate manorial demesnes, while many peasants paid money rents and attended seigneurial courts but were otherwise completely independent of the lords [7].

In the later Middle Ages, with pasture generally more profitable than arable, the commuting of services and leasing of demesnes proceeded further until they became generally established practices on larger estates. Some minor labour services lingered on into modern times as obsolescent appendages to farm leases, but such irksome obligations as the performing of carriage services or the making of gifts of produce at Christmas and Easter were normally commuted into money payments by the eighteenth century at the latest. Commutation of personal service, abolition of unfree status, and the alienation of demesnes did much in the later Middle Ages to improve the status and well-being of peasant farmers. Villein tenure was transformed wholesale into copyhold with money rents, and from at least the middle fifteenth century the protection of the equity courts, and even of the common law, was extended to copyholders. Indeed, many demesnes were leased on terms which gave the copyholder permanent rights of tenancy almost equivalent to a freehold interest in the land. Other tenants were less secure, holding leases which might not be automatically renewed or were renewable on certain conditions, and which could be terminated by the lord with greater or lesser difficulty. When, as in the sixteenth century, farming conditions became more attractive, some lords reverted to farming their demesnes themselves; in turn, they often leased them out again when conditions seemed less favourable. By the later seventeenth century most landlords, except the very smallest, had adopted a policy of permanently renting out the major part of their land, retaining in their own hands only the home farm, and that principally as a convenience for supplying fresh food to the mansion.

The extension of commutation and the wider leasing out of demesnes in the later Middle Ages owed a great deal to the secular deterioration in economic conditions which affected most of Europe in the fourteenth and early fifteenth centuries. The general economic decline seems to have been preceded by a period of population growth and expansion of the farm acreage involving a resort to poorer soils. By the thirteenth century this had resulted in declining yields, and a more precarious margin between food supplies and the demands of the enlarged population. The medieval economy came to be balanced on a knife edge. The crisis came in the fourteenth century when the fine equilibrium of supply and demand was disastrously disturbed by a series of exceptionally severe weather conditions and catastrophic harvests. A population weakened by hardship fell prey to the ravages of disease. Plague was endemic in the fourteenth century and the terrible Black Death, which struck the country in 1348, was only one, if the worst, of a series of destructive outbursts. In England plague reduced the population by something like a third. The effects were uneven, however, with some areas like the Winchester estates in southern England suffering little: vacant holdings were rapidly filled up by new tenants and revenue was swelled by the increase in entry fines. Elsewhere much of the labour force was destroyed or fled away, and it became difficult or impossible to continue cultivation. There are indications that some gentry were unable to keep up the cultivation of their demesnes, and some were in financial difficulties. In such areas pasture gained at the expense of arable, and poor land reverted to waste. In the long run a further impetus was given to the commutation of labour services and the inauguration of leases for lives or long terms of years. Leases of twelve, twenty or forty years were common, and Chertsey Abbey granted leases for 99, 200, and even 300 years.

Owing to labour scarcity wages rose, while from about 1320 prices of farm produce tended generally to fall because of reduced demand. Increasingly the shortage of labour enabled peasants to obtain commutation and personal freedom on easy terms, and for their part many landlords, faced by low prices and dear labour, were obliged sooner or later to offer attractive leases to such tenants as were willing to occupy their land. But the alienation of the demesnes was seldom abrupt: it had already gone some way before the end of the thirteenth century, and it proceeded only rather gradually and often uncertainly on many ecclesiastical and lay estates after the disasters of the fourteenth century.

'In the fifteenth century', remarked Duby, 'agriculture was in most cases, no longer conducted by the masters, but rather by the peasantry' [8]. However, it is an oversimplification to suppose that all landlords leased their demesnes and became rentiers, or that all the tenants of the demesnes were mere peasants who were just beginning to rise in the world. Research on estates in Kent and elsewhere shows that many demesne lessees were already substantial farmers, members of families that were well on their way to becoming gentry. On the Abbot of Westminster's estates some of the lessees were manorial officials, reeves, rent collectors and bailiffs, whose offices provided them with some degree of farming expertise and a little capital, as well as close knowledge of the lands in question. Others were already members of the gentry, small landlords, a knight of the shire for Worcestershire, and a merchant of Gloucester [9]. How far such relatively superior tenants worked the newly acquired land themselves, and how far they merely added the land to their existing holdings and sublet it, remains uncertain. At the lower levels of landownership there was possibly more direct farming by gentry landlords in the fifteenth century than has sometimes been supposed. In either case it seems that the economic climate which encouraged the leasing out of the larger owners' demesnes in the later Middle Ages was also one in which the lesser landlords were able to flourish.

The gentry and public office

By the fourteenth century the numerous body of middling and lesser landlords who made up the gentry was much broader than the ancient orders of knights. The heralds by 1370 had accepted the esquires, younger sons of knights, as belonging to the armigerous class; and the title of esquire was adopted not only by younger sons but also by the tenants of fragmented fiefs, whose fathers had not been knights and who themselves did not aspire to be knights. Possibly a shortage of knights after the Black Death, and the development of the 'use' as a legal device for passing property on to younger sons, may help explain the change. The esquires had begun by bearing, literally, the arms of their lord or knight; now in the later fourteenth century they were bearing their own coats of arms. Geoffrey Chaucer, who lived as a country gentleman in Somerset and Kent and had seen military service, was described in 1372–73 as *armiger* with a coat *per pale argent and gules, a bend countercharged* [10]. Numbers of these new country gentry had risen from the ranks of franklins or substantial freeholders and tenant farmers – the later yeomanry. Others began as lay clerks and rose to be judges, as did John Benstede and the Scropes. Then there were the manorial officials, and at a higher level members of the royal administration – the sheriffs, escheators, coroners, verderers, assistants to the royal justices, commissioners of array, keepers of the peace and tax-collectors. Such offices were sought for the fees which they sometimes yielded, for the social prestige they inevitably conferred, and for their ultimate value as political stepping stones.

The office of sheriff went back to Anglo-Saxon times, and both the sheriff and the later coroner were at the height of their powers about the early thirteenth century. As the agent of the king the sheriff was in control of the shire levies, the local defence force of militia made up of freemen, who under the 1285 Statute of Westminster had to provide themselves with arms according to the value of their property. The sheriff was thus responsible for local security and police matters. He was supposed to break up gangs of armed men, demolish unlicensed castles, and repress unruly students of the universities. He had to see that the ancient shire and hundred courts were duly held, and he was expected to arrest and imprison suspected felons and carry out the penalties decided by the courts. In addition he collected local revenues of the crown, and the opportunities this afforded him for oppression and extortion made him a highly unpopular figure. As a result it was decided in 1340 that the sheriff was to hold office for not more than a year, and by this time his authority was considerably diminished by the powers wielded by itinerant royal justices. His administrative functions, too, were reduced and given to specialised officials, while it was the recently established justice of the peace who acquired increased authority as the needs of local government expanded. The men appointed as sheriffs were frequently of rather humble rank, partly to avoid having to employ unreliable barons and so adding to their powers. Some sheriffs, such as Geoffrey de Clinton and Ralph Basset, found the office a means of rising in the world, and despite its burdensome nature men were often prepared to pay large sums for the privilege of having it [11].

The office of coroner was established in 1194, and in the thirteenth century the coroner held inquests on unexplained corpses, promulgated outlawries in the shire court and organised executions; he received abjurations of the realm made by felons in sanctuary and heard appeals and confessions; occasionally he dealt with wrecks and treasure trove. Until the reign of Henry VII the office was unpaid and the holder had to be a man of substance, not merely because of the prestige attaching to the coroner's powers but also because of the risk of incurring fines for neglect of duties. However, the coroners succeeded in exacting unofficial fees from those who came within their ambit, and they did so with increasing boldness in the later years of the Middle Ages [12].

In addition to the sheriff and the coroner many other officials were employed by the Crown and the wealthy magnates – local justices, escheators and verderers, constables of castles and keepers of gaols, stewards and bailiffs of honors, rapes and liberties, as well as feodaries, house stewards and land stewards. The growth of this administrative class provided a useful ladder of promotion for the lesser gentry and younger sons who commanded the appropriate education and ability. Henry de Bray, for instance, a country gentleman with some 500 acres, served as steward for a Northampton priory, and improved his fortune by exchanging and buying lands and rebuilding his farms. There were not enough knights to go round to fill all the offices, and even esquires and franklins were admitted as members of Parliament. The eagerness with which office was sought and clung to (witness the numerous ejections for old age, sickness and lack of qualification) demonstrates its importance for the wealth and prestige of gentry families. The fortunes of many Derbyshire gentry, to take only one county – the Arches, Bagshawes, Balguys, Eyres, Foljambes and Woodruffs, for instance – were founded on the holding of Crown offices in the royal Forest of the Peak in the early Middle Ages. The Foljambes, for example, first came into prominence as foresters at fee, holding land in return for defending the forest for the king. In the later thirteenth century Thomas Foljambe was bailiff of the Honor and Castle of the Peak, and built up an estate in that area. Another Foljambe, Sir Godfrey, who died in 1376, was a close associate of John of Gaunt and served the Dukes of Lancaster as Steward of Blackburn Wapentake, Steward of the Honor of Tutbury, and Chief Steward of the Duchy of Lancaster. By the fifteenth century the family had extensive properties in Derbyshire, Yorkshire and Nottinghamshire. Office continued to be important in the following century when the fourth Sir Godfrey Foljambe was Receiver and Feodary of Tickhill in the Duchy of Lancaster, Escheator of Nottinghamshire and Derbyshire, and three times sheriff jointly for the two counties.

Membership of the House of Commons offered similar attractions. In the fourteenth century the king instructed the sheriffs to obtain the election of two knights from each county to sit in Parliament. The gentry thus became directly represented in the national forum, and as Professor May McKisack has said, they brought into Parliament 'a wide range of administrative experience and knowledge of local conditions and, overlapping at one end with the nobility and, at the other, with the bourgeoisie, their presence there prevented alignment into rigid social or professional groups and made possible their own consolidation with the burgesses into a single *collegium*, or house of commons' [13].

Detailed studies have shown that the medieval county members of Parliament were usually, though not always, of the rank of knight; they were often connected with some powerful political figure to whom they owed their election; but they were also men of authority in their counties, often prominent in local administration as commissioners, assessors and collectors of taxes, coroners or sheriffs, and sometimes they held responsible military appointments, for instance as constables of castles. Such a one was Sir John de Morteyn, who frequently represented Bedfordshire between 1306 and 1330. He had seen military service in 1297, and at one time was constable of Rockingham Castle, and had experience as a commissioner of array and justice of the peace [14].

The electorate was very small, sometimes fewer than a hundred people, and this helped to keep the seats in Parliament the preserve of a few of the wealthier landed families. The tendency towards exclusiveness was reinforced by a statute of 1429, which laid down that the electors were to be resident in their shire with freehold lands worth at least forty shillings a year, a sum that then represented a considerable amount of land, and so effectively restricted the franchise to a very limited number of persons. There was a strong feeling that the parliamentary representatives should be elected by persons of their own social standing or near to it, and certainly that the office should be kept out of the hands of yeomen. Election came to be eagerly sought, since service in Parliament might bring a family to the direct notice of the Crown and result in various favours, such as grants of lands, awards of offices, wardships, hunting rights and gifts of jewels or of wine. Some gentry also sat for the boroughs which were under the control of the great political magnates, and these represented early examples of the later 'pocket boroughs'.

Knights frequently sat for shires in which they held no land and with which they had no obvious connection – evidence, no doubt, of the power of their patrons and of their own willingness to serve. 'Westminster was as attractive to ambitious men in the fourteenth century as it is today,' remarked Denholm-Young. Such was the local influence of some families that it was a matter of indifference whether they served for shire or borough. Possibly the old-established families showed a more conservative preference for a particular shire, and it may have been the ambitious upstart who migrated, as did John de la Haye who moved from Cambridge to Hertfordshire and then to Buckinghamshire, and Sir John le Rous who sat at different times for four shires. Many of the shires were controlled by magnates who nominated their own men as justices and M.P.s. Sir Thomas Hungerford, steward to the Black Prince and

John of Gaunt, was eleven times member for Wiltshire and four times for Somerset before he died in 1398. In 1377 he was made Speaker through the influence of Gaunt, and other members of his family appeared regularly for Wiltshire, Oxfordshire and Gloucestershire in the fourteenth and fifteenth centuries [15].

Just as the patronage of some great magnate could be decisive in elections to Parliament, so also his influence largely determined appointments of justices, sheriffs and under-sheriffs, bailiffs, stewards of hundreds and commissioners of musters. The justice of the peace gradually became the most important of these county offices, and as the powers of the justices grew so those of the sheriffs and other officials declined. The leading gentry already assumed the role of local keepers of the peace (where they were not disturbing it themselves), and had gradually assumed judicial powers; and in 1368 these powers were placed on a firm statutory base. As men of wealth, with strong local connections and knowledge, they could command respect and popular support, and in the absence of a class of professional administrators controlled directly by the Crown, the number of justices in each county was gradually increased, while the range of their powers was expanded. During the sixteenth century the number of justices doubled, and already in the previous century their powers included in addition to keeping the peace, control over sumptuary laws, regulation of wages and supervision of prisons, and inspection of beacons and coastal defences. To these functions sixteenth-century legislation added many more, especially in the spheres of industrial regulation and the administration of the Poor Law.

Decline of the great lords

As feudalism waned, the powers of patronage exercised by the great lords replaced the ancient military and protective bond between them and their vassals. Until the destruction of the old feudal nobility in the Wars of the Roses and the subsequent emergence of a more powerful monarchy, the great lords' control of offices remained a pervasive influence serving to keep the lower ranks of landowners under their sway. In the fifteenth century the role of the magnates was heightened by the recurring weakness of the Crown. They were not always concerned solely with selfish ends, however, and some magnates displayed administrative ability and a real sense of responsibility for the maintenance of government. Nevertheless they were able to manipulate the royal courts of justice and exert influence on the royal council, while many royal officers, the sheriffs, coroners, escheators and justices of the peace, were nominees of the magnates and took good care not to offend them. In 1439, for instance, Lord Fanhope rudely invaded Bedford town hall with forty or sixty armed men and brought a meeting of the justices to a sudden close. Fanhope was a member of the king's council and had little difficulty in securing a pardon for his action. After another incident twelve years later Lord Moleyns was able to employ the royal favour in escaping the consequences of an armed assault on another owner's manor [16]. In an earlier period, too, it was common to find gangs of robbers and bandits led by clergy and members of gentry families. Professor Hilton tells of Malcolm Masard who was involved in many brawls, assaults and robberies, but managed to avoid prosecution, and was even appointed chief forester of Fakenham, and in 1321 was made constable of Hanley Castle[17].

The king's reliance on the magnates in the Hundred Years' War, and in the internecine strife of the Wars of the Roses, increased the power of the magnates *vis-à-vis* that of the Crown. The reduced authority and the pressing military needs of the Crown encouraged the magnates to raise large bodies of liveried retainers which, originally part of the royal forces, eventually developed as private armies. John of Gaunt, duke of Lancaster, was the wealthiest magnate of his time. In the early years of Richard II's reign he had a following of one earl, three barons, 83 knights and 112 esquires[18]. A magnate could support his retainers and keep their loyalty only if his own wealth and political position were sufficiently strong. In consequence, he engaged in perpetual rivalry with fellow magnates in order to hold on to his power and improve his status. If his star waned his retainers would drift away, and eventually he lost following, influence, income, and possibly even his own life. Lesser men clung to prominent barons and changed patrons as circumstances warranted, and in this welter of unrest and instability the powers of feudal patronage increased as the authority of the Crown declined.

When, with the Tudors, a more stable monarchy was restored, many of the old nobility had been destroyed or impoverished in the struggle for power. The time was now ripe for the gentry to come more fully into their own. Numbers of them had grown in wealth through successful management of their demesnes, conversion of land to sheep farming, and perhaps through leasing watermills and exploiting minerals. Others had success in marriage, like Sir William Stonor, who married in succession two rich city widows. Such men were joined by wealthy merchants who bought estates and turned themselves into gentry, like the Verneys, Wottons and Boleyns. There is evidence of comfortable living standards at this time, and of substantial purchases of luxuries from London, such as spices, wine and fruit. In the sixteenth century the power of the great nobles shrank as the royal councils came to be composed of minor peers and knights, men devoted to the royal service. Under the influence of a strong monarch the council became an instrument for keeping the nobles in their place, suppressing livery, and crushing intimidation and violence. The Reformation gave the Crown mastery over the great lords of the Church, and with the Statute of Wales of 1536 the franchises of the marcher lords were abolished and the whole of Wales brought within the royal authority. The Tudors did not destroy the aristocracy as a rival to the power of the monarch, but they tamed it and made it serve a revised political system. The new order was symbolised by the appearance of the first layman, Thomas Cromwell, as the chief minister of the Crown, feared and obeyed by even the greatest nobles[18].

As the influence of the magnates waned under the Tudors so the independence of the gentry increased. In part, the enhanced position of the gentry was associated with the changing status of the House of Commons. Already by the end of the fourteenth century it had become accepted that representatives of the Commons should always be summoned to take part in Parliaments: earlier this was not so. Called originally merely for purposes of consultation and cooperation with the government, the Commons began to assert an independent role. Claiming to represent all the commons as an estate of the realm, its members assumed rights of submitting petitions and consenting to taxation. By the middle of the fifteenth century the judges held that no enactment could be a statute unless the Commons, as well as the king and the Lords, had assented to it. So influential was the Commons becoming by this time that there was great competition for seats, and the government sought the election of officials of the royal household and civil servants. As yet, however, the House of Commons was still only slowly feeling its way towards the eventual assertion of supremacy over legislation and the executive, and the claims of Parliament gave little trouble to Henry VIII, though they were to cause problems for Elizabeth.

Royal offices became a greater source of independence for the leading gentry as the powers of the magnates declined after the fifteenth century. The great lords found themselves increasingly bypassed in local administration. More and more duties, mainly connected with law and order and the regulation of trade and industry, were thrust on the justices of the peace, whose influence and status were thus enhanced. Unlike the great nobles, the justices had an interest in enforcing legislation that made for greater quiet and stability in the country, while the Crown kept direct supervision of their activities through the council and the courts. It is true that the leading gentry who filled the office of justice of the peace often owed their position to the support of some great lord, but as time went by such patronage became less important. Many great families had been sadly reduced by the Wars of the Roses and by subsequent rebellions and adventures. Estates were diminished by forfeitures and fines, while the Tudors succeeded in finding new exactions to impose on the nobles.

Moreover, the great lord's very way of life became increasingly expensive, impractical and irrelevant. The swollen bands of retainers, the maintenance of scattered castles and mansions, the princely hospitality and lavish extravagance, all became a costly display of magnificence without real advantage or justification. Some lords, finding their incomes insufficient, began to cut down on their households and reduced the scale of their hospitality. Castles were abandoned and allowed to fall into ruin, or were converted to less defensible but more comfortable residences [19]. Of course the great lords continued to fulfil a role of social pre-eminence, which has persisted into later centuries and on to the present. The lesser gentry, in particular, have always looked to the nobility for leadership and recognition. Patronage did not end with the close of the Middle Ages, but its trammels were weakened by the decay of feudalism and the growing autonomy of the gentry. With the old nobility gone down in self-destruction and the new brought within the framework of an ordered society, the stage was set for the gentry to emerge as a major force in the life of the nation.

The homes of the gentry

Few country houses have survived from the Middle Ages and not a great number of fortified houses or castles. One reason for this is that only a small number of landowners were sufficiently wealthy to build and maintain a really substantial mansion, even less a large stone castle. Most of the gentry were possessed of only modest estates: in fourteenth-century Leicestershire, for instance, Robert de Loland with lands, rents and manors in six villages, Roger Beler with four manors and other lands, Stephen de Segrave with five manors, and the Verdon family with three manors, were in fact the largest owners in the county. The Verdon manors in Lutterworth, Cotesbach and Newbold each had no more than a hundred acres of arable when Theobald of Verdon died in 1309, and as Professor Hilton has remarked, few landowners had manors of greater size, either in arable or other lands[20].

Medieval manor houses therefore began as modest affairs and were re-built and extended as their owners improved in means and status. They were sometimes fortified with a moat and drawbridge, or with a wall and watch-tower, and the house was surrounded by orchards, gardens, and perhaps a deer part. The earliest houses developed round the hall, which served as the common livingroom and meeting place of the household. Originally wooden in con-struction, later brick, half-timbered, or stone, the larger halls were divided into a number of bays by means of arched trusses known as crucks, a feature which also appears in a number of surviving medieval barns. The importance of the hall derived from its central role, not merely in the daily activities of the house-hold but in the life of the village. In the hall the justice of the manor court was dispensed, and there also the lord gave instructions to officials for the running of the demesne. 'The Hall' was consequently the familiar name by which many a manor house came to be known, and it has come down to us as the name still frequently used for the principal house in the village, as well as in the wider application of town halls, guildhalls, and the halls of schools and colleges.

From the evidence of surviving examples it appears that the hall origin-ally occupied two-thirds of the space on the upper floor of the manor house, the remainder of the floor being taken up by the private chamber or 'bower'. Access was by an outer staircase, and the ground floor, with its own external door, was devoted to storage, and possibly kitchens and other domestic pur-poses. As time went by it became increasingly common for the hall, now divided into nave and aisles by columns, to have its floor at ground level or slightly above and to occupy the whole of the height formerly given to both floors. The bower, cellar and kitchen were placed in adjacent buildings, and in this development lay the ultimate growth of the house on quadrangular or single block plans. A popular design was to flank the hall by two wings, a private wing containing bedchambers and possibly a chapel, and a servants' wing which included the kitchen, buttery and pantry. The hall remained as the most impressive feature of the house, open to the roof and forming the central con-nection between the two wings. The external entrance door was placed at one end of the hall, under a porch, and opened into a passage screened from the hall which gave access to a minstrels' gallery above and the domestic offices on the ground floor. At the opposite end of the hall, on a daïs, was set the high table for the lord, his family and guests, with tables for the officials and other inferior members of the household set lengthways down the body of the hall. A door behind or to the side of the high table opened on to a stairway leading to the private chambers, consisting of the withdrawing room or parlour below, and the solar or bedchamber above. A stone hearth was set in the centre of the hall, and a louvre or turret covering a hole in the roof directly above allowed the smoke to escape, an arrangement which may still be seen in the great medieval hall at Penshurst Place in Kent. Fireplaces set in the wall with chimneys soon provided an alternative to the central hearth, and became general in the fourteenth and fifteenth centuries [21].

In the houses of wealthier landowners the windows might be of glass, which was scarce and expensive, but more usually the window space was filled by a lattice of wood or metal and covered by shutters in bad weather. The walls of the hall and private chambers were plastered and painted in bright colours or covered with murals depicting scenes from biblical stories or popular romances. In the fifteenth century those of greater wealth draped their walls with costly tapestries and eastern embroideries. Vessels of gold and silver were displayed on the tables of the hall or on the cupboard, a term which was later applied to the chest in which the plate was locked away when not in use. By the fifteenth century, too, pewter tableware was replacing the wooden platters and 'trenchers', thick slices of bread on which meat was served. Both trenchers and bones were flung among the rushes on the floor for the dogs, and since the rushes were changed only infrequently the English hall was usually in an unpleasantly noisome and unsavoury condition [22].

As wall fireplaces and chimneys became customary the necessity of having the hall open to the roof disappeared, and from Tudor times onwards the space taken by the hall was commonly divided into two or three storeys. Houses increased in size and improved in appointments, and were often architecturally splendid. Nevertheless the design of the large house was still sufficiently similar to that of ecclesiastical buildings to make conversion quite possible. After the Dissolution a number of landowners transformed monastic buildings into mansions with little difficulty. The church and cloisters of Notley Abbey, for example, made an impressive residence of the fashionable quadrangular style for Sir William Paulet. Sir Thomas Wriothesley built a gatehouse tower on to the middle of the nave of Titchfield Abbey, and converted the refectory into a hall. And at Lacock in Wiltshire Sir Edward Sharington destroyed the nunnery church but preserved the cloisters, to which he added new upper storeys [23]. Renaissance art influenced architectural detail in many new houses and conversions, and craftsmen from Italy and France were in demand for their decorative skills, though they were seldom employed for planning and construction. The early Renaissance style of the first half of the sixteenth century was fundamentally a natural development of the traditional perpendicular Gothic overlaid with Renaissance detail. Elaborate wreathed chimney stacks, intricately carved high-pitched gables, mullioned and transomed windows piled up to form façades of glass, heraldic devices over doorways, and contrasting patterns of blue bricks in red brick surfaces added interest to otherwise plain and practical houses. The quadrangular plan maintained its popularity, which was one reason for the interest in converting monastic buildings. Elizabethan times saw a gradual move towards an open-ended quadrangle, or more radically towards the H-shaped house, where the cross-wings overlapped both ends of the main or hall block, with the entrance hall projecting from the middle of the hallrange front. A northeastern aspect was preferred, since it was believed that the south wind brought 'evil vapours' which a north wind purged, while a breeze from the east was 'fresh and fragrant'.

Life, leisure and education

As Dr Salzman observed many years ago, home life in the medieval manor house presents to modern eyes a curious combination of luxury and discomfort, splendour and squalor, compounded by lack of privacy. Members of well-to-do families slept on feather beds covered with linen sheets, with ample blankets, rugs and quilts; the embroidery of the bed hangings was often elaborate, and the value of both bed hangings and wall tapestries was great; books of etiquette made the regular washing of hands, face and teeth obligatory. On the other hand, baths were taken infrequently, and it was usual for all members of the family to use a single bedroom and to share beds, often with guests in addition. Servants made do in a common dormitory or bedded down among the odorous rushes in the hall. Despite the sharing of beds everyone slept naked, night clothes not becoming fashionable until the sixteenth century. Even in the household of the great Percy Earls of Northumberland, Salzman tells us, the chaplains at the beginning of the sixteenth century slept two to a bed, and the children three to a bed [24].

The two main repasts of the Middle Ages, dinner and supper, were taken about ten or eleven in the morning and at four o'clock in the afternoon respectively. A late supper was sometimes indulged in as well, but little is heard of breakfast. The number and variety of the dishes depended on the wealth and standing of the family, and in a great household there was a variety of soups, stews, pastries, fritters and jellies, together with fruit, nuts and preserves. Fish, again in great variety, was the staple fare in Lent and on fast days, and was frequently served at other times. There was an almost infinite range of joints and meat dishes, and the essential education of a gentleman included manifold skill in carving. Dishes were heavily spiced – possibly, it has been suggested, because of the need for disguising the rank odour of meat kept over the winter, though it seems more likely that highly seasoned food was attractive to the medieval palate. Food was washed down with home-brewed ale and imported wine. The shipping of wine from Bordeaux, in particular, was an important element in English trade. In the fifteenth century Dutch residents of London and the eastern counties introduced beer, brewed (unlike ale) with hops, and this new rival gradually supplanted the traditional beverage [25].

The great outdoor sports of noblemen and wealthy country gentlemen were hunting and hawking. Vast tracts of country were set aside as royal forests for the king's pleasure, and were made subject to rigorous forest laws enforced with doubtful efficiency by specially created forest courts and officials: foresters, stewards, warreners and verderers. Great nobles kept their own private parks and chases, and game laws protected the beasts and birds of the chase for the exclusive use of those holding royal grants of 'free warren', a kind of sporting licence giving rights to hunt over lands beyond the bounds of the royal forests. In the reign of Richard II a property qualification of land worth forty shillings a year – then a very considerable amount – was required if one wished to keep hounds or use ferrets, or employ nets or other means of taking deer, hares and rabbits. Justices of the peace were empowered to impose a penalty of one year's imprisonment for breach of the law. Ladies joined in the hunting of deer and hares, and possibly of foxes and other small animals; they were also depicted in contemporary illustrations as members of hawking parties engrossed in pursuit of pheasants, partridges and waterfowl. Spaniels and greyhounds were specially bred for these sports, while mastiffs were employed in the sterner work of tackling the wild boars, in which the ladies did not take part.

Vigorous ball games, such as handball, club-ball (possibly a form of fives), football and tennis, seem to have been the preserve of the menfolk, and were specifically prohibited for the scholars of Oxford colleges. Football was evidently a fiercely rough game in which accidents were frequent, and indeed sometimes fatal; by the sixteenth century it seems to have become a mainly plebeian diversion. By then the more gentle bowls and skittles had been introduced, and were popular among both the gentlemen and their inferiors[26]. In summer ladies spent much of their time in their gardens, reading a book of romances or legends, or playing with their pets – Maltese spaniels, larks and nightingales kept for their song, and magpies and popinjays or parrots valued for their powers of mimicry; sometimes squirrels and moneys were kept as well. Even highborn ladies devoted time to making sweetmeats and preserves, preparing home-made wines, and making up herbal remedies against sickness. The chief occupations of the ladies, however, were spinning, weaving, sewing, embroidery and managing the household. A sixteenth-century Bedfordshire landowner, John Gostwick, advised the appointment of a sober and discreet person as a waiting-woman, two women to look after a dairy of sixteen or twenty cows, and a third for the linen; a male cook would have the women's help as necessary[27].

Both men and women enjoyed the music and romantic tales which bands of minstrels offered as diversions in winter evenings. Professional musicians, harpers, jesters and actors provided a wide range of entertainment running from the recounting of epics and legends to juggling, tumbling, dancing, coarse songs and buffoonery. Performing dogs, monkeys and bears were popular, and at Christmas time families spent the holidays in dressing up, dancing and playing such games as 'hot cockles' and 'hoodman blind', the ancestor of blind man's buff. Recitations of romances tended to die out as books became more plentiful and both ladies and gentlemen were educated to read them at their pleasure. A variety of dice and board games helped to while away leisure hours – draughts, 'tables' or backgammon, and especially chess. The word 'chess' was derived from the chess king, the Persian Shah, the game having reached Europe from India by way of Persia before the year 1000. It was certainly played in England shortly after the Norman Conquest. In the European version the military character of the eastern game was somewhat modified: the eastern vizier became the queen, the horses knights, the chariots rooks, the elephants bishops and the infantry pawns. The game achieved enormous popularity, as illustrated by the fact that the second book to be printed by Caxton was a chess treatise. By the later fifteenth century, however, it was becoming eclipsed by the more recently introduced game of cards[28].

The growth of reading as a common pastime among the leisured people of the Middle Ages was a reflection not only of the consequences for book production flowing from the introduction of printing, but also of the wider diffusion of education. Originally such limited facilities as existed for learning were closely associated with the Church. At the elementary song schools the boys were taught hymns and songs in Latin, learned their ABC and some reading, and possibly some writing too. The monastery schools were designed primarily for boys intending to become monks, and were almost entirely concerned with religious instruction given under conditions of strict discipline.

Sons of gentry, intended for the Church, were sent to board in a monastery and were educated with the novices in the cloisters. However, the most important element in the educational arrangements of the Middle Ages was the grammar school. Here, as the name indicates, Latin grammar was taught, with 'grammar' defined broadly as the art of speaking and writing correctly, on the basis of the models provided by the masters of Latin prose and poetry.

From the earliest times grammar schools were a necessary part of every cathedral and collegiate church, and the teaching in them was performed by 'secular clergy', so-called because unlike the 'regular clery' they mixed with the world and did not live under monastic rule. Such schools existed, for example, at Canterbury, Bedford, St Albans, Bury St Edmunds and Lewes. The foundation in 1382 of Winchester school marked a new epoch, for it was not only the largest grammar school but also the first to be established primarily as a school and not as an adjunct of some ecclesiastical institution. Eton, founded in 1440, was the first grammar school to be called a 'public school', a term which simply meant that its scholars could come not merely from the immediate neighbourhood but from anywhere in the country. Eton was associated with Henry VI's other foundation, King's College, Cambridge, just as Winchester was established by William of Wykeham to prepare scholars for his New College, Oxford. The separation of schools from the Church was again emphasised when the re-founded St Paul's School in London was withdrawn from the supervision of the Dean and Chapter of the Cathedral and entrusted to the Mercers' Company. Another indication of the trend towards secular authority in education occurred in 1432 when it was ordered that the master of Sevenoaks school should not be a priest: and the introduction of Greek among the regular subjects taught at Winchester, Eton, St Paul's and Oxford marks yet a further breach in the monopoly that the Church had claimed over education.

Long hours, from six in the morning to five in the afternoon – hours whiled away in translation, repetition, essay writing, and the making of précis – were the rule in the grammar schools. Sunday was the only day of respite, when work ceased at eleven, the dinner hour, but fortunately holy days provided frequent and welcome breaks in the monotony of the school year. Leisure diversions were a curious mixture of the vigorous and the intellectual, with games of fives, hockey, tennis, football, and even cock-throwing, alternating with impromptu debates conducted in Latin on disputed points of grammar or logic. The study of logic and rhetoric might be followed up by some introduction to arithmetic, geometry, music and astronomy. Arithmetic was a late starter as a subject, partly because it was not until the fourteenth century that arabic numerals began to come into use and provided a much simpler basis for calculation than did the old roman numerals.

By the middle of the thirteenth century schools devoted to the pursuit of advanced knowledge were well-established at Oxford and Cambridge, with a system of laws and regulations, and a hierarchy of officials headed by a chancellor. It was obviously convenient and more orderly if students lived together in one house or hall, under the control of a master, and so there developed endowed halls or colleges. The first college was that founded at Oxford by Walter de Merton in 1263. For long no very clear line was drawn between the grammar school and the university, and boys might come up to Oxford and Cambridge as young as thirteen or fourteen, though a higher age was more usual. At the universities the grammar school subjects were taken further, and students were introduced to theology and law. Undergraduates obtained the degree of Bachelor on the strength of attendance at lectures given by Masters of Arts and their teachers' attestation of worthiness. Medieval students, it appears, were often unruly, ragged the lecturers and younger students, and went out of their way to pick quarrels with the townsmen, quarrels which often resulted in affrays, with swords and daggers used to grievous effect.

Universities, therefore, may have advanced learning rather more than polite behaviour, and for the sons of the wealthy their education was not completed without a period of residence in the household of a noble or bishop, where the emphasis was on training in courtesy. There the graces and refinements of polite society were cultivated. Carving and serving at table were regarded as particularly valuable arts: Chaucer names as one of the accomplishments of his squire that he 'carved before his father at the table'. Books of etiquette were available in Latin, French and English, and were pored over by both youths and girls. Young ladies acquired some skill in reading and writing by a stay in a nunnery or from tutors employed by the household in which they were placed. Good manners, it seems, have changed little over the centuries though the elementary nature of the advice offered in some early books of etiquette suggest that habits were not all they might have been, even in the best of families. The young person was instructed, for example, not to hang his head 'lumpishly' or scowl sullenly when spoken to by a superior; nor was he to puff and snort or scratch himself. At table he was not to burnish his teeth with the bones on his plate, nor pick them with his knife or fingers; he should not dip his meat into the salt, nor 'sup lowde of thy pottage'; neither was he recommended to scratch his head or spit over the table board.

Influence of the Church

The influence of the Church stretched far beyond its control of the meagre educational resources of the Middle Ages. As H. S. Bennett remarked, 'the building itself, standing commonly in the centre of the village symbolised the place of the Church in medieval life. The great moments of man's stay on earth – baptism, marriage, burial – centred in the sacred building' [29]. The peasant working in the fields and the lord gazing out from his manor house could hardly fail to be conscious of the soaring spire or the impressive walls of a nearby abbey or priory. Apart from its physical presence the Church entered daily life through its spiritual protection, which extended further than the customary services, and indeed included

exorcisms at every turn against evil spirits and sorcery. The church bells were tolled against the approaching storms, which had been conjured by some witch; and the priest would sometimes formally curse, with sprinklings of holy water, a plague of caterpillars or locusts. Villagers felt at home within the four walls of the church, and the difficulty was rather to prevent too great familiarity. Church councils had to forbid theatrical performances and dances and semi-religious beer-drinkings within the church or its precincts, and to prohibit markets in the churchyard. Here, moreover, the clergy themselves set an example of freedom, stacking corn or even brewing beer in the nave of their church [30].

Not that familiarity with the church did much for the ordinary villager's understanding of his faith. The illiterate peasant 'could only watch with dull comprehension "the blessed mutter of the Mass" ', and even the paintings on the walls of the church often had little to do with the Bible or related its stories only in a distorted form [31]. Many parish clergy were poorly paid stipendiaries and appallingly ignorant: some could not even sing the Mass, and scores, it was proved, could not tell who was the author of the Lord's Prayer or where it was to be found. Ignorance was not confined to the lower clergy: when Louis de Beaumont became bishop of Durham in 1316 he could neither understand Latin nor pronounce it. At his consecration he stumbled at length over his formal profession of faith, and finally had to give it up, remarking in French 'Let that be taken as read'. Many rectors were absentee pluralists, who served as clerks or agents for the king, a bishop, an abbot, or some lay magnate. Some appointed a salaried curate in their stead, but others neglected their duties and the Mass went unsaid for long periods; churches and rectory houses fell into disrepair; some priests engaged in common trade and usury, took to poaching and frequenting taverns, while charges of immorality against the clergy were commonplace [32].

There were no doubt many devout and high-principled clergy, but it is not surprising that the Church, as a whole, generally fell short of Christian ideals and failed to uphold truth and justice. Though supposedly treating all men as equal, Church courts allowed men of rank to escape due punishment: in Kent in 1292, for example, a distinguished offender, Sir Thomas de Marynes, was allowed to get away with a fine, as 'it was not seemly for a knight to do public penance' [33]. The priest was unlikely to stand between the peasant and his lord when it was the lord who often possessed the right of presenting the priest to his living, and who might give him support in the quest for preferment. The lord, or his ancestors, had often built the church in the first place, and took a leading part in its maintenance. The rector's tithes and glebe brought him into direct conflict with the peasants of the parish. Tithes, taken in kind, were in effect a comprehensive and pitiless tax on the farmer which, in Coulton's words, extended to 'even the down of his goose', and remained a constant source of rural grievance through the centuries. The parson's glebe, too, especially when scattered among other villagers' lands in the common fields, drew him into the daily annoyances and quarrels intrinsic in communal agriculture. The priest competed with the peasant in disposing of his surplus produce, sought an advantage over him, perhaps, in gaining an additional assart or a favoured close, and might have to appear before the manorial court to answer some degrading complaint of encroachment, neglect, or similar malpractice. All in all, the private interests of the priest were likely to be much closer to those of the lord than to those of his flock: he belonged, as Maitland said, to the manorial aristocracy [34].

Thus, early in the Middle Ages appeared the alliance between landlord and parson which was to endure over the succeeding centuries: an unequal alliance, no doubt, and one frequently producing its own frictions and conflicts; but, in general, the common persisting concern in property, in the

Church, and in the maintenance of good order in the village, prevailed over the ephemeral ill-will of individual, parochial disputes. Normally, squire and parson presented a united front against the propertyless classes in the pursuit of shared objectives. The clergy, in fact, were recruited from the families of gentry and free tenants. But at first the parson was very much subordinate to the squire. It was the squire who filled the influential local offices, and for long only he possessed the leisure, the standing and the education to do so. Both squire and parson were often enough the clients of more powerful lords, lay and ecclesiastical, but at the end of the Middle Ages, with the might of the nobility crumbling and the Church brought more firmly under secular control, the lesser local lords, the gentry, emerged as a significant power in the national as well as the local scene. It is with this enlarged role of the gentry, their part in the political, economic and social life of the country in the centuries of their consequence, that the subsequent chapters are concerned.

3 The rise and decline of the gentry

As we saw in the previous chapter, the origins of the political and administrative power wielded by the gentry were to be found in their assumption in the later Middle Ages of both the county representation in Parliament and the judicial and administrative functions of the justice of the peace. Thus, it has been remarked, the gentry in their counties 'provided the fulcrum for administrative action'. Their provincial strength lay not only in their capacity for undertaking the responsibilities of the commission of the peace but also in their appointment to such posts as captains of royal castles, vice-admirals, comptrollers, escheators and bailiffs of honors[1]. As early as the thirteenth century the knights and other men of similar standing were already the mainstay of local administration. As the major tenants and allies of the great landowners, and as proprietors in their own right, they provided the main link between the central authority and local affairs, and they acted for the Crown in the role of sheriffs, coroners, and members of Crown commissions.

Very early there developed a group of leading gentry who sought promotion and wealth through attendance at court and in Parliament, or who reached eminence through military offices – men who returned to their estates only when too old to defend castles and lead troops. The famous Sir John Fastolf was a case in point. Rather less prominent, forming a kind of second tier, were those county gentry who filled the local offices and were men of importance in a more restricted sphere. Below these came the rank and file of more modest country gentlemen. They lacked the wealth and connections to pursue distinguished political or military careers, or perhaps they preferred a quiet life in the country to the constant struggle for place and the alarms and excursions of war. They were satisfied with some modest local office, or engrossed themselves with their estates and the affairs of the neighbourhood.

The eventual result of the civil strife of the fifteenth century, we have seen, was to advance the political and administrative importance of the leading gentry. The great barons, the once powerful provincial warlords, destroyed themselves and impoverished their successors by their search for power and the effort of supporting great bodies of retainers. Their military strength and their provincial influence were whittled away by the Tudor monarchs, who relied more on men of middling or even humble rank as counsellors and administrators. At the same time the local role of the gentry was magnified as the justices of the peace became the key figures in county administration, and as the central government extended the scope of its social and economic legislation. The resident landowners of the counties emerged as the only figures with the necessary local knowledge, suitable education and leisure to undertake the role of a permanent unpaid bureaucracy. The nobility, tamed and shorn of much of their old power, ceased to be the great magnates around whom a client gentry clustered. True the old pomp and magnificence continued, castles were replaced by great mansions, hospitality often remained lavish, and the gentry still rode in the great lord's train. But the pageantry became mere display and ceremonial, and no longer symbolised the true relationship between the lord and his followers. It was still worth while for ambitious families to adopt a subservient posture. There was too much to be gained from estate and household appointments, from favours for younger sons, and all the minor benefits of patronage, for the old connection to be dropped. Nevertheless, the gentry as a whole felt, and showed, a greater degree of independence. Traditional personal loyalties gave way to closer identification with the county community of gentry, especially as the leading gentry families became more involved in the running of their county and concerned with its representation in the Commons. The spread of secular education and higher standards of learning among the gentry also helped to increase their competence and self-confidence. The Commons itself had long been rising in status, and its power increased further as the war expenditures of Henry VIII and Elizabeth, together with the inflation of the sixteenth century, eroded the financial independence of the Crown and made it more reliant on the Commons for supply. These developments directed attention away from the old provincial centres of power and towards the centre, towards Parliament, its relations with the monarch, and towards London as the capital and centre of government.

To some extent the patronage of the Crown, greatly expanded by the Tudors, replaced that of the great lord. In the sixteenth century there were grants of former monastic lands or Crown estates and offices to be obtained through ministerial or royal favour. Men of humble origins could well make their way to wealth through the royal household, if they had the requisite talent and could attract the right attention. Sir John Cheke, Sir Thomas Smith, and even William Cecil, built political careers on their ability in academic spheres. Similarly, John Harington, father of the better-known Sir John, the writer and poet, attracted the attention of Henry VIII – and hence an heiress to a Somerset estate – through his admission to the Chapel Royal where he studied with Thomas Tallis [2].

An age of opportunity

The prizes of the age were not limited to royal service or success in political and administrative spheres. Many gentry were able to advance their families by seizing the opportunities offered by an expanding economy. In the sixteenth century population and trade again began to grow rapidly after a century or more of decline, stagnation and slow recovery. The first half of the sixteenth century was marked by an extraordinary growth of the trade in woollen cloth, England's chief export. As a result, the manufacture of cloth necessarily expanded, production of wool increased and suitable lands were enclosed to make sheep-walks. The cloth trade, however, failed to keep up its momentum in the second half of the century, and there were signs of recession in the cloth industry. Nevertheless, it appears that the population continued to grow, if erratically; and prices, which had begun a marked upward trend in the earlier sixteenth century, continued to advance, the later inflation affecting especially wheat, meat and timber, while earlier the rise was more prominent in wool. Between the second half of the fifteenth century and the 1640s, indeed, the price of wool rose fourfold, timber more than fivefold, agricultural produce in general over sixfold, and some products, cattle, sheep and grain, more than sevenfold.

Clearly, those landowners and farmers who were in a position to take advantage of the market trends stood to make large profits. The first to benefit were the occupiers of land with large marketable surpluses of wool, timber, grain and cattle. As we have seen, in the depressed conditions of the fourteenth and fifteenth centuries many of the larger landowners had retired from direct agricultural production and had leased out their demesnes to copyholders and tenant farmers, and so become rentiers. The lessees of the demesnes were able to obtain their farms on very favourable terms, and when market conditions improved they were in the happy position of obtaining a higher return for their produce, while their rents, often fixed in advance for long periods, remained low. Many of these lessees were themselves men of substance, as prudent landlords saw to it that as far as possible their demesnes were let out to reputable tenants from well-to-do and well-established families. For example, of the lessees taking up the lands of the see of Canterbury between 1502 and 1532 a third were described as gentlemen, a half were yeomen, and only the remainder (apart from a few London merchants) were mere husbandmen [3]. Some of the yeomen leasing these lands, for instance the Knatchbulls, were to become important Kentish gentry in due course. Indeed, gentry families throughout the country could see their rise in fortunes beginning with some yeoman ancestor of the fifteenth or sixteenth century, or even earlier. The Cholwich family, whose members supplied a sheriff of Devon and a recorder of Exeter in the eighteenth century, could trace their origins back to a remote medieval farmstead on the edge of Dartmoor [4]. The 'great rebuilding' of gentry and yeomen's houses between 1575 and 1625, when additional rooms, internal staircases and other improvements were added to medieval structures, is clear evidence of the new wealth to be found among the farmers. More country house building, it is said, was undertaken in this than in any other comparable period.

If the tenants and yeomen prospered earliest, the landlords were not far behind. There were several ways in which they could obtain a higher revenue from their lands. First, they might revise the terms under which their property was leased, that is they might raise rents and entry fines, and turn long-term leases into shorter terms or annual agreements, when the land would be relet at whatever rent it would bear. The rent then became a rack-rent, one subject to frequent stretching, though the rent could go down as well as up, depending on the experience of harvests and prices. From the 1520s, however, the general trend of rents was certainly upwards. At the same time as revising tenures the landlord might take the opportunity to enclose open fields and throw small farms together, with the object of letting them out as large units to capitalist farmers producing on a big scale for the market, or even to farm himself. Despite contemporary complaints about the consequences of these changes – and certainly many thousands of small farmers and cottagers were displaced – enclosure did not necessarily have adverse effects on the rural population, especially where it led to improved cultivation through systematic alternation of grass and arable crops. On the contrary: as Sir John Brudenell argued when disputing with the rector the enclosure of Marston, enclosed land would not see wheat replaced by weeds and would be 'noe whit farther from tillage than in common fields'. Even when pasture did replace tillage and farms were engrossed, there was not necessarily a depopulation of the countryside. In some areas expanding industrial employment absorbed those displaced from farming. But in the lowlands of the northeast, Dr Kerridge tells us, the effects were more drastic. Sir Thomas Gray expelled 340 people from Newnham in one day; Robert Delavale threw all the land of Hartley into one great farm which was cultivated by a mere three teams in place of the previous fifteen; William Carr brought all the farms but one at Hetton into his own; and Edward Adams engrossed nearly half the farms at Little Houghton [5].

The possibilities for increasing rents depended greatly on the nature of the existing tenures. If the leases were for periods of years, or for three lives (i.e. for as long as three persons named in the lease should live), then they would eventually fall in and the farms would come into the landlord's hands. In many cases, however, the occupiers were copyholders of inheritance, that is perpetual tenants, and if the entry fines and rents payable by such tenants were fixed in amount, with no loophole for revision of the terms, then there was little or nothing the landlord could do to change matters. Even where copyholders of inheritance were subject to arbitrary fines, the revised fines levied by the landlord had to be 'reasonable' or compatible with custom, and copyholders could appeal to the courts against 'unreasonable' actions of the lords which cheated the heir of his inheritance [6]. Where the rents could be periodically revised, the tenant gained only during the period of the lease in which the rise in prices increased the margin between his income and his outgoings; but where the terms of the lease were fixed and the rents could not be revised, then all the advantage of the rising prices went to the tenant and none to the landlord. However, we do not have any precise idea of how much of the farmland was held under rigidly fixed terms by copyholders of inheritance; in some areas this form of tenure was commonplace, it is true, but in others it was uncommon or unknown. It is worth pointing out that not all the advantage of long periods of tenure at low rents went to the farmers: crown lands and the lands of religious houses were often leased to landlords on favourable terms, and they often sublet these lands to the farmers at higher rents, pocketing the difference themselves.

The extent to which a landlord could change the terms of tenure and raise his rents was also governed in practice by what tenants were prepared to pay. Clearly the landlord who wished to have his farms occupied by tenants had to offer such terms as the tenants felt enabled them to farm the land with profit. This point was well made in 1655 by Sir George Sondes, an east Kent landlord, when he replied to the charge of being a hard landlord:

It is said I am a hard landlord, and raise my rents. I confess as tenants' leases expired, I took no fines to renew, as my ancestors used to do, but let out my farms at improved rents, both the tenants and myself better liking of it. But I do not know that I let a farm to any tenant for more than I thought (and I had some little skill) it was really and honestly worth, nor for more than (had I been to have taken a farm) I would have given for it myself. Nor have I any tenant (though the times be now very bad) who shall say, sir, my farm is too dear, I cannot live upon it at the rent; if he leave it to me but as good as it was when he took it, I will take it again. Nay, notwithstanding corn is so cheap, I give any tenant I have liberty to leave his farm, and I will take it. I never did, or ever will, force any tenant to keep his farm. Neither in all this time hath any tenant come to me to take his farm again. Some indeed I would have ousted of their farms (being none of the best tenants), but could not persuade them. I never arrested or imprisoned any tenant for his rent, nor willingly used any severe course, if I could indifferently be satisfied any other way. I have scarce demanded my rents of late because of the cheapness of corn, but have made all the shifts I could to get money to serve my occasions, and spared my tenants, that they might not be forced to put off their corn at too mean rates. If these be the signs of a hard landlord, then I am one [7].

Of course the landlord, if he were able to take the farms into his own hands, did not have to renew his leases at all. He might prefer to keep the land in hand and farm it himself, and in the period of rapidly rising agricultural prices in the later sixteenth century there might be much more money to be made out of farming the demesne directly than from letting it out to tenants. We know that in East Anglia the profits from sheepfarming rose over threefold between the 1520s and the 1630s, and in Northamptonshire the Spencers of Althorp provide a good example of a family who rose in the world through their success as flock-masters [8]. Some landlords adjusted their policy according to changing circumstances, now farming more of their land, now leasing it out again. But in general there was a marked revival of demesne farming, and many landowners who assumed the role of agricultural capitalist did very well out of it. Gentlemen, commented Thomas Wilson, 'become good husbandes and know as well how to improve their lands to the uttermost as the farmer or country-man, so that they take their farmes into their handes as the leases expire, and either till themselves or else lett them out to those who will give most'.

The rise in prices also made it worth while to spend money on enclosing uncultivated land, such as forests, hill pastures, marshes and moors, in order to bring more land into cultivation. Large areas were deforested, drained and ploughed up in this period, especially in the Norfolk heathlands, the Lancashire plain, and – the outstanding example – the draining of the Great Level of the Fens, a vast morass which stretched through six counties from Lincolnshire to Cambridge. Lastly, much profit could be made from exploiting the resources of timber, stone, and minerals to be found on many estates. Timber became very profitable with the growing demand for wood for building purposes and for industrial uses, especially the making of charcoal in the expanding iron industry. The Pelhams of Laughton, Sussex, enclosed common land to increase their supply of timber. Bricks and stone, likewise, were in demand for the larger, more elaborate houses now in favour. Many of the growing industries of the period, brick-making, glass, lime-burning, salt-making and brewing, for example, were using coal for fuel, and coal was replacing wood in domestic hearths. Sir John Newdigate of Griffin in Warwickshire obtained a return of 8 per cent from his coal mine [9]. The Bugge family of Nottingham founded their fortune on coal mining; a change of name to the more aristocratic Willoughby, and eventually the building of a fussy Italianate mansion in

Wollaton Park, near Nottingham, signalled the arrival of the Bugges into the ranks of the gentry. Other minerals, iron ore, lead, copper, and tin, and the conversion of these into useful commodities, were also means to fame and fortune. In Derbyshire, for example, especially in the Peak district, the gentry were very much involved in lead-mining, as well as in coal and iron.

A good example of the enterprising industrialist squire of the period is provided by John Weld of Willey. Inheriting considerable wealth from his father, a member of the London Haberdashers' Company, Weld bought up in 1615 the Willey estate of the impoverished Lacon family, and subsequently acquired other lands in an area a few miles northwest of Bridgnorth in Shropshire. Willey itself had not only 'one fair house built most part with brick with all offices fit for the habitation . . . of a knight', but also valuable woods, a coal mine, deposits of ironstone, two mills and a forge and furnace. Others of Weld's newly acquired lands were also rich in coal and iron, and he set about replacing copyhold tenures by leases in which the mineral rights were reserved to himself as lord of the manor. He envisaged the introduction of water meadows, and the enclosure of commons and waste lands, but he was not interested in farming the land himself. His prime object was to exploit the mineral and industrial potential of his properties, especially the forge and the blast furnace which he rebuilt at a cost of £500. His estate would be well placed, he foresaw, if 'it may fall out iron may hereafter be made with pit-coal; then my coal will stand inside for my furnace and coals may be brought to my furnace by wagons, either from a place where coal breaks out on the other side of the hill, or from a place in the new Park . . . where a very firm coal breaks out'. It was not very many years before John Weld's business acumen gave him a high place in county society: in 1641 he became high sheriff, and in the following year he was knighted. Though a royalist his family comfortably survived the penalties of being on the losing side in the Civil War [10].

Thus, by revising tenancies, farming their demesnes, enclosing waste lands, by manufacturing, and by selling timber and minerals, many families revolutionised their income and mounted several rungs up the social ladder. The conditions of the age, and their consequences, did not go unnoticed, and as one ballad-writer had it

> Young landlords when to age they come,
> Their rents they will be racking,
> The tenant must give a golden sum,
> Or else he is turned packing,
> Great fines and double rent beside.

The dissolution of the monasteries and the weakening of the Crown

A further great factor in the rise of landed incomes and emergence of new families was the increased availability of land for exploitation. It is estimated that in the fifteenth century as much as a quarter or more of the country was in the hands of the Church and the Crown, the great bulk of this land being the estates of the bishops and monasteries. In 1536 and the following four years the monasteries were dissolved and ownership of their properties was assumed by the Crown. Immediately, the Crown began to sell off the former monastic lands, but only slowly at first. Then, between 1542 and 1547, under the financial pressures of war, some two-thirds of the lands were alienated by the Crown; by 1558 as much as three-quarters had gone. Some of the lands were presented as gifts or sold on very favourable terms to courtiers and statesmen, such as Suffolk, Cromwell and Audley, but the amount disposed of in this way was limited. The major part of the properties was sold in the normal way and at the accepted fair market price of twenty years' purchase.

In any one area the possibilities of acquiring this land were determined by the local extent of former monastic estates, but the general effect was to increase activity in the land market by swelling enormously the amount of property available for purchase. Presumably, too, the increased supply kept land prices lower than might have been the case in a more restricted market. In fact, the price of monastic lands remained fairly steady, even in the peak period of sales in the mid-1540s. Increased activity in the land market meant increased social mobility: a great opportunity was provided for rising men seeking to expand their estates, and for newcomers, mainly professional men and holders of government offices, who wished to establish themselves in the countryside. Those properties offering good sites for country residences, with former monastic buildings offering a convenient supply of building materials – such as the former granges and bartons – were eagerly seized upon.

Local studies, such as that of Dr R. B. Smith in the West Riding, suggest that after those closest to the administration – the courtiers and people connected with the Court of Augmentations – had made their choice, most of the purchasers were new rising men, younger sons of landowners, lawyers, merchants and successful farmers [11]. Professor Simpson has told us of Sir Nicholas Bacon, son of a Suffolk yeoman, who climbed to wealth by means of the law and office and finally rose to be Lord Keeper. Through his official position he had a direct concern with the disposal of monastic lands. He was able, no doubt, to take his pick, and with the money made in his official capacity and from the land market he built Redgrave Hall, and subsequently the first house to grace Gorhambury [12]. Many of the gentry of Lincolnshire, as elsewhere, served as stewards, bailiffs, and auditors of monastic estates before the Dissolution. The estates were often scattered in character, and so it was convenient for a local landowner to act as steward in return for a fee when he could easily oversee the monastic property that lay alongside his own. The fall of the monasteries gave such men a new opportunity of extending and consolidating their own estates by purchases of monastic lands, and among the former monastic administrators in Lincolnshire who were able to do this were the Tyrrwhits and the Heneages.

Members of these families, together with their neighbours the Ayscoughs, Maddisons, Missendens, and others, were involved in the Lincolnshire rebellion of October 1536, when the men of Louth rose in protest against the threat to their church and its treasures. 'Go ye and follow the crosses,' one of them urged, 'for if they be taken from us, we are like to follow them no more.' A party of the local gentry, meeting near Caistor, were captured by the rebels and forced to agree to present their demands to the king. But the gentry knew, or soon learned, which way the matter would end, and in preservation of their lives and lands all ended up on the king's side. Some, however, like Sir Christopher

Ayscough, remained under a cloud, and were discriminated against in the matter of disposing of monastic properties; while others, like the Tyrrwhits, Heneages, and Skipworths, who had more influence at court or were able to persuade the government that they were not implicated in the rebellion, managed to do well out of the business [13]. A similar rebellion broke out in Yorkshire at the same time, influenced by a like concern over the growth of the royal power (as expressed in the Statute of Uses) and the threat to the Church. It was led by Robert Aske, a combination of country gentleman and London lawyer, and ended less happily. Aske gathered the malcontents at his seat at Wighton Hall, and went on to occupy Hull. The rebels were in a strong position but made the mistake of believing in the king's apparent willingness to discuss their demands, and so gave him time to organise his forces and crush the revolt. A number of rebels were executed, and Aske himself was hung in chains at York.

In Norfolk the Crown's gifts of lands were confined to those prominent for their public or personal services, or who had incurred private expenditure in transacting government business. Thus the recipients of gifts included the Duke of Norfolk, who in return for his part in suppressing the Pilgrimage of Grace gained monastic properties worth £720 a year. Others in this category included Thomas Cromwell, Sir Thomas Gresham the London merchant, Sir William Butts the king's physician, and Sir John Spelman, who served at the trials of More and Fisher, as well as some eminent military men. Most of the purchasers of Norfolk monastic estates were gentry already prominent in the county, such as the Windhams of Felbrigg and the Townshends of Raynham, but there were also various newcomers. The latter included Robert Kett (of Kett's rebellion), and John Caius of Norwich, a distinguished physician who re-founded Gonville Hall at Cambridge as Gonville and Caius College. Lawyers who bought estates included the Recorder of Norwich, and there were citizens of Lynn and Norwich such as William Myngay, alderman of Norwich, who was sheriff in 1554 and mayor in 1561 [14].

Some of the monastic lands, but probably not many, were bought speculatively, to be sold again in the hope of making a profit; sometimes a property passed through several hands before coming to rest under a permanent owner. The picture is confused because some buyers made their purchases through agents, and this accounted for a proportion of the properties that were rapidly resold. The extent of speculation and the making of windfall gains from purchases and sales of monastic lands have been exaggerated, especially since most of the lands were put on sale at prices that offered little scope for immediate profit. A further curb on speculation was the existence on many monastic estates of long leaseholders whose terms of tenure provided no room for rapid revision of rents. In general, rents rose no faster on monastic lands than on those which had long been in lay hands. The greatest advantage from the sales of monastic properties was gained, first, by those purchasers who were prepared to hold the lands until leases expired and the rising market made it profitable to sell, and second, by the sitting tenants who were able to buy at moderate prices the lands they already occupied. The latter had frequently been in occupation since long before the Dissolution, for the probable course of events had been foreseen from the late 1520s when the monastic landlords, in anticipation, had begun to sell off their timber and offer long leases of their lands to neighbouring gentry and yeomen.

Reliable national estimates of the proportion of monastic lands obtained by the gentry are not available, but there is little doubt that the largest share came into their hands. Many of the former Church properties acquired by the nobility were resold to the gentry in the late sixteenth century, at a time when the latter were actively buying up also the lands of impoverished leaseholders and small copyholders. In Norfolk the gentry's share of the 1,527 manors in the county was increased from 977 to 1,094 by 1545; and by 1565 this figure had risen further to 1,181. At the later date the Crown had 67 manors in the county, the nobility 159, the Church 91, and colleges, hospitals and other institutions 30 [15]. The gentry's preponderance of manors in the county, though only a rough guide to their share of the land, thus rose to over three-quarters of the whole. It appears that relatively little monastic land went into the creation of new large estates. One of the exceptions was the empire carved out in central Essex by Sir William Petre in the reign of Henry VIII. A member of an old Devon family, Sir William was one of the commissioners appointed to examine monastic property in Essex: naturally he was in an excellent position to secure the choicest bargains for himself, and this he did with leases of the lands of Barking and Waltham Abbeys.

The existing gentry who bought did so mainly because they were the sitting tenants, or because the properties were particularly attractive to them as investments, or perhaps were adjacent to their existing lands and helped to round out their estates. It would be wrong to suppose that very many gentry estates were built up largely or entirely by purchases of monastic lands: other properties were also on the market and might be more attractive in situation and price. The conditions of purchase, too, might make monastic lands less desirable than private estates. Lands sold by the Crown were liable to payment of a reserved rent amounting to a tenth of the total annual value, and the lands were not freehold but held by knight service, and so subject to wardship (where the Crown was entitled to the revenues of the estate while in the hands of a minor). The market in private estates was active at this time because legal obstacles to the free disposal of land had been reduced: the feudal restrictions on estates had been loosened in the later Middle Ages, and by the Statute of Wills of 1540 all feudal tenants were permitted to devise two-thirds of their land by will. Landowners could now provide directly for younger children and other dependants but they had not yet come to tie up their estates in the restrictive coils of the strict settlement as it was developed after the Civil Wars. The monastic sales, therefore, added to and supplemented an existing land market; they did not create it, neither did they replace it.

Sales of land by the Crown continued erratically under Elizabeth I as severe financial needs made themselves felt from time to time. The total value of land sold in her reign was considerable: over £813,000; and James I by 1609 had disposed of a further £400,000 through lavish grants. While shrewdness in purchases, foresight in the taking of long leases, the opportunity of enclosing waste lands and forests and success in obtaining rewards of grants and beneficial leases from the Crown played a prominent part in the fortunes of the gentry, these were only some of the factors operating at this time. The majority of the new families seem to have risen through trade, industry or the law. Among the Elizabethan country gentry holding county offices in Sussex the flourishing families owed much of their success to marriage, legal practice, trade, and in particular the iron industry. The fortunes of the declining families were influenced by failure of male heirs, involvement in excessive litigation, and adherence to the Catholic faith. Two families were ruined by debts accumulated in consequence of their holding of crown offices [16].

Clearly a wide variety of factors other than success in the land market and estate exploitation might influence family fortunes. Some factors operated in both directions: profits made out of the law might be largely at the expense of other families who provided legal business and the fees, especially in tangled and protracted disputes over succession and rights over property. The Treshams of Northamptonshire were a prominent example of a family who hastened to destruction by pursuing an extravagant career of hospitality and costly litigation. The holding of Crown offices and attendance at court might produce a great income from salaries and profits of office, and offer a path to valuable sinecures and grants of Crown lands; equally, in return for what was often a meagre salary, office burdened its holder with numerous expenses, led him into rash speculation and debt, and kept him away from the care of his own property. No doubt there were spectacular profits to be made out of office. In the years 1540 to 1547 Sir Ralph Sadler received as much as £600 a year from the fees and favours offered him by seekers after Crown patronage, and his total annual income from office averaged £2,600, an enormous sum by contemporary standards. However he was one of the fortunate few; the majority were much less successful. Of 240 officeholders between 1625 and 1642, under forty acquired land worth more than £1,000 per annum. Office was at best a lottery where the prizes were great for the lucky few, the losses sometimes fatal to the disappointed many [17]. Perhaps the Marquis of Argyle had the best word on this subject. The court, he said, is 'a place difficult of access, shut up with rocks, shallows, and sands, and not an adventurer in twenty comes off a saver. Besides 'tis a place of a most uncertain air, full of damps and exhalations, spread with clouds and overcast, and sometimes again scorching hot, in the sudden rise and depression of favourites' [18]. Some factors, too, appear to have varied locally. For example, while recusancy was found to be an important element in economic decline in Sussex, it was apparently not so in Yorkshire.

The sixteenth and seventeenth centuries formed an age of great opportunities for those who had the means, enterprise, and shrewdness to benefit from them. It was a period when the cautious, conservative and unlucky were more likely to falter and be replaced by the numerous upstarts. Overall, the net effect was that the gentry increased their share of the land: indeed they may have doubled it to something approaching a half of the total. The great landlords did less well: they may have slightly increased their total share but not much more. The yeoman freeholders, despite contemporary lamentations of their decay, probably increased their share significantly. Numbers of yeomen were able to rise to the status of gentry. Thomas Wilson claimed to know

> many yeomen in divers Provinces in England which are able yearly to despend betwixt 3 or 5 hundred pounds yearly by theire hounds and horses and some twise and some thrise as much; but my younge masters the sonnes of such, not contented with their states of their fathers to be counted yeomen and called John and Robert, but must skipp into his velvet breeches and silken doublett and, getting to be admitted into some Inn of Court at Chancery, must ever after thinke skorne to be called any other than gentleman.

The great losers in these changes were the Church and the Crown, whose combined share fell from over a quarter to probably under a tenth. The significance of these major shifts in the distribution of landed property was that they accompanied and reinforced the changing situation of the nobility and the government relative to the gentry. The military power of the nobles had declined as their estates were broken up, while the personal loyalty of client gentry and tenantry was weakened by the landlords' absenteeism and the move towards a more strictly economic relationship in rents and tenures. The great lords' attempts to maintain their status and traditional way of life led to financial difficulties, sales of land, and further loss of local influence. Personal loyalties were strained still further when they eventually turned to screwing up rents in order to restore their financial position. Again, as constitutional and religious issues became more deeply felt and urgent, doubts grew round the question of the great lords' attitudes and objectives. The interests of the gentry shifted more towards the self-government of their county through the 'little parliament' of quarter sessions, and towards the voicing of grievances in the great Parliament at Westminster. The greatly improved education given to the sons of the propertied classes in grammar schools, universities, and inns of court fitted them to take a more influential and responsible role at the time when the powers of both justices and members of Parliament were steadily extending. The numbers of justices rose to cope with their enlarged responsibilities, and the preponderant gentry element in the expanded House of Commons became even more dominant.

As the personal attachment of the gentry moved away from the enfeebled leaders of the aristocracy it tended instead to gather round the charismatic figure of a great monarch, like Henry VIII or Elizabeth. At the same time the Commons was developing into a more powerful body where the actions of the Crown in religion, taxation and foreign policy could be debated and challenged. The position of the Crown *vis-à-vis* the Commons was weakened by its failure to secure a sound financial base. The enormous potential income of the monastic estates was dribbled away as sales were made to finance Henry's military adventures, and Elizabeth in turn constantly put off grappling with unpleasant but much-needed fiscal reform. When the Stuarts arrived on the scene it was too late to restore the Crown's financial independence without bringing on a major political crisis, and the clumsy financial expedients employed resulted in alienating much of the respect and affection that the Tudors had commanded from their subjects. The Commons, with its claim to control over taxation and legislation, developed a 'country' opposition to the extravagance of the court, its supposed popish tendencies which offended the growing Puritan sentiments of the propertied classes, and the arbitrary interference of the Crown in taxation, local affairs and Church matters. The prestige of the monarchy declined when the authority and magnetism of the great Tudors gave way to the more modest talents of the early Stuarts. The personal characteristics of James I and Charles I were not such as to make for much affection or compromise, and the disenchantment of the 'country' with the 'court' was intensified by the government's shifts and contrivances, and by the reactionary nature of the policies recklessly pressed forward by Laud and Strafford.

The fault lay not entirely with the Stuarts: they inherited a creaking political structure, resting precariously on an unpaid voluntary bureaucracy, a deficient and archaic system of Crown revenues and, with no standing army, an absence of the permanent military strength needed to enforce unpopular policies [19].

The great debate: the rise of the gentry

The gradual rise of the gentry to independent political power in the course of the sixteenth and early decades of the seventeenth centuries thus paralleled their increased control of the country's economic resources. The portentous change in the distribution of land in favour of the gentry and away from the Church and the Crown, together with the reduced relative position of the great landlords, formed the background to the gentry's greater control over local affairs, their newly acquired freedom of initiative, and their growing self-confidence in asserting the claims of the 'country' against the prerogative of the financially weakened Crown. But was their increased economic strength an essential factor in their enhanced political power, and if so, how were the two related? These questions have formed the nub of what is probably the most actively debated and bitterly contested historical controversy of the past quarter-century. The debate began in 1953 when Professor H. R. Trevor-Roper published his monograph on *The Gentry 1540–1640* [20]. This was a detailed attack on the thesis put forward by R. H. Tawney in his famous article of 1941, 'The rise of the Gentry' [21]. Tawney had suggested that in the breakdown of the personal rule of Charles I and the ensuing Civil War, prior shifts in the balance of landownership played a significant part. In the century before 1640, Tawney argued, a new class of gentry, 'bourgeois' in their attitudes towards the exploitation of land, had risen through close attention to the possibilities of revision of rentals, profits from demesne farming, enclosures of wastes and exploitation of estate resources. As they rose, so the more conservative landlords, particularly the nobility, declined. The latter went downhill through their inertia and their respect for social convention: they failed to show that entrepreneurial spirit which recognised the existing opportunities of estate exploitation, and they clung to a traditional way of life of great establishments, impressive bodies of servants and retainers and lavish hospitality, which proved crippling in the age of the price revolution. The débâcle of the 1640s represented an adjustment of the political structure to the realities of the changed balance in the distribution of property. That such a change involved a change in the balance of political power was the doctrine of a number of contemporary philosophers, and James Harrington's famous phrase summed up its effect: 'A Monarchy devested of its Nobility has no refuge under Heaven but an Army. Wherefore the dissolution of this Government caus'd the War, not the War the dissolution of the Government.'

The theory of the balance, thus expressed, and the changes in the distribution of property that Tawney supposed gave the theory its concrete meaning, were both challenged by Trevor-Roper. In fact, he argued, 'power does not necessarily follow property: property – as the economic rise of the office-holder shows – often follows power'. Further, 'the gentry did not rise as a class, nor at the expense of the aristocracy, nor on the profits of agriculture'. Some landowners did suffer from the squeeze imposed on traditional standards of consumption by the rise in prices, but these were the 'mere gentry', the small and middling owners whose sole source of income came from estates of severely limited resources. The men who rose did so not primarily through land, but through the profits of the growing number of government offices, through favour at court, and through the law. Thus arose the division between 'the court' and 'the country', the prospering peers and gentry who enjoyed the spoils of office and luxuriated amid the splendours of the royal circle, and the impoverished backwoods squires, hastening towards economic collapse and social extinction. It was the latter, the mere gentry, who formed the radical core of the great rebellion: it was they, as the Independents, who 'executed the King, abolished the House of Lords, purged and repurged the City, abolished wardships and purveyance, abolished the centralised Church and preserved from Church and peasantry alike their cherished tithes' [22].

The dissatisfaction of the mere gentry was not aimed at the monarchy itself, Professor Trevor-Roper added subsequently. It was aroused by 'the vast, oppressive, ever-extending apparatus of parasitic bureaucracy which had grown up around the throne and above the economy of England'. It was, he argued in a controversial article, part of a 'general crisis' of the seventeenth century, of a general European attack on Renaissance courts and their extravagance and inefficiency. The attack was not necessarily irresistible: on the continent it was warded off. But in England under the Stuarts there was

a fatal lack of political skill: instead of the genius of Richelieu, the suppleness of Mazarin, there was the irresponsibility of Buckingham, the violence of Strafford, the undeviating universal pedantry of Laud. In England, therefore, the storm of the mid-century, which blew throughout Europe, struck the most brittle, most overgrown, most rigid court of all and brought it violently down. . . . Had James I or Charles I had the intelligence of Queen Elizabeth or the docility of Louis XIII, the English *Ancien Régime* might have adapted itself to the new circumstances as peacefully in the seventeenth century as it would in the nineteenth. It was because they had neither, because their court was never reformed, because they defended it, in its old form, to the last, because it remained, administratively and economically as well as aesthetically, the last Renaissance court in Europe, that it ran into ultimate disaster: that the rational reformers were swept aside, that more radical men came forward and mobilised yet more radical passions than even they could control, and that in the end, amid the sacking of palaces, the shivering of statues and stained-glass windows, the screech of saws in ruined organ-lofts, the last of the great Renaissance courts was mopped up, the royal aesthete was murdered, his splendid pictures were knocked down and sold, even the soaring gothic cathedrals were offered up for scrap [23].

The distinction drawn by Tawney between the declining aristocracy and the rising gentry was, according to Trevor-Roper, a false one. Both aristocracy and gentry, he argued, had the same manner of life, faced the same problems and, in particular, had to meet the same rise in the cost of living. The differences between them were merely differences of degree. The fundamental difference was between those families, whether aristocracy, gentry or of humbler origin, who succeeded in prospering through office, court and the law, and those excluded from these avenues to wealth by lack of education, opportunity or means, and so doomed to decline. Moreover the statistical underpinning which Tawney had relied on to support his thesis was shown to have fundamental flaws. His figures were those of the numbers of manors held by the two groups of landowners in seven English counties between 1561 and 1640. But as was demonstrated by J. P. Cooper [24], this basis for assessing rise and decline was open to the objections that manors were not uniform units of property but varied enormously in size, and more important, in the income produced; that sales of manors might be due solely to demographic accidents, the failure of male heirs and collateral descents of the property; and further, that many of the families included in the calculation owned manors outside the counties studied, so that the figures were in any case incomplete and misleading.

Tawney's argument was revived in a somewhat different and much more precise form by Professor Lawrence Stone. In his *Crisis of the Aristocracy* Stone argued that the incomes and property of the peerage did decline sharply in the middle and later sixteenth century, and that this decline was followed by a strong recovery in their financial position during the early seventeenth century owing to a combination of rising estate revenues and royal favours. This financial recovery, however, while it enabled the aristocracy to retain their way of life in its old magnificence, could not make good the decline in their position relative to that of the greater gentry. In wealth, possessions and influence the aristocracy had lost ground; and perhaps more important, as J. H. Hexter pointed out [25], they no longer commanded the military power that was once at their beck and call. In the fifteenth century the great lords could bring to the battlefield not only their own tenants but an array of lesser lords and their followers, who were bound to the magnate by ties of blood, interest, fees, and gratitude for past favours. By the early seventeenth century (and indeed earlier) the private retinues of armed men had disappeared, their place taken by the county trainbands under command of lords-lieutenant appointed by the Crown. As Raleigh commented, 'The Great Seal of England . . . will serve to affront the greatest lords in England that shall move against the King. The force, therefore, by which our Kings in former times were troubled is vanished away.' As for the train of lesser lords, it was still the case that around each magnate there circled a ring of major and petty satellites, but the ties between them had been weakened by the great lords' loss of military power and by the economic and social levelling-down they had suffered. The gentry had thus come to assert themselves and show a spirit of independence, and although they might find it wise to keep on good terms with the magnates, the ties between them were more tenuous and more easily broken than before.

The reduced power of the aristocracy, and the growth in stature of the greater gentry, boded ill for Crown and Church when loyalties were placed under mounting strain by the highly unpopular policies espoused by the early Stuarts. Too late, according to Professor Stone, the Crown realised the danger created by the reduced strength of the aristocracy and vainly tried to restore the situation. The increased power and independence of the gentry, and their control of Parliament put them into the political saddle; a long story of mis-judgment on the part of the monarchs, especially in their management of taxation and Crown revenues, the growing hostility in the country towards the extravagance, corruption, favouritism and general way of life of the court, and most important, the alienation by the Church of England, with the support of the Crown, of a large and influential section of the population, at last brought down Church and Crown together.

By 1640 the Court had contrived to arouse the same resentments as those of the Continent, but had failed to create a vested interest large enough to protect it against the legion of its enemies. Such were the consequences of half a century of ineptitude by three very different monarchs in the handling of the patronage system [26].

Some conclusions

In the greatly oversimplified terms employed here we are thus presented with three very different theses on the social changes occurring in the century before the Civil War, changes which according to their authors produced the preconditions for the Puritan Revolution. First, according to Tawney, the rise of a new class of gentry with 'bourgeois' attitudes towards the exploitation of land changed the balance of landed property and resulted in a consequential change in the balance of the constitution. Second, we have the declining mere gentry of Trevor-Roper, who, cut off from the refreshing draughts of office and court, stumbled and fell under the crushing burden of an inexorably rising cost of living, and finally brought their grievances, and their consequent radicalism, to the point of revolt and revolution. Thirdly, the relative decline in the wealth of the aristocracy, and their absolute decline in prestige, authority and military power, was in the view put forward by Stone the factor that left the Crown too weak to meet the consequences of its own recklessness.

Now, it is clear that each of the three theses depends for its plausibility on two basic conditions. The first of these is the assumption that it is possible to identify with reasonable accuracy the groups under discussion. Stone is probably on the strongest ground here because the numbers of the nobility and greater gentry were relatively small. There is the difficulty, however, that the nobility were not a fixed group but changed considerably in number and composition over the period discussed; further, the dividing line between the nobility and greater gentry was not clearcut, and the two overlapped considerably in income and influence. Professor Stone's vast detailed research leaves no doubt but that the peerage did decline in terms of landholding and income between 1559 and 1602, but it seems doubtful whether it can be argued that the great landowners as a whole declined similarly in that period. The problem turns on what proportion of the great owners was represented by the peers – and there are indications that they may have been in a minority – and whether the peers' experience was typical of the great owners as a whole, and over this there is disagreement.

Similar problems of identification apply both to Tawney's rising class of middling and small gentry, and to Trevor-Roper's declining mere gentry. That *some* gentry rose, and *some* declined, is indisputable, but neither protagonist produced firm evidence that would indicate the size of the respective groups, or showed that they were sufficiently homogeneous in character to make up a 'class' of gentry sharing the same outlook and the same aspirations. In the nature of the matter it is unlikely that sufficient sound statistical evidence can ever be produced to support conclusions drawn from the broad fact that some gentry rose and some declined; and in view of the wide range of purely local, as well as general, factors operating on the process of rise and decline, it would seem improbable that a broadly pervasive class-consciousness of common economic interests and political purposes could have developed among groups of people so artificially and variously constituted.

The second condition underlying the three theses is that it should be possible to connect the supposed key social change with the course of events of the Revolution itself. Tawney hardly attempted to do this, beyond suggesting that some contemporary commentators themselves connected the shift in the balance of property with the political upheavals. But whether Harrington and the other writers really understood what changes in the balance had occurred, whether their writings had any important influence, and whether indeed the theory of the balance has any validity at all, have all been questioned.

Stone's original argument was that the reduced power and status of the aristocracy was not itself a cause of the Revolution but an essential precondition which allowed the financial and religious policies of the Crown to become *effective* causes of Revolution. He was of course correct in emphasising the fact that by 1640 the Crown had alienated so many groups and interests that it could no longer command that general body of support and loyalty that formerly nipped dissension in the bud, or at least made open unrest unlikely to succeed and easy to overcome. But why was the weakened position of the nobility an *essential* factor in the collapse of the autocratic monarchy? Why is it impossible to suppose that the conservatism of the Tudors, Elizabeth's misjudgment in the matter of patronage, followed by the ineptitude and obstinacy of the early Stuarts, their espousing of unpopular causes, unwise financial expedients, and choice of unsuitable advisers, do not constitute an accumulation of error so collectively enormous as to explain, by itself, the events that followed? And why should it be assumed that the nobility as a social class, were the traditional and natural defenders of the monarchy? Why should they not share the same fear and dislike of arbitrary government as the gentry and not show the same degree of independence?

More recently Professor Stone has broadened his approach so as to include preconditions additional to that of the decline of the aristocracy, and 'to stress the interconnections of forces and events, to demonstrate the way everything affects, and is affected by, everything else'. He identifies four 'most salient elements' as being of prime importance: in brief, the failure of the Crown to acquire a standing army and a reliable paid bureaucracy; the decline in the aristocracy and the corresponding rise in wealth, status, education and political and administrative power of the gentry; the spread through large sections of the propertied and lower middle classes of Puritanism, and a consequential sense of the need for changes in Church and State; and the loss of confidence in the integrity of the holders of high offices in both Church and State. These preconditions, together with a number of secondary factors, did not, he adds, make the collapse of government inevitable, but did make almost essential some redistribution of political power and, very probably, reform of the Church too, whether by peaceful means or by force of arms [27].

As for the changed position of the nobility, it might be argued that both they and the greater gentry were inexorably caught up in the web of interests spun round the monarchy, through the ramifications of office, patronage, monopolies and the court. And Professor Aylmer has pointed out that although the numbers of officeholders were not large in relation to the total numbers of the gentry, in the 1630s they received as much as between £250,000 and £400,000 a year in fees and gratuities alone, and the total income drawn from offices was about equal to the whole of the revenue of the Crown [28]. Typical of the men whose rise in status and wealth depended entirely on success in office and the court was Francis Cottington, who began humbly enough as third son in a family of Somerset clothier-gentry [29]. Officeholders made up the court party which stood for the *status quo*, though when the breach between court and country became a threatening chasm some officeholders deserted the Crown. Again, was there in fact a connection between the declining gentry and the parliamentary cause? The geographical factors seem to be against it, for although there were declining gentry in every county no doubt, the fact was that the areas where it is believed the gentry were most wealthy and independent, in the south and east, rose for Parliament, while royalist support was strongest among the less well-off gentry of the economically backward, more highly agricultural north and west. Within counties, though, the taking of sides does not seem to have been much influenced by economic factors. In Yorkshire, for example, it has been found that 'resistance to the Crown . . . was far more closely associated with growing prosperity than with economic decline' [30]. Within regions the ports and industrial areas were predominantly for Parliament, though the top layer of wealthiest merchants tended to side with the king; one might suppose that the bulk of the mercantile and industrial classes had more in common with rising gentry than with those in an advanced stage of decay.

Professor Trevor-Roper saw the declining mere gentry as forming the radical backbone of the Revolution in the shape of the Independents. But, apart from the basic problem of identifying the Independents as a coherent group, there are the difficulties that by no means all the Independent members of Parliament were gentry, or were gentry in evident financial decline, and that in any case the vital steps in the breakdown of the old order, the legislation of 1640–41 and the outbreak of the war in 1642, occurred a considerable time before the emergence of the Independents as an influential group. Further, as Hexter and others have pointed out, the Trevor-Roper thesis (and, it may be said, the original Stone thesis also), by emphasising the supposedly central role of one group of landowners, neglected the part that was played by the great mass of middling gentry, neither markedly prosperous nor gravely declining, without whose support the Revolution must have fizzled out as the feeble action of an unrepresentative minority.

It was essential to the Trevor-Roper attack on Tawney, and to his analysis of a court party of wealthy officeholders opposed to a country party made up of declining gentry, that the court (including office, patronage and the law) was the only important road to wealth, and that the mere gentry were declining because they could draw only on the meagre income provided by their estates, and had no means of tapping the wealth of the court. In contrast to Tawney, Trevor-Roper held that the exploitation of land was in fact only a limited, exceptional means of rising in the world. This is a view that did not lack contemporary support. Sir John Oglander of Nunwell in the Isle of Wight was one of those 'mere gentry' who believed that land alone could never make one's fortune:

> it is impossible for a mere country gentleman ever to grow rich or raise his house. He must have some other vocation with his inheritance, as to be a courtier, lawyer, merchant or some other vocation. . . . By only following the plough he may keep his word and be upright, but he will never increase his fortune [31].

The country party, however, did not consist solely of declining, or even of lesser gentry: it included peers and others of substantial fortune and assured position. As Perez Zagorin has remarked, 'because the Court and Country were formations within the governing class no rigid barrier separated the two. It was possible for men connected with the Country to pass over to the Court'; moreover, 'what made the Country so formidable was that its adherents were pillars of society' [32]. It must also be noted that recent investigations of landed incomes indicate that revenues from land could be an important source of increased wealth: land revenues were moving upwards from the second quarter of the sixteenth century, rose considerably, in some cases more than doubled, between 1560 and 1590, and rose very sharply indeed, by much more than did prices, from about 1590 to the 1620s. The overall increase between about 1530 and 1620 was commonly more than threefold, and quite often very much more than that [33].

There is evidence that the major rises of incomes on the great estates was usually delayed until the 1590s, which suggests that it took the great landowners longer to reorganise their more scattered estates and rearrange tenancies, or perhaps that they only slowly and reluctantly came to recognise the necessity for such changes and put off as long as possible the unwelcome business of engrossing small farms and displacing old tenants. If the latter explanation holds, it supports the view of Tawney that the great proprietors were conservative in their estate management as in their way of life and allowed their finances to deteriorate gravely before attempting to change either. Tawney argued that the gentry who prospered through more flexible estate management and direct farming of their demesnes were those of a newly adopted bourgeois mentality, businesslike in their dealings and progressive in outlook, in contrast to the hidebound, tradition-ridden attitudes common among the old-established class of large proprietors. The bourgeois character of the rising gentry sprang too, it was supposed, from their close connections with the business world, from which they had only recently emerged. Some support for his view is provided by recent evidence which shows that it was the gentry with close London connections who tended to support Parliament in East Anglia and neighbouring areas.

There is an obvious plausibility in the contention that men of business origins, or still connected with business, were more likely to show a businesslike attitude in their handling of landed estates. It does not follow that old landed families were necessarily lacking in business sense, or were less alive to the possibilities of profit in the booming agricultural markets of the later sixteenth and early seventeenth centuries. There was no special mystique about the new forms of estate exploitation, and nothing that could not be handled by a competent estate steward or lawyer. The true situation might indeed have been the reverse, for certainly in the eighteenth century it was generally the old landed families who were the most enterprising, simply because their estates were more in need of enclosure and reorganisation, while the newcomers from business preferred to buy properties already bearing their full economic rent and not requiring a lot of money to be spent on them.

There seems no good reason why the majority of sixteenth-century landowners should not have done well out of the rise in prices and the many opportunities of increasing estate revenues. There is no need to invoke the bourgeois capitalist spirit to explain why some landowners rose further or faster. The factors affecting a family's income and expenditure were many and complex, and the way in which they managed their estates was only one of these, although frequently an important one. Other things being equal, the families who failed to take advantage of the times were, we may hazard, those who lacked the necessary capital or who were too heavily burdened with family or other debts to hang on to their land long enough; or they may just have been unfortunate in having small estates of severely limited possibilities, or perhaps estates leased out very largely to irremovable copyholders of inheritance. In any case there seems no good reason for supposing that the declining landowners were especially numerous or especially hard-hit in the fifty years or so before the Civil War; the trends of rents and estate revenues would suggest the opposite. Dr Cliffe's study of the Yorkshire gentry supports this conclusion. He found that the causes of financial decline were extremely varied: they included, certainly, failure to raise rents in due time; but also important were the heavy outlays on jointures, portions and annuities, extravagance in building, excessive household expenses, lavish hospitality and, inevitably, litigation. Taxes (except for wardship fines) were seldom burdensome because estates were generally undervalued by the feodaries, while Catholic families had in practice a variety of ways of escaping or minimising the various additional fines and penalties to which they were subject [34].

The distribution of landownership

The value of detailed local studies, such as that of Dr Cliffe, is that they reveal how excessively oversimple are explanations of complex changes which turn on some single key factor, whether it be the rise of a new 'bourgeois' gentry, the debasement of the nobility, or the discontent of 'mere' gentry. The true situation was nowhere near as clearcut as these explanations suggest, for the experience and the motives of landed families were subject to a much wider variety of conflicting factors and influences than any one theory can encompass. It is of the nature of history that the great conception is self-destructive since it inspires the patient work of detailed investigation which gradually qualifies, undermines, and eventually overthrows it. At present enough of such work has been done to make us more than a little sceptical of existing theories, but it is too soon to indicate a new orthodoxy. The best we can do for the moment is to offer some suggestions which may help to keep the problem in perspective.

First, it may be urged that with so much emphasis on change, crisis and division the essential stability and conservatism of landed society have been unduly neglected. Recent investigators, notably Professor Everitt, have sought to restore the balance by emphasising the reality of the existence of the 'county community', the closely interlinked society of the ruling families of the county. The independence of the leading landowners and their rooted loyalty to their local interests had always constituted a major limitation on the powers of the central government, and remained a fact of political life that thwarted Charles and Cromwell alike. Of course, the solidarity of the county community was more marked in some counties than in others. The existence of extensive areas of royal forest to be obtained by grants from the Crown, the availability of monastic lands, and the possibilities of enclosure from forest and waste, meant that some counties had a large proportion of newly established landed families. This made for a more positive attitude towards the issues of the day, as in Northamptonshire, which in Everitt's words was 'on the whole energetic, puritanical, and decisive'. Kent, on the other hand, offered far fewer opportunities to newcomers, and was 'obstructive, conservative, and Anglican'. Despite the proximity of London, the disrupting influence of the metropolis on Kentish society was limited and was largely confined to the county's western region. In the county at large, 'where the native community was deeply rooted, highly inbred, and remarkably cohesive, where manors and estates were small and seem to have come on to the market in scattered parcels, only one-eighth of the gentry were newcomers since Queen Elizabeth's reign' [35].

Kent was perhaps an extreme example: in other counties landowners were often less interrelated, less clannish, less tenacious of their land and interests; but the difference was only one of degree. The forces making for stability were inherent in the very structure of landed society, and the ability of the local community to resist intrusion and to absorb newcomers as they appeared was one of its enduring features. Shifts in religious belief and political allegiance inevitably occurred, but their extent and effect were profoundly influenced by the character of the local community and its degree of cohesion. This must go far to explain the varying role played by the provinces in the Civil War.

Secondly, there seems little doubt but that in the century of heavy disposal of Crown lands after 1536 the main beneficiaries were the gentry, considered as a whole. If Mr Cooper's ingenious calculations are to be relied on, it may be estimated that the gentry increased their total share of the land from about a quarter in the fifteenth century to some 45 or 50 per cent in the late seventeenth century. The major part of this change certainly, and perhaps all of it, had taken place by 1640. In this sense there was indeed a rise of the gentry. The sufferers were apparently not the yeomen owner-occupiers, who on balance probably also increased their share of the land substantially, but the nobility, the Church, and the Crown. The absolute share of the nobility may not have been much changed, but the position of the nobility *vis-à-vis* the gentry was much weakened; while the combined share of the Church and the Crown fell drastically, and perhaps disastrously. These changes are indicated in Table 3.1, and the word 'indicated' is used advisedly since at best the figures represent intelligent guesses from a variety of unsatisfactory and disparate sources.

If these figures are reasonably near the truth then we may suppose that Stone was right in emphasising the weak *relative* position of the aristocracy. (There was indeed the peer who said in 1628 that the House of Commons could buy out the Lords thrice over.) The greater territorial strength of the gentry was accompanied by an accession of political power, as in the course of the fifteenth, sixteenth and seventeenth centuries landed gentlemen invaded the representation of the corporate boroughs and so augmented their position in the Commons. It is now argued, that already by the middle decades of the sixteenth century, before the development of Stone's aristocratic crisis, a shift of political balance between the nobility and the gentry was in train. The destruction of the great warlords gave the gentry a greater independence and freedom of action, and gradually created a new court staffed by gentry who took over offices formerly held by clerics. Moreover, as Professor Stone has recently stressed, the second half of the sixteenth century saw a significant rise in the power of Parliament 'as a great engine of political action', and Lords and Commons were filled by members of the ruling class who were becoming not only better educated, but educated to govern, a change that had its effect on the tone and strength of Parliament [36].

Table 3.1 Distribution of landownership in England and Wales, 1436 to 1873

Percentage of land owned by:	1436 (England only)	c.1690	c.1790	1873 (England only)
I. Great owners	15–20	15–20	20–25	24
II. Gentry	25	45–50	50	55
III. Yeoman freeholders	20	25–33	15	10
IV. Church and Crown	25–35	5–10	10	10

The figures for 1436 and *c.*1690 are derived from J. P. Cooper, 'The social distribution of land and men in England 1436–1700', *Econ. Hist. Rev.* 2nd ser. xx (1967); those for 1790 and 1873 from F. M. L. Thompson, 'The social distribution of landed property in England since the sixteenth century', *Econ. Hist. Rev.* xix (1966), and *English Landed Society in the Nineteenth Century* (1963); and G. E. Mingay, *English Landed Society in the Eighteenth Century* (1963).

What emphasis, however, should be given to the great *absolute* decline in the Crown's stake in the country? Sales of Crown lands were resorted to as an obvious solution to short-term financial difficulties, but of course they had the effect of solving the problem of the day at the expense of the income of the morrow. And it was after all the growing financial difficulties of the Crown (in which the reduced income from Crown lands was, it is true, only one factor) that necessitated unpopular measures such as the sales of honours, knighthood compositions, wardship, purveyance, forced loans and ship money, and finally led to the calling of the Long Parliament.

There was a shift in the balance of property, and that shift helped to force the Crown into expedients that were not only unpopular and degrading to royal authority, but were also of highly dubious legality in the constitutional sense. But was this, by itself, enough to bring about the conflagration? The decline in the political authority of the Crown was of long standing and paralleled the decline in its economic position. From the 1560s the nobility and gentry were gaining in initiative over the Crown. Before 1603 Elizabeth found the royal authority increasingly checked, as in the matters of purveyance and monopolies. But with the Stuarts the process accelerated. The image of kingship itself became tarnished. Grave errors of policy further weakened the Crown's position and bit deeply into the fund of respect and loyalty on which the throne was ultimately based. What damage was done by James to the pride of the old aristocracy and titled gentry by his indiscriminate showering of grants and honours? What damage was done to kingship by the opulence of the court, the extravagance, the corruption? Above all, what damage was done by the Crown's support of high church tendencies, by the lenient treatment of Catholics after 1620, and finally by Archbishop Laud? For although the country appeared to divide on economic lines, the wealthier and more economically advanced south and east against the more rural north and west, the divisions were never clearcut. The war raised issues of politics and religion that ran across economic boundaries, that divided counties, towns, and families.

In Yorkshire, according to Dr Cliffe, religion was a more reliable line of division than wealth and economic interests, although some moderate Puritans, as well as Catholics, sided with the king. There were no major differences between royalists and parliamentarians in landed incomes and methods of estate management; nor, on the whole, in their attitudes to commerce and the professions. There was also no marked social distinction between the two sides, and the gentry who supported Parliament were far from being entirely a collection of *parvenus* with connections in the professions and trade. Among those who took the side of Parliament on the outbreak of the war were gentlemen like Sir John Hotham, Sir Matthew Boynton, Sir Hugh Cholmley, Sir William Constable, Sir Edward Rhodes, and Sir William Lister, all of whom had served as deputy lieutenants under Wentworth. While on the Parliament side it was Puritans who made up by far the most important element, the main body of royalist support consisted of conservative Catholic families, together with a smaller group of families, a court party element, connected with Wentworth, with the Crown's most controversial measures, or partly dependent on the Crown for income.

> There can be no doubt that many of the participants sincerely
> believed that they were fighting over important issues of principle,
> whether it was the defence of the king's person and authority, the
> safeguarding of the public liberties, the preservation of the Church of
> England from Puritan designs or the triumph of a Geneva-style
> Protestantism over both the Catholic and Laudian parties [37].

When it came to the crunch, men had to make a choice that involved their deepest private loyalties and sensibilities. It might be an agonising choice between an irrational but sincere attachment to the Crown that transcended the petty irritations of arbitrary taxes and impositions, and a hostility to a Church that seemed false and unfaithful in its deliberate restoration of the idolatry of Rome. In this kind of choice, personal questions of finance and social status, whether improving or declining, might seem hardly relevant. A powerful sense of honour, involving ancient loyalty to the monarch, or on the other hand perhaps, overriding belief in the sanctity of faith and liberty, were profound motives in men's actions [38]. No doubt, too, the choice of the greater gentry influenced the lesser, and much depended on the attitudes of the leading families in each area. It is hardly surprising, after all, that an issue that was basically constitutional and religious should cause men to divide along the lines of politics and faith, not economics.

The conflict and the county community

The legislation of 1640–42 ended the eleven years of Charles's rule without a Parliament and went far towards abolishing the prerogative powers of the Crown, and with these momentous developments the old groupings of court *versus* country disintegrated. The issue of the control of the army in Ireland brought the breach between Crown and Parliament to the point of open conflict, and when civil war was imminent there were many who searched their conscience to decide whether their rightful place was with the king or with Parliament. Some of the officeholders went over to Parliament, while many of the country gentry who had supported the legislation restricting the powers of the Crown now thought that things had gone far enough and joined the royalists or took a moderate neutral position.

It was remarkable that the small backwoods squires of the more remote rustic counties, such as Cornwall, Merioneth or Lancashire, rallied to the Crown. They had received no particular notice from the king – on the contrary their local interests, such as the defence of the Cornish coast, had been sadly neglected; but they were perhaps too far from the capital to be much aware of the extravagance of the court or of their own economic and social backwardness. Certainly they had grumbled as much as any about the exactions of ship money, wardship and the rest. But when resistance was replaced by revolution they were basically conservative. Their loyalty rested on the simple logic: no Crown – no squire. Other more prominent figures among the gentry were bound to the Crown by past favours and personal association. They had supped too long at their master's table to turn away when the crisis came. Such a one was Sir Edmund Verney, Knight-Marshal of the Palace, and a patentee of tobacco and London hackney coaches. When war seemed inevitable Sir Edmund sent for his armour and ordered Claydon to be put in a state of defence, with carbines, powder and bullets ready: 'for I feare a time maye come when Roags maye looke for booty in such houses; therefore bee not unprovided; but saye noething of it, for that maye invite more to mischeefe that thinck not of it yett.' Sir Edmund fell defending the king's standard at Edgehill; his hand, still holding a piece of the standard, was recovered and buried in the crypt of Middle Claydon church [39].

In many counties there was a large, perhaps predominant, neutral element. Men of property were naturally afraid of the destruction that active warfare brought in its train. They joined in declarations decrying violence, and advocated peace negotiations. Many of them were reluctant to take sides and stayed close to home, preferring to do no wrong than to risk doing any good, as their more active associates complained. Some moderate Royalists were averse to seeing either side triumph completely, Lord Savile declaring that 'he would not have the King trample on the Parliament, nor the Parliament lessen him so much as to make a way for the people to rule us all [40]. Detailed enquiries into the composition of the two sides show conflicting results. In Yorkshire the division tended to be along religious lines; in Derbyshire the parliamentarians were broadly men of wealth but of little landed property, while the royalists were the reverse; in Cumberland and Westmorland, as in Kent, the Parliamentary party was drawn from men of low position in county society. In general, the dividing lines are difficult to distinguish. The two parties possessed an essential homogeneity, as witnessed by the splitting of families into rival factions, and the continuation of friendly relations, even intermarriage, among families on opposing sides of the conflict.

The geographical alignment of the conflict, south and east *versus* north and west, was in some respects more apparent than real. Counties which were nominally for the one side or the other contained large numbers of dissidents whose activities were closely watched by the controlling party, while in time moderates gradually changed their position and moved from one camp to the other. Analysis of marriages in Lancashire has shown that as many as twenty-two brides of Roundhead families came from future Cavalier families, while a much smaller proportion of Cavalier marriages were with women whose fathers or brothers supported Parliament in the Great Rebellion. Typical of the latter was the Cavalier Robert Hesketh of Rufford, whose father-in-law, Alexander Rigby of Goosnargh, was one of the most dedicated leaders of the Roundheads. Marriage connections were certainly one of the factors causing gentry to change sides during the conflict [41]. Generally the lower middle classes in the towns and countryside – the artisans, small shopkeepers, small freeholders and yeomen – tended to side with Parliament; the wealthy merchants and the aristocracy leaned more towards the Crown. There was not, however, any clear alignment of entrepreneurial or 'bourgeois' class against the rentier or 'feudal' class in society. And the ordinary labourers in both town and country remained uninvolved, or at least as much as they were allowed to be. As the Civil War went on and the political situation became more confused by the fissures within the ranks of the victorious parliamentarians, it becomes difficult, if not impossible, to say how far the split between Independents and Presbyterians, the radicalism of the army, and the failure to achieve a political and religious settlement within the parliamentary framework, reflected shifts in opinion and divisions within the gentry at large.

On the local level, Professor Everitt's studies of the county gentry of Kent, Suffolk and Northamptonshire throw valuable light on the changes in political loyalties. In Kent the old-established gentry families were closely knit and clannish: 'they are all first cousins', it was said. Originally moderate in their views, the old gentry had become mildly royalist by 1642, but not sufficiently so to leave their estates and join the army of the king. The war and its aftermath of radicalism and Puritan rule pushed these families more firmly into the royalist camp, and by 1660 they were heartily in favour of the Restoration. It was the lesser gentry in Kent, particularly those more recently established in the country, who provided the active support for the Parliamentary cause and they became more extremist as time went on. They obtained the control of the county committee, through which Parliament sought to keep the county loyal to its cause, and through which it also raised troops, money and supplies. The strength of the extremists on the county committee rose with the domination of the Independents at Westminster, and they managed to keep a hold on the county to the end despite a series of royalist plots and risings. The abortive major rebellion of 1648, which began the second Civil War, was led by the old-established families, 'the ancient, indigenous gentry . . . rooted in their lands, moderate, anglican, county-minded [who] had been embittered by sequestration if they were royalists, and elbowed out of their natural leadership of Kentish society if parliamentarians'. The natural independence and moderation of the vast majority of the county's gentry, both great and small, made them hostile to the rule of the Commonwealth and the Protectorate, and although the power of the major-general and the efficiency of the army kept royalist plans from becoming more than pipedreams, the eventual weakening of the republican grip on the county went hand-in-hand with the collapse of central control following the death of Cromwell and the unpopularity of the Rump. When finally Charles II landed at Dover, amid 'great acclamations of joy and rejoicing for his Majesty, and crying out, God save the King', it was not only the King but the old gentry families of Kent who came into their own.

The history of the Protectorate showed, said Professor Everitt, that

Oliver Cromwell could neither dispense with the support of the county gentry nor subdue the independent spirit of provincial life. Ultimately, the very success of his policy of centralisation created a craving to return to older forms of government whose genius was essentially local: just as the autocratic rule of Laud and Strafford had ultimately forced Charles I to summon that parliament of angry countrymen which overthrew his régime between 1640 and 1642 [42].

In contrast to the persistent moderation of many Kentish gentry and the opposition of the old families to the Parliamentary cause, the Suffolk gentry were more clearly divided. The royalists in Suffolk were sufficiently enthusiastic to do more than stay at home and foment plots, while the great majority of strongly Puritan gentry put their 'dread of popery' into effect by savage pillaging of the property of Catholics. The county was so strongly Puritan indeed that under ten per cent of the estates of Suffolk were sequestrated as compared with over sixty per cent in Kent. The enthusiasm for the Parliamentary cause may be connected with the fact that, unlike the gentry of Kent, the majority of Suffolk gentry were of relatively recent origin, and many of even the older families, such as the Barnardistons, were closely connected with trade. Certainly it seems that trade and Puritanism went together, as did agriculture and Anglicanism, again emphasising the broad regional economic divisions that we have already noticed. In Northamptonshire, too, there was a connection between the recent origins of most of the gentry families and their marked affinity with the Puritans and support for Parliament. The result of the Civil War, however, was to give the Northamptonshire gentry a greater concern with stability: they closed their ranks and became a more conservative, tightly knit community [43].

The Restoration and after

The Restoration restored the monarch to his throne and power (now constitutionally restricted), produced a Cavalier Parliament and Cavalier court, and reinstated the Church of England with its hierarchy of bishops and deans. But what did it do for those gentry families who had spilt their blood, spent their money, and perhaps lost their estates in the royal cause? The answer is, very little: in part because the king was reluctant to dissipate the general goodwill with which he had been received by embarking on a course that would involve too great an upheaval of landed property. The lands of the Church and the Crown which had been confiscated by the Commonwealth were restored by statute, but private owners whose estates had also been confiscated could only petition to have them restored, or attempt to sue for them in the courts. The peers, with their greater influence, were best able to take advantage of the situation, and some of them obtained special Acts of Parliament for the return of their estates. Protestant adventurers in Ireland were confirmed by statute in the properties they had acquired.

Numbers of royalists had suffered not confiscation but sequestration: their estates had been fined by the county committees according to the degree of their delinquency. These fines varied considerably, and could be as high as eight years' value of the delinquent's estate. A fine of two or three years' value was much more common, however, and in some cases the fine was moderated by the terms of a military surrender. Further, the county committees allowed a wide variety of deductions from the gross value of the estate before arriving at the figure used for calculating the fine. Frequently, therefore, the fine was in practice equal to less than one year's total income from the estate. Moreover, as H. J. Habakkuk has pointed out, landowners could borrow in order to pay the fines, and they might prefer to do this and avoid sales of land because of the weak and uncertain nature of the land market during the Interregnum. Delinquency fines by themselves rarely resulted in sales of land. It was only those families who were already heavily indebted before the Civil Wars who were forced to sell: they 'were already so precariously poised that any straw would break their back'. Even so, they often managed to hang on, until eventually the mounting debts forced sales on them some considerable number of years after the Restoration. But 'sales were less important among the permanent consequences of the Interregnum than a period of impoverishment, denuded estates, possibly poor marriages for a generation or more. As Sir John Culpepper, whose estate had been sequestrated, wrote in the decade after the Restoration: "May not this Kingdom be presumed still to feel the effects of the late Civil War, as men do sometimes old bruises or the sins of their youth very long after"' [44].

Of course, the changes in ownership resulting from the wars were still considerable. The government sold land during the Interregnum to repay its debts; some royalists lost their estates outright by confiscation; more, some 3,000, were subject to delinquency fines, although as we have seen only the already heavily indebted families were forced to sell land. Such families emerged at the Restoration with their estates reduced and indebted, and without any means of redress. In contrast, some of those who took the risk of purchasing land during the Interregnum (and these included officers of the New Model Army, Puritan merchants, and similar upstarts), were able to hang on to it. Some of these new gentry had lent money to impoverished royalists, and others were Parliamentary soldiers who received land as a reward for their services. One such newcomer was the notorious Colonel Philip Jones, who bought the Fonmon Castle estates from the St John family during the Commonwealth. Jones was a friend of Cromwell, and became one of the best-hated men in Wales. With old and respected families replaced by arrogant *parvenus*, there was plenty of ground for bitterness, recrimination and envy when the nature of the Restoration land settlement became clear. Feelings were further exacerbated when royalist squires found their loyalty going unrewarded while erstwhile Parliamentarians went forward to new honours and greater wealth.

Nevertheless, overall the changes in landownership were less than might be expected. Most royalists who had suffered confiscation were able to regain their estates, although sometimes only after considerable outlays, and perhaps at the cost of continuing the Interregnum purchasers as sitting tenants with long-term leases. Other royalists had made private agreements with the new owners before the Restoration, and some had already purchased back their lands before 1660. The men who had bought Crown, Church or private confiscated estates during the Interregnum were not, Habakkuk has said, those who had an eye to building up a permanent estate for themselves: such estate-builders still bought their land in the private market. Those who acquired confiscated land were rather men who were prepared to accept the land in settlement of debts, or were often tenants who took the opportunity of buying the lands they occupied. In any case, much of this land was subject to long leases, so that the purchasers were merely buying the right to receive the rent or enjoy the property until the lease fell in. Such purchasers were not greatly upset by the land settlement for they had largely anticipated the outcome, and at least they had enjoyed some years of income from their property.

Quite apart from the families affected by the Restoration land transfers there were also many moderate gentry who managed to steer a skilful middle course between the worst rocks and shallows of partisanship, and so succeeded in bringing their property safely into port. Such gentry failed to secure the offices, grants and beneficial leases of Crown lands that were handed out by a grateful monarch to faithful supporters, but through the careful management of their estates they often showed a capacity for survival that in the long run proved more advantageous. In Kent it was the older gentry families who best weathered the storm:

> not a single family of importance was established in the county as a result of the Restoration settlement. Of the families who had established themselves in Kent since 1603, only 29 per cent retained their hold till 1688; whereas 87 per cent of the gentry of medieval stock survived into the eighteenth century. More than two-thirds of the properties sold by the newer families, moreover, were now purchased by those who had been established in the county since before the Tudor period [45].

But for almost all landowners, whether old-established or new, the period between the Civil War and the 1720s was a difficult one. Many came out of the Interregnum with estates reduced in size or heavily burdened with mortgages incurred to meet the compositions imposed by hostile county committees. Cornish royalists impoverished by the wars included Sir Richard Vyvyan, who spent nearly £10,000 in the king's cause, and Jonathan Rashleigh, who lost over £8,000 by the plundering of Menabilly. The royalist gentry of Devonshire, Professor Hoskins has told us, were already indebted before the wars, and had to pay fines equivalent to between two and eight years' value of their property. As a result some spent long years in reduced circumstances, forced to practise the strictest economy, with their children's prospects of making a good match or following a lucrative career not a little blighted. One such was Henry Bidlake, who was fined £300 – the equivalent of five years' value of his estate. To meet this sum Bidlake was forced to borrow from friends and neighbours, and his son was still struggling to make ends meet in 1669: 'For my life I know not what to do if you cannot help me fifty shillings or three pounds' [46].

The problems of survival were compounded by adverse economic conditions. In the latter half of the seventeenth century and opening years of the new one estate revenues ceased to show their former buoyancy. The generally downward trends in agricultural prices, associated with a less rapid growth of markets as population increase slowed and came near to halting altogether, put pressure on rents. In the years of particularly low prices, and also in unusually bad seasons, tenants fell into arrears with their rents, and some went bankrupt and decamped. Landlords, for the most part, gave up demesne farming as too risky and unprofitable, and concentrated their efforts on improving their farms so as to keep good tenants in occupation and attract new ones when farms fell vacant.

The period was, however, one of important agricultural improvements. Convertible husbandry, the alternation of grass and roots with arable crops in order to effect higher yields, reduction of fallows, and heavier stocking, was spreading in areas where the soil conditions and farming structure were suited to it. In certain areas the new root crops and grasses were becoming well established: turnips in Suffolk from about 1650 and in northeast Norfolk by 1670, sainfoin in the Cotswolds again from about 1650, and clovers in a wide variety of districts during the latter part of the century. Experiments with improved breeds of livestock were in train, water-meadows had become common in some grazing districts by the middle of the century, and lime and marl were widely employed to improve the fertility of soils. Drainage of marshes, deforestation and enclosures of waste land were continued in order to bring new land into cultivation. Alongside these developments, landlords and farmers were taking steps to make farms more compact, efficient and easier to work by arranging exchanges of lands, undertaking piecemeal enclosure of portions of common fields and commons, rebuilding farmhouses and barns and introducing drainage schemes and embankments to control flooding. Also in train was a general attack on obsolete forms of tenure in an effort to secure better farming and to restrict the depredations of careless or inefficient tenants.

A leading figure among the improving landowners of the middle seventeenth century was the Surrey squire, Sir Richard Weston. His understanding of agriculture was enlarged by his sojourn in the Low Countries during the Civil War, and led to the publication in 1650 of his book, *A Discours of Husbandrie used in Brabant and Flanders*. Weston was particularly concerned to improve the cultivation of poor soils (which characterised part of his own estate), and to this end he experimented with the cultivation of clover and was a pioneer in establishing new crop rotations in England. Before this, as early as 1618, he had developed plans for greatly extending, by over 100 acres, the area of water-meadows on his Sutton Park estate. This involved cutting an artificial channel three miles long from the river Wey, which was completed by 1619. His new water-meadows produced luxuriant crops of early grass and hay, and Weston was able to sell well over a hundred loads of hay a year at nearly £3 a load. On his return from the Low Countries full of new ideas about inland navigation he proceeded to push ahead with his old plans for making the Wey navigable, and the work was started in 1651 and was completed after his death in May 1652 [47].

In some areas transport improvements of significance, like Weston's river Wey navigation and the improvement of the Great Ouse in East Anglia, were features of the period, and these had the effects of reducing costs of carriage and of widening markets. Specialised production for distant markets became more marked, and land could be turned to more profitable uses. Rivers were improved for navigation by getting rid of rocks and shoals, and by making cuts across the necks of the loops formed by meandering river beds. Better facilities were provided at river and coastal ports, and these, together with the road improvements carried out by turnpike trusts (mainly after 1695), made for cheaper and speedier outlets for goods of all kinds. Not only farm produce was affected, but also other kinds of estate products such as timber, lime, bricks, stone, gravel, coal and other minerals. The advantages of better transport mitigated the effects of low prices, and encouraged estate development and specialisation. This was especially marked in the home counties and regions further afield which possessed good water and turnpike communications with the great London market of over half a million consumers. In other areas, especially where water communications were lacking and clay soils meant that roads were almost impassable in winter, conditions remained backward. It was in the notorious Sussex weald that Defoe saw a lady 'of good quality' brought in to church in her coach drawn by six oxen: 'nor was it done in frolic or humour, but mere necessity, the way being so stiff and deep that no horse could go in it.' And some years later another traveller asked: 'Why is it that the oxen, the swine, the women, and all other animals are long-legged in Sussex? May it be from the difficulty of pulling the feet out of so much mud by the strength of the ankles that the muscles got stretched, as it were, and the bones lengthened?'

While agricultural improvements and transport developments helped to keep many estates afloat, the economic weather took a distinct turn for the worse with the heavy taxation required to fight the wars of William III and of Anne. Between 1689 and 1714 the navy increased its tonnage by two-thirds and became by far the largest in Europe, the existing dockyard establishments necessarily expanded, and a new dockyard was opened at Plymouth. The army too, although still small by continental standards, increased rapidly in size. To pay for the swollen naval and military establishments, to keep the navy at sea and to send troops all over the continent, new taxes were required as well as increases in old ones. Particularly onerous was the land tax, introduced in 1692. Originally designed as a kind of general tax on incomes, it soon came to fall, through administrative difficulties, almost entirely on land. In war years the tax was levied at the rate of four shillings in the pound, and in the south and east of the country, where the assessments were up to the full value of the properties, landowners had to pay away a fifth of their income. The tax fell with particular severity on the smaller gentry estates, whose proprietors had few or no other sources of income but rents. The larger owners, with their more varied estate revenues and greater access to government offices and perquisites, suffered less; in some instances, too, they had sufficient influence to secure lenient assessments from the commissioners of the land tax.

With low agricultural prices, stagnant or falling rentals, periodical crises among the tenantry, debts hanging over from the Civil Wars and Restoration period, and now a heavy burden of taxation, numbers of the lesser gentry and yeoman proprietors found themselves compelled to sell. No doubt more of them would have sold, had it not been for the greater security and lower cost of borrowing. Before the late seventeenth century borrowing on mortgage was a risky procedure because the courts were inclined to take a strict view of any default or minor infringement of the terms of the mortgage. Fortunately for many owners, the Court of Chancery modified this strict interpretation of the law, and as the untrammelled right of the mortgagor to reclaim his land was established, borrowing on mortgage involved little risk of ending in sales of land. Mortgages, together with personal bonds, became a standard means of financing purchases of land, payment of dowries, building schemes, elections and repayment of debts. In addition, rates of interest fell from the six or seven per cent common in the later seventeenth century to a moderate five per cent in the early eighteenth century, making mortgages even more attractive to borrowers.

A further factor helping to keep estates together was the development of the strict family settlement. This was a legal device by which the interest of an owner in his estate was limited to that of a life tenant, the original object being to reduce the damage to an estate arising from possible imposition of fines and forfeitures during the Interregnum. In these arrangements a proportion of a family's land was reserved for the purpose of paying jointures, portions, and annuities to members of the owner's family. As the legality of the strict settlement became fully established by a series of court decisions in the later seventeenth century, so family settlements became the usual instrument for securing the passage of the estate intact from one generation to the next, and for securing also the interest of widows, daughters and younger sons in the property. Sometimes, indeed, the owner of the estate found his hands too securely tied, and mounting debts and interest payments might oblige him to seek a private Act of Parliament in order to break the settlement, or he might put his estate in the hands of trustees with powers to bring about a thorough reorganisation and financial restoration of his affairs.

Nevertheless, despite the family settlement and the greater ease of borrowing, it is clear that many smaller proprietors came to grief in the long and arduous period between 1660 and 1725. The Catholic gentry, in particular, often found it difficult to survive. Loyalty to their faith subjected them to an additional and severe burden of taxation as well as legal disabilities, and despite the help of Protestant friends numbers of them succumbed, or struggled through with reduced estates and a more straitened way of life. Some owners, however, may have decided to sell land because they decided that trade or some other form of investment was a better proposition. The net return on land rented to tenants was low – only about three per cent, which was well below the cost of borrowing on mortgage – and farming was in the doldrums. So as the range of alternative investments widened and became more secure, the attractions of land considered purely as an investment declined. Selling of land was especially likely if it was already heavily encumbered with mortgages or other liabilities, and if it descended through the female line; then the property might come into the hands of daughters, sons-in-law and nephews, who were free to sell it, and who might have little interest in retaining it when their own property might be at a distance, or their business was in a town and not connected with land at all [48].

Sellers were seldom deterred by lack of purchasers, for the land market was kept active by the steady demand emanating from two main kinds of buyers. These were, first, the larger landowners, men with substantial estate revenues, often augmented by officeholding, who were always interested in land that helped consolidate their existing properties, improved their parks or increased their influence over electors; secondly, there were the new men, from trade and the professions as always, but with a fair sprinkling of rising politicians and officeholders, war financiers, contractors and industrialists, and naval and military officers, who had done as well out of the wars as some of the sellers had done badly [49]. The newcomers were usually looking for established small or medium estates with a suitable house, though often they had to settle for a nucleus of a farm or two around which to build up a new estate by piecemeal acquisition. This was the way in which the Cowper and Grimston families built up substantial holdings in Hertfordshire in the seventeenth and early eighteenth centuries. It is interesting that their new estates of Panshanger and Gorhambury were accumulated from successive small purchases of neighbouring properties, ones that had come into the hands of absentee owners, and for want of male heirs had passed through the female line into the hands of persons living at a distance. They were not bought from impoverished yeoman freeholders [50]. Hertfordshire, however, may not be typical in this respect, for the county had long been marked by a high turnover of property, a characteristic which arose, no doubt, from its proximity to the business metropolis of London.

Ascendancy of the great landowners

The period between the Restoration and the accession of George II was thus one that saw some further shifts in the distribution of landed property, although on nothing so grand a scale as in the hundred years before 1640. In this period the gentry as a whole probably lost no ground, and may have gained a little: sales of property by declining families were made good by purchases on the part of the more prosperous and the newcomers from outside. The main losers of land were the yeoman freeholders who sold to both new and older gentry families and to the owners of the great estates. The very approximate estimates of land distribution suggest that the freeholders' share of the land may have fallen at this time by as much as a half, from between about a quarter to a third to as low as some fifteen per cent. The great owners' share, on the other hand, rose from perhaps a fifth to nearer a quarter, while the gentry held on to, or perhaps even improved on, their share of about fifty per cent. Whatever the precise figures might be, it does not seem that the shifts were very great, except for the yeomen owners, whose share apparently sank rapidly towards that reduced position so alarming to the land reformers of the late nineteenth century. Certainly the changes created no new class of landed proprietors, nor any great new rift among the ranks of the existing landowners. Landed society showed its ancient ability to assimilate the newcomers. The main effect was to widen the gap between the great landlords and the county gentry, to accentuate differences in wealth and therefore, as it happened, to widen differences in influence and political power.

These changes were indeed very much interrelated with political developments. The Restoration had re-established in addition to king and Church the old electoral system of the forty shilling franchise in the counties and the heterogeneous electorates of the boroughs. The county gentry, with all their provincial independence and obstinacy, seemed to be once again in the political saddle. In various subtle and gradual ways, however, the reality of power was slipping away from them. The times were characterised by great uncertainty and sudden political changes. The matter of the Protestant succession to the secretly Catholic Charles II and the overtly Catholic James II, the numerous plots and open rebellions against the established order, ranging from those of Titus Oates and Rye House to the Fifteen, the bewildering shifts and fluctuations in foreign policy, and above all the still unsolved question of the respective weight of Crown and Parliament in the constitution, produced a chaos of changing allegiances and an atmosphere of distrust and suspicion. The problem of the constitutional powers of the Crown had not been solved by the Restoration. Charles attempted to secure a greater influence over elections by confiscations and remodelling of boroughs' charters, and towards the end of his reign the questions of the calling of Parliament and the duration of its sittings again became critical issues. Indeed, Charles managed to rule for four years after 1681 without calling a Parliament at all.

The deep significance of the unsettled political issues made for violent partisanship, and elections were frequent and bitterly contested. The electorate was now much larger than in the past, partly because of the growth of population and partly because the franchise had been widened by elastic interpretation of the qualifications, and by monetary inflation. The medieval limitation of forty shillings had come to mean no more than a mere handful of acres, and the county electorate included not only little freeholders but those who possessed only leaseholds for lives and rent charges, or had even less impressive qualifications. With the increased size of the electorate there came also a greater sophistication in the organisation of the elections and control of the electors themselves by the contestants. Further, the close connection between success at the polls and the profits of patronage, and perhaps most important, the longer period for which election secured enjoyment of office after the passing of the Septennial Act in 1716, made powerful families willing to invest ever larger sums in securing seats. The cost of fighting an election rose greatly, not least because of the surprising degree of independence shown by the electorate, as recent examination of Suffolk poll books has shown [51]. Gradually, all but the great magnates and the wealthy gentry were forced out of the competition for seats by the sheer size of the costs involved in electioneering. As a result election pacts became common in some counties, and seats were divided by agreement between the magnates and the leading gentry.

The exclusion of the lesser gentry from direct participation in politics, and their consequent loss of influence and reduced participation in the spoils of office, were aggravated by the ability of the Crown to control directly certain seats and influence the elections for others. As the growing political power of the Crown became more evident, and as the country squires became increasingly resentful of the political strength and powers of patronage exercised by the great families, so division within the landed classes, already shaped by economic forces, began to take a definite political form. The aristocrats and greater gentry who dominated government and court through their wealth and their control of seats in Parliament became the Whigs: they favoured, after 1694, the strengthening of the royal authority and an enlarged naval and military establishment, both of which made for extended powers of patronage. The county squires, heavily taxed and shut out from court and office, were for an increase in the power of Parliament. They wished to counter the renewed power of the Crown, and they wanted peace and a reduction in the armed forces, which would mean lower taxes. Some remained uncommitted and prided themselves on their independence of party; others, 'honest Churchmen', leaned towards the Tories. But whether independent, Whig, or Tory, the county gentry shared certain common views. The influence of Parliament, they believed, and of their representation in the Commons, would be strengthened by frequent, preferably annual, elections. In Parliament the county members worked also to counter the power of the great lords by attempting to secure the detachment of all placeholders from Parliament, the imposition of heavy penalties for corruption and bribery at elections, and insistence on a substantial qualification for MPs in terms of land.

The Revolution of 1688–89 was the grand occasion for the assertion by the Tory squires of their principles of parliamentary supremacy over the powers of law-making, taxation and the forces, and the restatement of their demand for restriction of the royal prerogative. The House of Lords had already conceded that money Bills could be introduced only in the Commons, and that they could not be subsequently amended in the Lords. Now in William III's reign the Commons began to state the specific purposes to which the money collected in taxes was to be put, and this represented the start of effective parliamentary control over government spending. The scope of the king's expenditure under the Civil List was gradually reduced, and the Crown's powers of borrowing came to be subject to strict parliamentary control. But although in the immediate reaction to the follies of James the squires could secure for their principles the approval of all the propertied classes, they could not subsequently put them into effect. It was the Whig aristocracy, not the Tory squires, who resumed the monopoly of court and government, who gradually extended their powers of patronage and control of Parliament, and who determined the general course of events.

By Anne's reign the great constitutional issues had largely receded into the background. The uncommitted country members, still largely consisting of landed gentry with a few professional men and merchants, did not constitute a cohesive 'country party'. Rather were they a haphazard group of independent individuals, linked by a concern with common interests. A contemporary explained to the Elector of Brandenburg that these country members never joined with Whigs or Tories but 'speak and vote in the House according to their rights. . . . The principles which govern their reasoning' included in addition to religion and the liberty of the individual, 'the trade which enters the value of their produce, and the cultivation of their lands. No matter which is the party in power, and no matter how eloquent its appeal may be, it will never win over these members unless it can convince them that one of these four points is under attack' [52].

The country members' interests followed old antecedents in revolving round the extravagance of government expenditure, opposition to the presence of military men in Parliament (and incidentally to the use of the press-gang), and not least, hostility to the growing number of placemen in the Commons.

Protests against the government's reward of Marlborough echoed the earlier hostility exhibited towards William's grants of land to his Dutch and other favourites; and local squires who had lost their seats to army officers could hardly fail to agree with John Lowther's view that the people of Cumberland 'ought to be appris'd of the unreasonableness of having three in six of the parliamentary representatives of the shire officers of the army. . . . Country gentlemen are fitter to be Knights of the shire than officers of the army' [53]. Above all the country members persevered in their protracted campaign against the undue 'influence' represented by the large body of officeholders and pensioners in the Commons. Their more general Place Bills failed, but they were successful in securing the exclusion from Parliament of certain office-holders, such as revenue officers, and in securing the rule that acceptance of an office involved re-election of the member to his seat. It was as a consequence of this that many ministers and rising politicians sat for close boroughs or in the Lords. While fulminating against the sinister role of placemen, many country members saw nothing inconsistent in attempting to secure from the government places or favours for their relatives or friends; their 'independent' idealism was always moderated by a degree of practical materialism. On the other hand, there were not a few of them who pushed their distrust of government and all its works as far as persistent refusal of lucrative offices for themselves. Inconsistent, factious and unpredictable, the country gentlemen provided some check on the growing power of the executive, and, while rarely powerful, they remained an influential element that governments in the early years of the new century had to take into account.

Meanwhile the political hegemony of the great Whig lords grew with the widening of the economic gap between them and the country gentry; their alliance with merchants and financiers paralleled the ramification of their interests in commerce and industry. The independent Tory squires, divided among themselves and lacking sound leadership, were reduced to near-impotence both in their counties and in Parliament. The county representation tended to be dominated by a few leading families whose tenants formed the majority of the freeholder electorate, and in some counties a contested election became a rarity. In time the small squires became either Tory diehards, old-fashioned and discredited, tainted with the suspicion of Jacobitism, and dis-trustful equally of placeholders, the Whig wars and the governmental inefficiency and corruption the wars revealed, or they acquiesced in the economic and political facts of the age, made their peace with the magnates, and in due course accepted some minor office and perhaps a place on the justices' bench. By the 1720s the Whig management of Parliament and control of place had been developed into a fine art, and in the hands of such masters as Walpole and Newcastle the country at last emerged from a century of turbulence into a new era of political and social stability.

The problematical position of the independent gentry in the changing conditions of the early eighteenth century may be illustrated from the career of Sir Edward Knatchbull. During the seventeenth century the Knatchbulls, a very old-established Kentish family, had gradually risen in status. Sir Norton Knatchbull, the first baronet, was chosen to represent the county in the Short Parliament, and sat for New Romney in the Long and Cavalier Parliaments. Sir Edward, the fourth baronet, with whom we are concerned, first entered Parliament in 1702 as the member for Rochester, an Admiralty borough. He lost his seat in 1705, but eight years later was returned again for Kent in company with another high Tory. A supporter of Bolingbroke, Sir Edward was defeated again in 1715 with the Hanoverian succession, and was not elected again until 1722. As Walpole increasingly dominated affairs, Knatchbull shifted from opposition to support for the administration, and so joined the ranks of the numerous country gentlemen who came to terms with the new regime. He was one of those important county members whom Walpole succeeded in detaching from the hostile ranks of diehard Tories and dissatisfied Whigs to the side of the court and Treasury party. Sir Edward's changed position, however, lost him the support of many Kentish friends, the result of 'my regard for the public service and my particular attachment to you', he told Walpole. The loss of his county support meant that in the election of 1727 he had to be brought in by the government for a Cornish seat. Three years later he died. 'An ambitious, capable Parliamentarian, Knatchbull had no future in the opposition', Dr Newman has remarked. His life showed well the nature of the dilemma which faced the independent country gentleman of ability, who after the collapse of the old Tory cause in 1714 could make some mark on the course of events only by deserting old friends and comprising old principles [54].

The gentry in the age of reform

In the second quarter of the eighteenth century England settled down under the rule of the Whig aristocracy. The great landowners dominated the House of Lords, and for the most part were able successfully to 'manage' the House of Commons. With the issue of the Protestant succession settled, and questions about the powers of Parliament and the extent of the royal prerogative in abeyance, much of the old violence and rancour disappeared from politics. It was an age of moderation and accommodation, when expediency ruled over principle, and when control of seats through the exercise of influence over voters, and control of supporters through the power of patronage, became the normal way of political life. Men perforce accepted the system and got out of it as much as they could. Compromise extended, too, into the religious sphere. The Church of England was supreme, and the Dissenters and others outside its pale were kept from Parliament, the universities and public office. But this did not prevent them from obtaining a good education or from following careers in commerce and industry. Even the Roman Catholics, who nominally laboured under more severe disabilities, experienced in practice a large measure of toleration. They were able to worship in their houses without undue interference, and the numerous Catholic gentry of Lancashire, for example, maintained friendly relations with the Protestant clergy and justices. Through the skill of their lawyers and the good offices of Protestant friends the Catholic gentry were now better able to protect and develop their estates. Nor were they ostracised even by the Protestant clergy, for Parson Woodforde recorded an occasion when he dined at his squire's house with the Bishop of Norwich and some Roman Catholic guests.

Politics revolved around the unstable groupings of factions and connections which the politicians who were in a position to dispense favours to their 'friends' built up around themselves. Government, in turn, was exercised by alliances of the leading men who could obtain the support of the monarch: this gave them, in addition to their own following, command over the king's supporters and dependants in Parliament and the vital control over patronage, a combination that was usually sufficient to keep a grip on the Commons and maintain stable government. In addition to the Crown's direct hold over some twenty-five or thirty Treasury, Admiralty, or Ordnance boroughs (where the electors depended for their incomes on Crown offices), there were some 200 placemen in the Commons of the middle eighteenth century. These were not always easily controlled, for their places were usually rewards for past services or had been obtained through influential connections, and a particular place-holder was not necessarily tied to the government. The art of managing the placeholders lay in a constant wooing of their support and in the judicious distribution of new or vacant places.

The situation was further complicated by the existence of 'interests', groups of influential men inside and outside Parliament who were bound in a loose alliance by common economic concerns; such were the city financiers, or the East India and West India merchants. The wars of the period continually breached the links between the various interests. The landed interest was opposed to the heavier taxation and greater difficulty of borrowing which wars involved, while the moneyed interest welcomed the wartime rise in interest rates and the greater demand of the government for funds. Compromises between rival factions and conflicting interests were made by the handful of powerful men meeting in their London houses or country mansions. 'From some eighteenth-century memoirs', as Habakkuk has remarked, 'one might suppose that England was a federation of country houses' [55].

The entrenched position of the great aristocrats in the political system remained a fact not only in the eighteenth century but even in the more demo-cratic era after 1867, as a glance at the cabinets of Gladstone and Disraeli will confirm. The most able leadership derived from a succession of great com-moners – Walpole, the two Pitts, Peel, and Gladstone – but they were glad to lean on the political talent and influence commanded by the Newcastles, the Grahams or the Salisburys of their age. Certainly the great landowners' share in government was disproportionate to their stake in the country. The gentry owned collectively twice as much of the land, but apart from the inclusion of a few of the most wealthy gentry families in the governing circle and a substantial and influential representation of country gentlemen in the Commons – some sixty or eighty out of over 550 – they had little direct control over the broad course of politics.

Some of the independent country gentry still remained important, how-ever, if only because of their independence. Such members sat in Parliament as the representatives of their county, which they and the other gentry of the shire regarded almost as a self-governing community. For them the matters affecting the county were all-important, and they expected to be consulted on them, whereas the wider questions discussed at Westminster were frequently of only peripheral interest. Sir James Lowther, member for Cumberland, once spoke of his county as though it were a separate state, declaring that if certain pro-posals became law they in Cumberland would reserve their position [56]. A number of these independents remained true old-fashioned Tories: they ignored the Hanoverians and still kept holy the 30th of January – the martyr's day, on which the Denbighshire magistrates refused to undertake county business. Some of these diehards, like Bagot of Staffordshire or Rolle of Devon, extended their conservative independence almost to the point of creating a third party. William Drake of Buckinghamshire told the younger Pitt that he and his would not be 'the spaniel of a minister'; no doubt he would have agreed with Squire Western that all lords 'are a parcel of courtiers and Hanoverians – my daughter shall have an honest country gentleman' [57]. William Drake's power and source of independence lay in the borough of Amersham which his family had represented in Parliament from the early seventeenth century. He owned a large proportion of the town's property, nearly a hundred houses, or over a third of the total in the 1770s, and many of the town's craftsmen and tradesmen relied on his tenants and his Shardeloes estate for their income.

Like the Drakes, the strength of the peers lay in the control of urban electorates. In the middle eighteenth century only forty-seven of the 203 boroughs (providing a total of 417 members) had more than 500 electors. It was true that it was landowners who formed the majority of the Commons, and continued to do so until late in the nineteenth century, but most of these – Irish peers, sons of English and Scottish peers, and wealthy gentry – may have had little connection or even much sympathy with the more commonplace body of country gentry at large. Even the growing number of members who hailed from trade or the law were associated by family or by business interests more with the great landowners than with the gentry. The enormous cost of disputing an election put the question of an increased gentry representation, one in line with their stake in the country, quite out of court. Only great property magnates such as the Grosvenors could afford sums like the £6,500 they spent at Chester in 1732, or the £8,600 spent on food and drink alone in the election of 1784. Of necessity the great majority of politically ambitious gentry had to restrict their activities to local affairs. When they entered the lists a parliamentary career could spell financial ruin. Sir William Gostwick, who represented Bedfordshire from 1698 to 1713, accumulated debts of £26,700, and his heir was forced to sell up and leave the county [58].

In local affairs the gentry's role was by no means unimportant, for matters affecting the county and parish were generally of far greater import for the lives of ordinary people than were the debates and resolutions in Parliament. In the county the post of lord-lieutenant was usually filled by the aristocracy, and among the gentry the high sheriff's office was rarely popular or eagerly sought since the expenses attached to it were heavy, while its influence was small. But the Commission of the Peace, the stronghold of the gentry, was still the fulcrum of local administration, for it was well into the nineteenth century before new legislation and new administrative authorities impinged seriously on the justice's sphere of operations. Here, on the justices' bench, the leading gentry found an outlet suited both to their position in county society and to their pocket.

Like the sheriff, the justice was unpaid, and if he undertook his duties conscientiously he found himself out of pocket well beyond the four shillings a day allowed for expenses, as well as short of time for his own affairs. But there were the valuable compensations of added local prestige and some considerable degree of influence and minor patronage. If he were so minded, the determined justice could seek to maintain high standards of public probity and a healthy respect for law and property. Such a man might take great pride in his energy in pursuing lawbreakers, and in bringing down the weight of his justice on the thieves, drunkards, poachers, keepers of disorderly houses and other miscreants put before him. On the other hand he might choose to set an example of humanity by careful distinction between major and petty offences, and by looking into the conditions of the gaols, houses of correction and workhouses, and making what improvements were possible.

Indeed, the economic and social conditions of the age were extending the justices' influence in a variety of ways. The maintenance of law and order, prevention of riots, and supervision of alehouses became more onerous when the rural population grew considerably after about 1750. Such problems were multiplied as new industrial settlements appeared in the countryside of the Midlands and north, arousing the hostility of the workers in the old hand trades. The expansion of industry and agriculture put increased pressure on communications, and gave a new urgency to the justices' concern with the condition of roads and bridges, and the regulation of markets and of carriers' rates. Above all, the growth of rural population and the decline of some rural industries, such as cloth manufacture and iron making, intensified the problems of local pauperism. The Poor Law had long been a rich field for local experimentation: in the various forms of outdoor relief, the licensing of beggars and apprenticeship of poor children, the attempted organisation of workhouses on commercial lines, and such relaxations of the law of settlement as were provided by the granting of certificates of movement and extra-parochial pensions. It was the justices of rural counties, Oxfordshire, Berkshire and others, who in 1795 introduced the so-called Speenhamland system, a scheme for subsidising the wages of able-bodied men by reference to the price of bread and the size of their families – a crude forerunner of our presentday supplementary benefits. Equally, it was the justices who in the twenty years of scarcity and soaring food prices after 1795 decided whether or not the Speenhamland scale, or something like it, should be applied within their jurisdictions throughout rural England. In the years after the wars, in reaction to the supposed evils introduced into poor relief by Speenhamland, the Southwell justices in Nottinghamshire, and others elsewhere, experimented with new deterrent policies, such as the work-house test and 'less eligibility', and so foreshadowed the infamous harshness of the Poor Law reform of 1834. Even after 1834 the New Poor Law, with all its apparatus of control and inspection operated from Somerset House, could not secure uniformity of practice nor abolish local preferences. The justices, in their new guise as guardians of the poor, were too stubborn and independent, too down to earth, too knowledgeable about local conditions, and perhaps too humane, to try and administer the law in all its Benthamite rigidity.

In fact much of the long rearguard action fought against the modernis-ing, centralising and standardising tendencies of national legislation was inspired by the old tradition of local independence among the country gentry and their sympathisers in the provincial towns. It was an action doomed to eventual failure. The logic of industrialisation and of creeping democracy was necessarily in favour of central regulation and national uniformity. The shire hall had to give way to Whitehall, the amateur administrator to the professional civil servant and local government officer. Thus the gentry declined even within their ancient stronghold of the county from which they had resisted the demands of both autocratic monarchs and upstart Protector. And finally, on the new county councils after 1888 they eventually found themselves increasingly outnumbered and outvoted by urban representatives with an alien background and a totally different outlook.

The ultimate decline of the gentry, as of the once all-powerful aristocracy, was associated with the greatly reduced place of land in the national economy and the reform of the franchise. The new era was foreshadowed by the declining importance of placeholders in the old unreformed Parliaments. The enquiries into the methods and organisation of government departments in the 1780s followed on provincial demands for 'economical reform'. The consequent abolition of places and sinecures resulted in a decline in the monarch's influence over Parliament. But this was only one of the anachronisms whose days were numbered by the new concern with equality and rational reform. A demand for a general reform of Parliament, the franchise, and the distribution of seats in the Commons followed from the Wilkesite agitation and Wyvill's county associations of the later eighteenth century. To these were added the radical rumblings of the corresponding societies and the demand for universal suffrage which Tom Paine and the fall of the Bastille encouraged among the more aware of the working classes. And this in time was supplemented by the growth of a middle-class sentiment in the industrial towns in favour of a more direct representation of commercial and manufacturing interests. The evident absurdity in the new conditions of the nineteenth century of a representative institution whose members sat for tiny Cornish fishing villages, an uninhabited sheepwalk, and even a town that had been lost for centuries under the sea, to say nothing of the undue pressures applied to electors that a system of public hustings made possible, all this could not but attract the fire of reformers of a wide variety of hues and motives.

The reform of 1832 was severely limited: the new electorate was still only about the same proportion of the increased population as it had been in Anne's reign – that is, under five per cent; and while the more obvious abuses were removed, the power of the landed interest remained largely unimpaired. Of course, the reform was intended not to destroy that power but to preserve it. The middle classes were brought formally into the constitution, but were still to be subordinate to the landowners. Indeed, the numbers of county constituencies were increased and a large number of country pocket boroughs remained in being. It was, declared Grey, 'the most aristocratic measure that ever was proposed in Parliament'. The reformed House turned out to be 'just like any other Parliament', as Greville noted [59]. This was what made the subsequent issue of the Corn Laws crucial, for in 1846 the 1832 constitution, as well as protection, was at stake. But the reform of Parliament, however conservative, did bring some changes of consequence. It made control of the Commons by the old methods more difficult, encouraged the registration of electors and hence the rise of party agents, and made governments more dependent on the views of the enlarged if still miniscule electorate.

The concessions made in 1832 were only a beginning, a first limited attempt to stifle the reform agitation by bringing Parliament into line with new political circumstances and with the changed circumstances of the country itself. In the eighteenth century and earlier the leadership of the landowners was the natural and obvious corollary of the enormous importance of land as the basis of political power, wealth and status, as well as the major source of production and employment. A hundred years before 1832, perhaps as much as two-thirds or three-quarters of the whole population derived their livelihood in one way or another from the land. Even the more limited numbers directly engaged in the business of farming accounted, probably, for over half the population. But very soon this great pre-eminence of land was on the wane. By the end of the eighteenth century the proportion of the country's labour force directly engaged in agriculture was not much more than a third; by 1850 a fifth; by 1900 under a tenth, and today a mere three per cent. And as agriculture lost its ancient dominance of the economy so it had to surrender its old and valid claim to a special place in the life of the nation. Reform could not be halted at the 'aristocratic constitution' of 1832. Loss of agricultural protection marked the turning point. True, in 1846 the aristocracy and gentry still dominated Parliament, and a Tory landowner was in possession of 10 Downing Street. (It should be noted, though, that according to one definition of 'gentry', nearly a third of their numbers in the Parliament of 1841–47 was made up of either businessmen or lawyers, and as many as two-fifths had connections with business through directorships of railway, insurance and banking companies, or had interests in mining, docks, canals and similar enterprises) [60]. The gentry's apparent stranglehold over Parliament, and the continued enthusiasm for protection of the mass of country gentry, did not, however, obviate the necessity of repeal. The Corn Laws had to be sacrificed in order to hold back for a while the rising tide of industrial democracy, protection was abandoned in order to remove a focus for a renewed assault against the political power of the landed interest, and against the limited franchise and control of seats on which that power rested.

The Corn Laws were jettisoned, too, because as Peel saw, and he had experience as an improving landlord, they were not essential to the survival of those landlords and farmers who marched with the times and farmed efficiently for the market. In the 1860s the landowners, with repeal behind them, enjoyed their Indian summer. Free trade did not prove disastrous. Rentals were higher than they had ever been, were indeed more than twice as high as a century before, and were still rising. Tenants were prosperous, and the techniques of 'high farming' made the capitalist agriculture of England and Scotland a model for the world. Society still revolved round the great houses with their hunts and shoots, their garden parties and balls, and their political weekends and literary *soirées*. The great families still dominated in cabinets and at court; the gentry still ran county affairs much as ever; younger sons still proliferated in the Church, the army, and the law. But this apparently stable and serene world, its niceties of rank and etiquette minutely mirrored for us in the pages of the novelists, was on the edge of final decline. It could not withstand the combined effects of the partial collapse of English agriculture after the 1870s and the political changes that followed from the extensions of the franchise. One turning point came with the Reform Act of 1867, a more ominous one in 1884 when the county franchise was brought into line with that of the boroughs, and many of the small pocket boroughs were finally abolished. The old methods of controlling elections were made impossible by the secret ballot, and more important, the Corrupt Practices Act of 1883; while the introduction of compulsory, and eventually free, education was a portent of the coming of universal adult franchise. Henceforth it became increasingly unlikely that the old independent county members, chosen from among the ranks of the greater gentry, would again be seen in Westminster.

The pace of decline thus quickened from the 1870s, when political changes were accompanied by the fall in farm prices and hence in rents. The Conservatives were impotent to stem the tide. The steady growth of the urban population and the country's increasing dependence on overseas trade took return to protection out of the realm of practical politics. Meanwhile the Liberals succeeded in driving a wedge between landlords and farmers, enacting in 1880 the Ground Game Act (allowing farmers to destroy hares and rabbits), in 1882 a more effective Settled Lands Act to permit greater flexibility in the disposal of estates, and in 1883 an Act which gave tenants rights to compensation for improvements, a measure that quite overshadowed the Tories' ineffective predecessor of 1875. In some respects the weakened position of the landed interest was far from obvious. Country houses and country sports retained their social vitality, though not a few houses and their sporting amenities were let out to urban plutocrats. As late as 1883 Bagehot was moved to complain that Parliament still had 'an undue bias towards the sentiments and views of the landed interest'. Cabinets were still studded with aristocratic titles and, as Bagehot remarked, 'the series of Cabinet Ministers presents a nearly unbroken rank of persons who either are themselves large landowners, or are connected closely by birth or inter-marriage with large landowners' [61]. It was not until the Liberal administration of 1906 that the political influence of the great landowners was clearly seen to be on the wane.

Before the 1880s the changed position of the landed interest was also obscured by the apparently unimpaired resilience of landed incomes, though the evidence of decay was accumulating when Trollope wrote his searing satire on the money-grubbing, degenerate aristocracy who peopled *The Way We Live Now* – the dissipated young bloods of the Bear-garden, Lord Alfred, the waster and sponge who lent his name and respectability to the schemes of the swindler Melmotte, and the plotting, haughty, but hard-up Longstaffes, who kept up a pretence of lording it over their acquaintances on a precarious basis of borrowed money. Perhaps only a small minority of the aristocracy were driven to the lengths described by Trollope – he himself thought his picture overdrawn and ill-natured – and indeed many landowners showed more foresight, prudence and integrity than did his characters. Many of the old families found it possible to stave off disaster by adjusting gradually to the new circumstances, by diversifying their interests, selling land and buying shares, renting out country houses and shooting rights, and some had followed this precautionary course for a considerable time. For others survival lay through a career in business or the professions, or eventually in the kinds of specialised farming that a state subsidised agriculture made possible from the 1920s. Not a few were saved by the modern middle-class snobbery that makes a title a desirable appendage to a reputable board of directors. Despite the introduction of a crippling level of death duties and the gradual disappearance of cheap labour from the countryside some have managed to cling on to their homes and a remnant of their estates, if only at the cost of transforming them into an attraction for the tourist. In these and other ways the landowners have come to terms with the twentieth century, but the gentry as a meaningful term, as a social class respected for its economic strength, its political responsibilities, and its traditional way of life, has disappeared.

4   The estates of the gentry

The predominance of agriculture

Until the nineteenth century agriculture remained the backbone of the economy and the major source of employment. As industrialisation produced its vast urban conglomerations so the consequence of land declined, but in 1811 agriculture still employed a third of the country's labour force, and even as late as 1891 there were more people working on the land than in the metal manufacturing industries, or in building or textiles, or even in the whole of transport and communications.

Two centuries earlier, according to Gregory King, well over half the population were directly dependent on the land. Landowners and their families numbered perhaps 150,000, but the freeholders and tenant-farmers, together with their dependants and labourers, were far more numerous. Landowners, farmers and labourers together accounted for some three million souls out of a total population of five and a half million. Furthermore, in King's time, as earlier, many important trades and industries were based on agriculture, using as their raw materials wool, flax, leather, timber, tallow, vegetable dyestuffs and malting barley, and often employing much rural labour. Nearly half the nation's income went on food and drink, and one-third of this outlay went on beer [1]. The mining of coal and other minerals, as well as quarrying, brick-making and iron-making, were carried on under the patronage of landowners, often with the aid of their capital, and sometimes under their direct control.

The gentry as farmers

The pre-nineteenth century economy, therefore, although one in which trade and industry had long been advancing, was still firmly rooted in the countryside. The larger part of the 38 million acres of England and Wales was by the seventeenth century in the hands of the gentry. Their hegemony, however, was more marked in some areas than others. The whole of Wales, much of the West Country, Yorkshire, and most of the south and east of England were dominated by gentry estates. Of course, proud mansions of the nobility could be found everywhere, but it was only in certain districts that the great owners occupied a pre-eminent position, as did the Derbys in Lancashire, the Devonshires, Newcastles and Rutlands in the Midlands, and the Northumberlands and Lonsdales in the north.

The gentry estates themselves varied greatly in size. At the upper end they merged into the vast accumulations of the great proprietors, at the lower they consisted of a modest house and its adjoining farm, with a few scattered parcels in neighbouring parishes. In Devonshire, Professor Hoskins tells us, the small backwoods gentry with £50 to £100 a year in the seventeenth century possessed some six to twelve farms besides their own home farm[2]. For the modest country gentleman the home farm was a major source of income, perhaps his only important income. The home farm of the greater gentry served primarily as a convenient means of supplying fresh food to the mansion and its inhabitants: it was only secondarily a commercial venture. Nevertheless, sales of produce often went far to meet the expenses of the home farm and might even produce a substantial profit. Sir John Banks, one of the richest businessmen of the post-Civil War era, built up between 1657 and 1671 an important estate in Kent which passed on his death to the future earls of Aylesford. From his home farm at Aylesford on the Medway, Banks sold wheat, peas, rye and bullocks. Some of his produce went to London, some was sold to the Navy, and more went to provide victuals for his trading venture to the Mediterranean, the good ship *Virgin*. He dealt also in hops, and sold timber and reeds to the naval dockyards at Chatham[3].

Elsewhere in Kent the old-established gentry, unlike the *parvenu* Banks, had tended their home farms for generations. Sir Norton Knatchbull, whose family had farmed in east Kent in the Middle Ages, fattened sheep in Romney Marsh, and in 1671–72 he made over £1,500 from sales of sheep and wool, with some cattle, wheat, barley and skins. One of his neighbours in the Marsh, Nicholas Toke of Godinton, rented several hundred acres of pasture there as well as other grazing land near Ashford[4].

In Northamptonshire Sir Thomas Tresham of Rushton obtained more than half his income in the 1590s from sales of farm produce. This consisted mainly of wool and sheep, but there were other livestock, corn, hops, cheese, hides, timber and lime. Even sales of rabbits formed a profitable business on this and other estates of the period. Owners with an excess of grazing land let off their surplus pasture and sold grass and hay. In the late 1590s Thomas Grantham was selling more than 170 acres of grass each year on his Lincolnshire estate, although he himself was running some two thousand sheep as well as cattle. His hay was sold unmown at 10s an acre, and in 1598 his hay and grass sold at Lincoln brought in nearly £100. Grantham also received an average of £130 a year for his timber. On many estates timber was a valuable asset, producing income either from proceeds of direct sales or from rents paid by timber dealers for leases of woodland. In Huntingdonshire the Cromwell family sold timber worth several hundred pounds a year, and between 1611 and 1614 Sir Thomas Leigh at Leighton Buzzard had sales of over £130 a year of his spires, bark, underwood and faggots. On the Buckinghamshire estate of Sir Henry Lee timber sales over the period 1639 to 1650 realised almost £3,000[5].

In East Anglia, particularly in Norfolk, sheep were of especial importance. In 1489 the Townshend flocks totalled over 9,000 sheep, while in the 1550s John Corbett of Sprowston had over 5,000 sheep. The twenty flocks of Sir Henry Fermor totalled over 15,000 in 1521, and these numbers were matched in the 1540s and 1560s by the flocks of Sir Richard Southwell of Wood Rising. Flocks were smaller in the late seventeenth and early eighteenth centuries, but those of Sir Robert L'Estrange of Hunstanton and the Walpoles of

Houghton still ran to two or three thousand in some years. Profits from sheep might rise to some hundreds of pounds, depending on the size of the flocks and the ruling price for wool. Sir Richard Southwell, who was in a very large way of business, made £328 in 1544–45, and as much as £553 in 1561–62. Much of the Norfolk wool was sold to middlemen, the wool-broggers, and some went direct to the clothiers of Suffolk and Essex. From the mid-sixteenth century the growing food demands of Norwich and more distant London encouraged specialised mutton production. By the later seventeenth century the market for Norfolk mutton had fostered the introduction of new fodder crops and advanced crop rotations: the Walpoles' sheep, for example, were bought in the autumn, wintered on turnips, and sometimes finished on early grass in the spring [6].

Large-scale sheep farming was also found in the Cotswolds and the enclosed portions of Northamptonshire, Warwickshire and Leicestershire. Flocks totalled up to 10,000 or even 20,000, and transactions in sheep ran into hundreds, sometimes thousands, of pounds. In Northamptonshire as many as 2,060 sheep changed hands on one occasion, and the price agreed between Dame Elizabeth Hatton and William Knight of Holdenby came to as high a sum as £2,820 [7]. Some families, indeed, like the Spencers of Althorp, owed their rise into the peerage principally to the profits of sheep-farming. The Spencers had begun as graziers in Warwickshire, where in 1497 John Spencer was farming the manor of Snitterfield. The profits of grazing, marriage to a local heiress, and the help of influential relations enabled Spencer to acquire estates in both Warwickshire and neighbouring Northamptonshire, and in 1508 he purchased the manor of Althorp from the Catesbys for £800. Three years later Spencer was High Sheriff of Northamptonshire, and in 1518 he was knighted by Henry VIII. The less well known Eyres of Hassop in Derbyshire also rose as agricultural capitalists through their stock farms, land speculations, and activities in the lead trade. But these families were exceptional: more generally income from direct farming formed a useful supplement to other resources, but it was seldom sufficient in itself to lever families far up the social scale. Marriage, office, law and trade were generally much more important [8].

Growth of the landlord-tenant system

Commercial farming entailed risks of loss as well as prospects of profit. The vagaries of the weather, the periodically high incidence of animal disease and the uncertainty of the markets made it a highly speculative business. An income from rents offered a more certain, if lower, return from one's land, and when the mortgage became safer as an investment in the later seventeenth century it seemed wiser to many landowners to put spare capital into land rather than farm stock. The returns on land let out to tenants, although secure, were low. The demand for land was influenced considerably by the political power and social influence that landownership conferred. Consequently the competition to buy land kept its price high and correspondingly reduced its yield as a pure investment: in the middle eighteenth century the average annual return on land represented by rent was only about 3 or 4 per cent when deductions were made for taxes, repairs and expenses of management. Mortgages were a little more profitable, yielding between 4 and 5 per cent, and since they were almost as secure as land itself, involved no outlay for taxes or repairs, and were less troublesome to manage, they became a popular form of investment among all the propertied classes. It is much more difficult to gauge the average net return on farming because the evidence in farm accounts is less easy to interpret, and because the return varied according to the soil and type of cultivation, the harvest, and weather conditions, and the level of prices. It seems that farmers in general made a minimum of 10 per cent on their outlay, and in favourable conditions considerably more.

It may have been the higher returns, but also a personal interest in agriculture and sense of vocation, that kept many gentry in commercial farming. The majority of those who went in for farming for the market were the smaller country gentlemen who could not have lived on their limited income from rents and the funds. In the East Riding Arthur Young was impressed by the 'great number of landlords the occupiers of their own lands . . . gentleman farmers from £200 to £500 a year; who, cultivating their own property, do it with a spirit that very few leases will permit. Within a few years there are a great number of well-built brick houses, with inclosed and well-managed gardens, many new cottages; much planting.' Some of the farming gentry, in fact, were in the forefront of agricultural progress, and in the eighteenth and nineteenth centuries exhibited at the county shows and contributed technical papers to such journals as Arthur Young's *Annals of Agriculture, The Farmer's Magazine* and the *Journal of the Royal Agricultural Society*. For them farming was not just a source of income but a way of life. The wealthier gentry treated farming more as a hobby, and relied on other sources of income – rents, mortgages, canal shares, the Funds – to cushion the impact of periodical agricultural depressions. That such depressions could play havoc with farming finances is made clear by bank records. The bank accounts of Oxfordshire gentry, for example, dropped dramatically in the severe depression of 1821–22, when fat South Down wethers sold for less than their price as lambs, and a gloomy Cobbett predicted that 'the present race of farmers . . . must be swept away by bankruptcy' [9].

The majority of the greater gentry seemed to have abandoned large-scale commercial farming in the course of the late seventeenth and early eighteenth centuries. In Norfolk the Walpoles and Townshends, among other local owners, were still actively farming for profit in the early decades of the eighteenth century, but in general the larger proprietors moved away from direct participation. They retained a home farm for its convenience but seldom regarded it as primarily a profit-making enterprise. The bulk of their land was let out permanently to tenants, and so far were they from wanting to engage in farming that their estate policy was consciously directed towards avoiding vacant holdings. If by some mischance a farm did fall into hand, it was re-let again as soon as was feasible. In part, this policy arose from the expense and inconvenience of having to find farm stock and a bailiff to run a vacant farm for a short period, although sometimes it was necessary to do this in order to bring a neglected farm back into good condition for letting again. It was widely held that farming through the agency of a bailiff invariably involved a severe risk of fraud and loss (although it must be said that this does not seem to have discouraged their forbears from demesne farming). In 1737 when Henry Purefoy, squire of Shalstone, Buckinghamshire, had a farm fall into hand he found his customary days of leisure replaced by discomfort and 'great hurry':

with his servants away looking after the farm and his horses all 'workt down', entertaining and visiting were out of the question. 'Wee are in great hurry', he wrote, 'having a ffarme of an hundred pound a year fell into our hands, which, joined to this other misfortune [his mother's illness], makes it impossible for us to entertain anybody' [10].

Possibly the sharp fall in agricultural prices in the later seventeenth century, and the continued low levels that ruled in the first half of the eighteenth century, had much to do with the larger owners' loss of interest in commercial farming. The price fall occurred when other forms of investment in mortgages, the Funds, and the great trading and financial companies, were becoming more secure and readily available; and no doubt the attractiveness of the new investment possibilities was enhanced by the bleakness of the agricultural outlook. It has been argued recently that the growth of absenteeism among landowners contributed to the decline of demesne farming in this period. Marriage alliances often meant that land was acquired at an inconvenient distance from the main estate, and in addition landowners absented themselves from their seats in order to attend Parliament, take up a political career, hold a colonial governorship, or merely indulge a taste for living abroad. As a result farms were let out to tenants and supervised by stewards, with possibly harmful effects on farming efficiency [11]. In this connection it is interesting that Sir William Coventry, writing about 1670, attributed the 'want of tenants' to the landowners' habit of living in London: 'When the nobility and gentry lived in the country they kept a considerable demesne in their hands, which, since they have lived much in London, they have strove to let even to the very door of their mansion houses' [12].

Whatever the reasons, the distinction between the function of the landowner and that of the farmer became quite marked. In a sense farming became a joint operation between landowner and tenant farmer in which each made his own contribution. The landowner provided the land, farmhouse, barns, stables, fences, embankments and other essential facilities, and he generally provided wood and other materials for repairs. Usually he undertook to pay the land tax, introduced near the end of the seventeenth century, but he left the parish rates for the tenant. A good landlord concerned himself with improvements that would benefit the property and help the tenant to be more efficient. Thus landowners took in waste and commons for additional farmland, consolidated holdings in common fields, rebuilt farm buildings, undertook flood control and drainage works, encouraged tenants to enrich their soil with marl, and involved themselves in promoting turnpikes, river improvements and canal schemes in order to obtain easier access to markets.

The tenants, for their part, provided the working capital for the farm – the stock, plough team, implements, seed – and of course paid the labourers and provided the skill and enterprise in cultivation. Where tenants held their farms by lease there might be detailed husbandry covenants which regulated the rotation of crops and use of pasture; but such leases seem to have been rather exceptional, and in practice farmers had a great deal of latitude in how they cultivated the soil. Naturally the landlord kept an eye on them to see that the farm was not seriously prejudiced by improper practices, and that the buildings were kept in repair, but he tried to prevent difficulties from arising by making a careful choice of tenant in the first instance. When considering applicants for a vacant farm the points that most exercised the landlord did not concern obtaining the highest possible rent but centred round the tenant's character, his experience in farming and, above all, his possession of adequate capital to stock the farm in question. To have an experienced, sober and substantial tenant on the farm, even without the formal security of a lease, was safer than to take the highest bidder and hope to keep him up to the mark by restrictive covenants. Landlords, especially when letting their large farms, therefore made careful enquiries of the previous landlord and neighbours of a prospective tenant. 'James Greaves rents £39 a year of mee, most of it ploughed land & leaves my Bargain at Lady day next', wrote Henry Purefoy in 1747 to a fellow landowner; 'I heard hee had a mind to take a Grazing Bargain, for lesse Stocks that than ploughed land & I believe him sufficient to rent your Bargain of £50 a year. Hee is a very civill ffellow & I hope hee will make you a good Tennant' [13].

Sir Joseph Banks, the famous botanist and enthusiast for African exploration, was in addition a landlord with progressive ideas on estate management. He held that the rent, after deducting tithe, land tax and poor rate, should be divided into four parts. One part should be reserved for the landlord 'for his maintenance and the support and placing out of his family'. The other three parts should go to the tenant and be divided as follows: 'one for the ordinary expenses of his household in food, clothes'; another 'for the purchase of seed and cost of labour and materials of farming'; and one 'for improvement of his premises . . . and for providing Portions for his daughters and Capital sufficient to enable his Sons to take farms'. Sir Joseph also held that no farm should be worth less than £50 a year

because a Family cannot Live upon Less decently even if they Labour in the Field as all the Children ought to do, nor should a Farm exceed £200 a year, for if it does the Father will educate some of his sons as clergymen or merchants, and by so doing rob the state of as many farmers as he is able and turn them into Gentleman Consumers and not Providers of Food.

Furthermore, maintained Sir Joseph, 'unlearned' tenants should be prevented from competing for farms and paying rents they could not afford. He summed up his creed in these words:

A Landlord like a Monarch or a Father of his Tenants ought to Live among them delighted at their happiness and meeting their benedictions whenever he sees them. His care must be first not to destroy them by exhorbitant demands of Rent, and secondly not to suffer them to grow rich enough to make their sons into Consumers of the Producers of the Earth as Lawyers, Parsons, Doctors, etc., etc. Certainly these classes should be taken from the younger branches of Gentlemen's Families, and Farmers suffered to save enough out of their Farms to make their sons Farmers and their Daughters Farmers Wives, and be happy and cheerful and will produce to their Landlord sufficient to enable him to Live as well as a man of his Landed Property ought to Live [14].

The happy combination of a fair-minded, improving landlord and a competent, substantial tenant was not always achieved, of course; but where it was it helped to account for the efficient and progressive character of English farming. It made also for stability. Tenants would not lightly give up the farm of a just and enlightened landlord; equally, landlords would not readily part with tried and trusted tenants. This mutual confidence meant that many tenants went on for years, even generations, without the formality of a lease, and were not afraid to engage in long-term improvements to their farms. On the Yorkshire estate of the Roman Catholic Constables the Quaker Stickney family had already farmed for a century in 1841, adding 500 acres by drainage and improvement without ever possessing a lease[15]. A nineteenth-century enquiry showed that in Glamorgan farmers without leases had been in occupation of their farms for much longer periods than those holding leases: cases were noted of farms held in the same family, merely by annual agreements, for periods of 80, 180, and 'upward of 100' years[16]. And when tenants were in difficulties, as in times of exceptionally low prices or severe outbreaks of animal disease, landlords came to their aid with rent abatements and improvements to the farms, or helped to pay their local taxes and husbandry expenses. All this was not sheer altruism: the last thing landlords wanted to see was their farms unoccupied.

While much farming was assuming the progressive and stable character engendered by the landlord–tenant system, it has to be remembered that many farmers were 'yeomen', independent owner-occupiers of farms of varying size and efficiency. The bigger of these independent cultivators were men of capital and highly enlightened in their ideas, as the *Tours* of Arthur Young show us; but the smaller yeomen, for a variety of reasons, were in decline. The evidence suggests, indeed, that a substantial shift away from smaller owner-occupied holdings and towards larger estates and the extension of tenancy occurred between the later seventeenth century and the middle of the eighteenth. It is impossible to be sure what were the major factors in this shift, but no doubt the inefficiency and poverty of some small owner-occupiers was an element in the situation[17].

Not all gentry estates were progressive or even up-to-date in their methods of management. Many estates were still dominated by ancient tenures, copyhold, leases for lives, and in the north 'tenant right', all of which had the effect of restricting the landowner's control over his property and inhibited the undertaking of improvements. The replacement of unsatisfactory tenures by leases for terms of years or simple annual agreements was usually a lengthy procedure, which on some estates stretched into the nineteenth century. Even in well-established areas of commercial farming, such for instance as east Kent, the twenty-one year leases of the early eighteenth century still retained old provisions for the tenant's performance of carriage services for the lord and payment of rent in kind.

Antiquated conditions of tenure survived in more remote areas until quite recent times. In northern England old manorial rights still pertained, but the landowners' neglect, and the tenants' virtual independence under the system of 'tenant right', meant that these ancient dues were difficult to collect; and sometimes a new owner found it impossible to ascertain just how, or under what conditions, his tenants had come to occupy the farms. In Wales there were farms let on perpetual leases 'for as long as the sun rises and water flows'. In Pembrokeshire payment of rents in kind and in services to the landlord were commonplace. Tenants were required to present their landlord with gifts of hens, geese, capons and eggs; they were obliged to help get in his harvest and carry coal from his mines; they paid a heriot of their best beast on succeeding to the holding, ground their corn at the landlord's mill, and kept a sporting dog for his use. Even in the more developed Glamorgan of 1789 Robert Jones of Fonmon Castle required his tenants to carry two sacks of coal for him from the pithead, and he obliged them also to ship their corn to Bristol from the harbour at Aberthaw, where he claimed exclusive rights[18].

More systematic and efficient methods of estate management were slow in appearing. The bigger gentry owners followed the practice of the great proprietors in employing a full-time steward or agent to manage their estates and relieve them of the burden of keeping regular accounts and maintaining day-to-day supervision. Lesser gentry were more likely to look after their property themselves, although they sometimes paid a local attorney or a farmer to collect their rents and inspect their farms on a part-time basis[19]. Some gentry families had themselves originated from estate offices and had prospered in the service of a great lord. In Gloucestershire the Smyths of Nibley, in Staffordshire the Bill family, in Lancashire the Greenes, in Westmorland the Porters of Weary Hall, and in Derbyshire the Eures, Everinghams, Babingtons, Brights and Saviles were examples of this widespread process. Others rose from holding similar administrative offices in the household of a great proprietor. Such was William Farington of Worden, who in 1572 became steward of the household to the fourth Earl of Derby, and subsequently receiver-general to his heir. Connected with the Derbys by marriage, Farington eventually became a justice and a deputy lieutenant of Lancashire.

Perhaps an aptitude for administration and accounting became inherent in such families, and certainly it was quite common for a son to succeed his father as steward of a great estate. Two generations of the Fillingham family, for example, served as stewards to the Duke of Rutland in the later eighteenth and the early nineteenth centuries. They acted also for other families in the Belvoir area, and William Fillingham, the father, officiated as an enclosure commissioner for twenty-three parishes in Nottinghamshire and elsewhere. In 1792 he was rich enough to find £12,000 in ready money for the purchase of Syerston Manor, and he then proceeded to enclose the open fields of Syerston. His son, George Fillingham, married a Leicestershire heiress and completed the building of Syerston Hall. George was a meticulous keeper of accounts; all the members of his family had to keep their own records of household and personal expenditure (down to 'pence lost' and 'pence found'), which he duly inspected and signed at the end of each year. When in 1800 he worked out his liability for the new income tax he had a net income of £142 from land in his own occupation, £403 from rents, £286 from interest on mortgages and Consols together with dividends on canal shares, and a net £256 from his estate agency. Of the total of £1,087 he calculated that £532 was chargeable to income tax after allowing for his payments of interest on mortgages, bonds, and promissory notes, an annuity, and his assessed taxes[20].

All prudent members of the gentry kept a wary eye on their financial position and were obliged to keep some form of accounts. From the 1760s to the 1790s, Gervase Powell of Llanharan, Glamorgan, kept separate accounts of his income, money lent out to relatives and neighbours (in sums of a few hundred pounds at 5 per cent), and his transactions with his bankers, Messrs Hoare of Fleet Street. The last included his purchases of stocks, and payments to jewellers, goldsmiths, cabinet makers, upholsterers, wine merchants, silk mercers, drapers and milliners (he had four daughters) [21]. Sir John Oglander of Nunwell in the Isle of Wight found it rather an alarming exercise to add up his annual expenses. The total for 1632 came to £684 9s 6d:

> By this account I spend almost £1,000 *per annum*, for I account that my corn and such other provisions of my own, as some 12 beeves, 100 sheep, butter, cheese, milk, bacon, pork, poultry and other things of my own and that are given me by my friends and tenants, cannot come to less than near upon £300. This proportion is too large for my comings in.

In another year his expenses amounted to £716 14s 10d. This, he remarked with nautical similes, was 'too much for my estate, having so many poor children: therefore it behoves me to tack about and lay by, or shift my course. If I spend as much this year as I did the last, I shall be like a man in a storm, not well knowing what course to take.' His accounts included £20 for 'my wife to find her apparel and other necessaries for the whole year', £3 'lost at cards to the sea captains at several times and spent in their company', six shillings paid 'to Mistress Brassbridge for tending of Bridget when she was sick of the pox', and two shillings for a bottle of wine given 'at my Brother Bromfield's marriage'[22].

Accounts were frequently supplemented by memoranda. Notes were made, for example about the misbehaviour of tenants, details of useful covenants for inclusion in future leases of farms, proposals to exchange lands or engross farms, dealings with tradesmen, household matters and all the miscellanea of country life. Correspondence seems to have centred round the family's state of health, social excursions and the visits of friends. Only rarely were there references to national events or market conditions, as when in September 1730 the Reverend Patrick St Clair of Sustead, Norfolk, remarked to his old friend Ashe Windham of Felbrigg, 'there is great scarcity of money in the country and nothing sells'. And again in February 1739, 'I am sorry you have such a farm to let now, when every thing is so low, and a prospect of the prices of grain falling yet more'[23]. A hundred years earlier Sir James Oxinden, Lord of the Manor of Makinbrooke in Herne, Kent, ran into the same kind of trouble in May 1640. Apologising for his inability to send more money to his nephew, Sir James commented that

> according to my old wont, I went among my fewe tenants in Hearne for my rent, where I founde so much want of money as I never did all dayes of my life; tho they confessed they were not without that was worth money, yet they protested to me that unless they should be very great Loasers they could not get any money for their commodities [24].

From their accumulated experience some landowners felt the advisability of leaving detailed instructions for their sons when they came into their patrimony. The staple items of advice included the prevention of frequent changes of stewards and tenants, encouragement of the tenants to state their grievances, real or imaginary, the importance of keeping regular accounts and memoranda of business affairs, frugality in personal expenditure, and above all avoidance of entanglement in the law. 'Be advised by me', wrote Sir John Oglander. 'Have no suits in law, if possibly thou mayest avoid them. . . . So many inconveniencies hang upon a suit of law that I advise thee, although thou hast the better of it, let it be reconciled without law.' James Bankes, who about 1595 purchased the Winstanley estate near Wigan, left a memoranda book containing a variety of instructions for his heir, including the advice to abandon leases in favour of annual tenures: 'When any lease shall fall to thee, let the same to the tenant again for a yearly rent, and in God's name take not too much rent nor yet too little, for a mean is the best, so shalt thou be best able to live' [25].

Yet despite the well-known expense, uncertainty and vexation of law-suits, it was difficult for landowners to keep out of the courts. Questions of title to property, the extent of manorial rights, boundaries of estates, interpretations of the terms of leases, wills and marriage settlements, recovery of debts, dis-traints for rent upon insolvent tenants and a host of other sources of dispute were inherent in the transfer and management of landed property. Further, the overweening pride of gentry families, their consciousness of status, susceptibility to slights and a deep belief in the rights and privileges of property, all made them reluctant to give way, even in the most petty matters. It was therefore an everyday occurrence to have a lawsuit in train, perhaps several at once. The more irascible of them had a passion for what a Denbighshire man called 'lawying', plunged headlong into new disputes, and were always at loggerheads with their neighbours. Sadly, a taste for litigation rarely benefited an estate as much as it did the lawyers.

It was partly to resolve disputes over boundaries, and to facilitate exchanges and enclosure of land, that the gentry began to demand accurate maps of their estates. Such maps might run from rough sketches to elaborate works of art, expensively embellished with a decorated title, coat of arms, and illustrations of scenes of husbandry and the chase, like the famous 1635 map of Laxton. Alongside the necessarily utilitarian purposes of estate surveys there developed a more general interest in the mapping of the county. About 1572 Thomas Seckford, a wealthy Suffolk lawyer, commissioned Christopher Saxton to survey and map all the counties of England and Wales, and Seckford had the maps engraved and published at his own expense. Similarly, the work of subsequent generations of county map-makers was encouraged by the patronage of the gentry, the marking of whose seats formed a prominent feature of the finished work.

Running an estate was not exclusively the responsibility of the male members of gentry families. Unavoidable absences of the proprietor at court, attending Parliament, or at the assizes and quarter sessions, together with illness and premature death, meant that estate affairs were often temporarily or permanently in the hands of wives, daughters, or widows. The Paston family of Norfolk was supposed to suffer under an ancient curse which pronounced that one of the family would always be a fool 'till it is become poor'. In fact it seems that the family's decline was due more to its losses in the Civil Wars, but certainly Sir Edward Paston was so affected, and it was his wife who with great ability took charge of affairs and managed the property. John Allen of Cresselly, Pembrokeshire, gave instructions to his daughter while away from home: 'I am very glad to hear the collieries go on briskly; push 'em on with all the care and frugality that is possible. . . . Let me beg you will all live in the frugallest manner, and take all the care very early and late of everything in your power'[26].

Another eighteenth-century gentleman, John Noble, a justice of Herefordshire, left detailed instructions for his wife to observe when he was away on business. Her daughters were to be up by six to get on with the housework, while she organised the transport of coals from the Forest of Dean, supervised the bread-making, and attended the vestry meetings to see that nothing was done to involve the parish in expense[27]. It is clear from Mrs Purefoy's letters that she, too, was no mean businesswoman in managing her sales of butter and purchases of livestock. Nor was she unacquainted with the procedures of law but could tell an attorney that his clerk had made a mistake in the engrossing of a bond assignment[28]. If we knew more about the role of the gentry's womenfolk we would no doubt find many a good lady deserving of the encomium paid his wife by Sir John Oglander:

> I could never have done it without a most careful wife who was no spender, never wore a silk gown but for her credit when she went abroad, and never to please herself. She was up every day before me and oversaw all the outhouses: she would not trust her maid with directions but would wet her shoes to see it done herself. Yet I always kept a good house, not much inferior to any in the Island. I pray God they that follow me may do as well[29].

The expansion and management of estates

Detailed studies of individual gentry families suggest that their history was marked by an alternation of periods of progress with years of decline or, at best, stability. Fluctuations in fortunes were partly due, of course, to family circumstances. The periods of a family's progress were often connected with a fortunate marriage to a rich heiress, succession by the accidents of death to the estates of relations, or a minority when the heir was under age and guardians reorganised the estate and revitalised family finances; or again the head of the family might be a shrewd opportunist who took full advantage of what opportunities for advancement were open to him. Decline, on the other hand, accompanied a preponderance of daughters who had to be dowried out of the estate, or the longevity of a well-jointured widow; or the family might be brought down by feckless extravagance in building, electioneering or high living. While such family circumstances were general factors accounting for the ups and downs of a family's progress, national conditions in politics and economics might have a crucial influence too, working with or against the family's circumstances to accelerate advance or to hasten decline. For example, the dissolution of the monasteries, sales of Crown lands, and the great rise in prices in the sixteenth and early seventeenth centuries provided opportunities for the favourably situated to make very large increases in their estate incomes. Later the expanding investment market and the development of trade and industry in the eighteenth and nineteenth centuries offered comparable opportunities. In agriculture itself the rising prices of the years between 1760 and 1813 gave scope for increased farm profits, large rent increases, and participation in the contemporary form of lucrative land development, enclosure. On the debit side of the balance sheet were wardship, the confiscations and sequestrations of the Interregnum, the post-1660 burden of taxation, and for the Roman Catholic gentry of that era the special fiscal penalties and disabilities imposed on recusants.

Naturally, the family's good or bad luck in the chances of birth, marriage and death affected all in some degree, while only a proportion of the gentry gained or lost very much through other influences, depending on their alertness to opportunity, resilience in times of difficulty, availability of capital, and, simply, the geographical situation of their estates. Although the dissolution of the monasteries did not create very many new gentry families, there is little doubt that the transfers of land from the Church and Crown in the course of the sixteenth and early seventeenth centuries greatly augmented the estates and incomes of existing gentry. It has been estimated that in Kent the gentry increased their territorial holdings by over a third [30], and this was perhaps on the low side for the country as a whole. Numerous families used the lands they acquired as the sites of new houses. In Norfolk, for example, Sir Robert Southwell built where Bermondsey Abbey once stood; in Dorset, according to a county historian writing in 1732, the Benedictine house of Abbotsbury was purchased by Sir Giles Strangways, who built 'in place of the Abbie a faire Mansion House' [31]. In Devon William Abbot, of the King's household, bought Hartland Abbey and turned it into a gentleman's seat, while over the border Sir Richard Grenville was the most prominent of the Cornish gentry who went in for Church property. In the reign of James I the Roberts family of Truro, with a fortune made in the tin trade, established themselves on a former monastic barton at Lanhydrock [32]. And in his *Itineraries* Leland noted many similar conversions: Milwood Park for example, a former Carthusian monastery in Lincolnshire, and Cateley Priory near Sleaford, occupied by one Car, 'a proper gentilman, whose father was a rich merchant of the staple' [33].

Not only monastic lands but the greater part of the monastic income from tithes went into the hands of the county families. Even before the dissolution many gentry had managed monastic estates and acted as farmers of the tithes. At the dissolution they were the best placed to take advantage of opportunities of investing in both monastic lands and leases of tithes. Such investments not only added to their incomes but also increased their social importance, particularly when they acquired the right of presentation to livings. Large profits could also be made from leases of the properties retained or acquired by the Church of England. The estates of the Dean and Chapter of Canterbury, for example, were persistently let below their economic rents, and the lessees were able to sublet or farm the properties themselves to great advantage. The farm rents of the Dean and Chapter of Durham remained unchanged for more than a century after the Restoration. In Wales, too, the gentry were eager for leases of glebe and tithes, for which they paid low rents, while squeezing the incumbents with meagre customary stipends that remained unchanged over long periods.

In addition to beneficial leases and periodical revisions of the conditions of tenure, one of the major ways by which landowners could increase the income from existing estates was to go in for enclosure. This term covered a wide variety of land improvements, not all of which were harmful to the farmers and labourers concerned. It was only where a scarcity of pasture was accentuated by enclosure of rough grazing land or commons and wastes, or where enclosure was associated with engrossing – the throwing together of small holdings into larger farms – that the farmers' grievances festered into unrest and open hostility. Other forms of enclosure – the extinction of common grazing rights over common fields, and the gradual consolidation of inconveniently scattered holdings into compact farms separated from each other by hedges, fences, walls or ditches; the creation of new pasture closes out of the arable common fields to relieve shortages of pasture; and the bringing into cultivation of useless heath, moor, or marsh – all these generally caused little or no disturbance, and were often supported and even initiated by the farmers themselves.

Much depended on the local conditions, on how rapidly the changes were made, and how equitably they were carried out. Until fairly recent years enclosure has received a bad press from historians who were unduly impressed by contemporary complaints of loss of employment, depopulation and distress. The obviously beneficial effects for farming efficiency, farm incomes and, not least, employment, of cultivating the land more effectively and of bringing uncultivated land into production have been neglected, although they were clear enough to some contemporaries. For example, a Welsh gentleman, Charles Hassall, replied in verse to the old slur that 'it was a sin to steal a goose from the common but not the common from a goose':

> He stands in need of no excuse
> Who feeds an Ox where fed a Goose,
> Expels a base, encroaching crew,
> And gives each honest Man his due,
> Who bids the Ocean keep its Bounds
> And not intrude on People's Grounds,
> Witness the Marshes near this Town
> So lately cloathed in dreary brown;
> But now are always to be seen,
> In gay and everlasting Green [34].

In its various forms enclosure went on for centuries from the Middle Ages to recent times. For much of this long stretch of years it gave rise to little or no outcry. It is significant that the two outstanding periods of concern, the sixteenth century and the fifty years after 1760, were both times of increasing population and rising food prices. In these two periods the acceleration of enclosure seemed the more calamitous because it occurred when greater numbers were seeking employment on the land, and when standards of living were under pressure from dearer food. Modern opinion holds, however, that it is unlikely that enclosure was more than an occasional local factor in the growth of more widespread rural distress. In the sixteenth century the government's alarm over the supposed effects of depopulation and unemployment through 'decay of tillage' was concentrated consistently on the counties of Leicestershire, Lincolnshire, Warwickshire, Northamptonshire, Bedfordshire and Buckinghamshire. It was these counties which were mentioned again and again in the measures designed to check enclosure. This was not because there was little or no enclosure elsewhere, but rather because it was in the Midlands, particularly, that enclosure of commons and conversion of arable to grass had severe consequences. In the Midlands the combination of mounting population pressure, shortage of land – especially of commons and waste for grazing – and the relevant circumstance that the Midland clays were much better suited to pasture than to arable, meant that enclosure inevitably meant some decay of tillage, with the consequent unemployment, land hunger and unrest that the government so feared[35].

Some enclosures had the effect of converting farmland or common grazing into uncultivated pleasure parks, thus depriving local people of their livelihood. Among the tyrannical park-makers of the sixteenth century were Sir John Rodney, who enclosed 200 acres of common on Mendip and a part of Brent marches, and Guy Willistrop, who was accused of destroying the whole town of Wilstrop for his park. Numbers of rising gentry, like John Spencer of Althorp, had to answer charges of causing depopulation, and while Spencer could make a satisfactory reply, other gentry showed a heartless disregard for the poor inhabitants whom they evicted. John Palmer, emparking in West Angmering, replied to a complaint with the contemptuous remark: 'Doo ye not knowe that the kinges grace hath putt downe all the houses of monks, fryers and nunnes? Thierfor nowe is the tyme come that we gentilmen will pull downe the houses of such poore knaves as ye be'[36]. Emparking continued in subsequent centuries, but often in areas of poor land unsuited to intensive farming and better fitted for rough grazing or timber, such as Sherwood Forest, the Yorkshire wolds and the chalk downs of the southeast. In consequence the extent of disturbance and depopulation was frequently quite small, and some park-makers provided displaced cottagers with a newly built model village close at hand.

The enclosures of the eighteenth century were again largely concentrated on the Midlands, because despite the activities of the sixteenth-century landlords, it was still there that the largest areas of remaining common fields were to be found. In this period, however, much of the enclosing was for improved forms of mixed farming: the alternation of arable and fodder crops which made it possible for the land to carry more stock and produce larger crops of grain. Unlike the conversion of arable to permanent grass, which reduced labour requirements and was still going on in some districts, the adoption of improved convertible husbandry made for a larger labour force than could find employment on the former common fields. Enclosures elsewhere in this period were mainly of waste, and over the country as a whole some millions of acres of additional land were taken into cultivation, thus greatly increasing local demands for labour. The worst rural unemployment and poverty were to be found in old-enclosed areas of southern England and East Anglia, which saw little new agricultural development.

Over large parts of the country enclosure of commons and waste land was never a serious problem, either because it occurred when the local population was still very small and large alternative areas of waste were available, or because common rights were not important in the system of cultivation. In much of northern England, Wales and the southwest, the predominant farming was of a pastoral kind and the arable was seldom extensive; great stretches of mountain and moorland provided grazing; and the population was generally sparse. For the small cultivators in the pockets of arable, however, enclosure of common lands could give rise to anxiety because common pasturage was essential for their sheep and cattle and was a necessary element in the successful cultivation of the ploughland. Consequently there sometimes occurred the same kind of disturbances which marked enclosure in the Midlands, with the small farmers tearing down the newly formed walls and hedges, and issuing threats of further action if the landlords did not desist[37].

From the landlords' point of view enclosure was a profitable rationalisation of the use of existing farm land, making possible more efficient farming, more viable tenants and higher rents. It was also a means of converting waste land into more advantageous arable or pasture, and of securing claims to exclusive use of woodlands and minerals. Throughout the centuries, indeed, enclosure was basically concerned with improved exploitation of the land, putting the soil to its most profitable use and securing rights of individual ownership and occupation. With enclosure went a number of other developments: drainage, flood control, improved farm buildings, transport projects, revision of tenures, and increased interest in methods of cultivation and improved breeds of livestock. All these were interconnected, for it hardly made sense to spend time and money on enclosing when the advantages were vitiated by poor drainage, inadequate means of transport or low standards of husbandry. The years of most intensive enclosure in the eighteenth and early nineteenth centuries were influenced by the growth of urban food markets, especially in London, and by improved conditions of transport. Further, it was a period when landlords had more money available for estate development as new capital came into the land from industry and commerce, and as the level of rents rose very markedly, nearly trebling between 1750 and 1815. The earlier decline of landlords' interest in large-scale direct farming must also have released capital from farm stock for other purposes, including investment in permanent improvement of the land itself. It would be misleading, however, to exaggerate the extent of landlords' investment in land improvement, taken as a whole. Under particularly ambitious owners progress could be very marked, and the total investment over a period of years might run into many thousands of pounds. Investment was especially heavy in the period when parliamentary enclosure was in vogue in the late eighteenth and early nineteenth centuries, and during the enthusiasm for under-drainage in the middle decades of the nineteenth century. Both of these were costly forms of improvement running from a pound or two to £10 an acre, so that enclosure or under-drainage of a property in only one village might involve sums of several thousand pounds. Generally, though, the pace of improvement was slow, and from the Middle Ages onwards the proportion of landowners' incomes that went into permanent improvements was fairly modest, rising from as little as 5 per cent to 30 per cent or so on progressive estates.

It was natural that the interest of landowners in maximising the returns on their land should spill over into the techniques of farming; as countrymen and the keepers of home farms the gentry could hardly fail to have some knowledge of agriculture and its problems, even when they were not themselves directly engaged in farming for the market. Thus the scholarly Sir Roger Twysden laid aside his treatises on government and the Church to make careful notes on his tenants, the tithes, and the care of his woods[38]. A number of Twysden's Kentish contemporaries wrote on various aspects of husbandry. Sir Edward Dering, for example, produced *Orchard, or a Book of Planting*, with detailed notes on some 150 varieties of trees to be found in his orchard grounds near Ashford[39]. In the Isle of Wight Sir John Oglander was another expert on fruit trees and gardening in general. At Nunwell he planted with his own hands a hundred Portugal quinces as well as

pippins, pearmains, puttes, hornies and other good apples and all
sorts of good pears . . . cherries, damsons and plums. In the upper
garden, apricocks, mellecatoons and figs. In the Court, vines and
apricocks: in the Bowling Green, the vine and infinity of
raspberries. . . . When my successors hereafter reap the fruits of my
labours, let them remember the founder [40].

The gentry were prominent in the practical experiments on which
agricultural progress was founded. The leading figures included Rowland
Vaughan, a Herefordshire squire, who compiled the first account of water
meadows; Sir Richard Weston, who based his *Discours of the Husbandrie used in
Brabant and Flanders* on a personal study of Flemish methods of using flax, clover
and turnips; Sir Thomas Gresley of Drakelow near Burton-on-Trent, a pioneer
stockbreeder from whose Drakelow cattle all the improved longhorns traced
descent; and the great Tull himself, the Berkshire landowner whose *Horse
Houghing Husbandry* epitomised the empirical, practical approach to the age-old
problem of soil fertility. The new industrialist squires of the eighteenth century
also made their mark as agricultural improvers. John Wilkinson, the iron-
master, reclaimed a thousand acres of peat bog on his estates near Grange-over-
Sands, and experimented with 'sweet coal' as a manure on his lands in north
Wales [41]. The Peels put £138,000 of their profits from cotton manufacturing
into an estate at Tamworth, installing five steam engines and making numerous
other improvements, while another Lancashire cotton master, Samuel Oldknow,
manured the meadows of his Mellor estate with urine pumped from his factory
and apprentice house. In the next century, but still in the same tradition,
William Marshall, son of John Marshall, founder of the Leeds and Shrewsbury
flax firm, employed the celebrated Josiah Parkes to drain a thousand acres at
Patrington, built new roads, imported steam engines and promoted the cultivation of flax; and John Joseph Mechi used profits made from his patent razor
strop to convert 130 acres of waterlogged Essex clay into a famous demonstra-
tion farm, showing that even that unpromising soil could be made to pay: he
also attracted much attention by the publication of his annual farm accounts
with explanations of his occasional losses as well as the general success of his
intensive farming.

Few of the old country gentry, and probably few of the industrialist newcomers, could afford to pour large sums into spectacular but highly uncertain
projects of reclamation. The examples mentioned were exceptional: the
majority of new arrivals among the squirearchy preferred an established estate
with farms which were already a going concern. But there were a considerable
number of gentry who kept up with the latest technical discoveries, attended
the county shows, wrote papers for Young's *Annals of Agriculture*, and ran
advanced model farms.

Many of the farming gentry joined together to form local agricultural
societies, some of them, like the Bath and West of England, developing into
permanent institutions which published their proceedings, and held well-known
shows. Others, though less conspicuous, have survived down to the present, like
the Canterbury Farmers' Club. Frequently they tried to encourage the adoption of new practices by exhibiting implements and machinery and by holding
trials, offering premiums or prizes for the best results and for labourers who
performed long and meritorious service. The distinction of being the oldest

surviving society (as distinct from farmers' dining club) is claimed by the Brecknockshire Society, founded in 1755. Its leading figure, Charles Powell, held that such societies, if widely established, would draw landowners from 'idle and expensive Diversions, such as Cocking, Horse-racing and Gaming' to more worthwhile objects:

> the encouraging and establishing Manufactures, and the promoting Improvements in Husbandry, and consequently exciting an honest Spirit of Industry, and a laudable emulation among the lower Class of our fellow Creatures and at the same time extirpating those Banes of Society – Idleness, Party Rage, and Narrowmindedness, and in lieu thereof cultivating a true publick Spirit, a Spirit of Universal Benevolence [42].

Among the most celebrated figures in the scientific advances of the nineteenth century were Pusey and Lawes. Philip Pusey, who succeeded to his Buckinghamshire estate in 1827, was a many-sided character, a connoisseur of art, hymn writer and member of Parliament. As editor of the leading publication on scientific agriculture, the *Journal of the Royal Agricultural Society*, he played a central role in the progress of English farming. His technical expertise was based on personal experience, for his farm was a well-known trial ground for advanced experiments. He would rise at dawn to supervise the operation of his water-meadows, and he succeeded in quadrupling the size of his sheep flock and doubling the yield of his corn. Sir John Bennett Lawes made a greater and more permanent contribution with his work on the new science of agricultural chemistry. He inherited his Rothamsted estate in 1834, and with the assistance of J. H. Gilbert, a student of the great Liebig, Lawes carried out a long series of strictly controlled experiments designed to ascertain the precise effects of various fertilisers on the growth of crops and livestock. In 1842 he set up a factory at Deptford for the manufacture of superphosphate of lime, and the success of this famous fertiliser led to his establishing larger works at Barking Creek and Millwall. On his death Rothamsted was endowed as the permanent centre for agricultural research which it remains today.

Pusey and Lawes were outstanding examples of a general if much more conventional interest in agriculture among the gentry. Even in backward Wales the 'spirit of improvement' was beginning to appear in the eighteenth century as the Welsh squires founded agricultural societies, experimented with rotations, imported grass seed as well as ploughs and harrows from England, crossed their native sheep with the New Leicesters, irrigated meadows, drained bogs and planted belts of trees as windbreaks. In the less developed areas of England, too, the squires were active. In Yorkshire the Sykeses and the Legards did much to reclaim the bleak moorlands of the wolds. Sir Christopher Sykes sold his interests in stocks and shipping to raise money for the project, while in Young's words, Sir Digby Legard was 'known all over Europe as one of the most accurate of cultivators'. Other Yorkshire improvers included Thomas Elliot of Fremington, the Vavasours, Stricklands and Hildyards. Everywhere improvements made by the gentry and great landlords were reported on by the experts of the day. A plan of Sir Lawrence Palk's carefully designed farmyard at Haldon appeared in Vancouver's 1808 account of Devonshire for the Board of Agriculture. In Norfolk Arthur Young reported in 1804 that the first steam engine designed solely for agricultural purposes was in course of erection by Colonel Buller at Haydon: it cost £600 and was to perform the work of ten horses in threshing, grinding corn and cutting straw. In 1793 a Society for the Encouragement of Agriculture and Industry was founded at Canterbury by two prominent members of the Kentish gentry, Sir Edward Knatchbull and Filmer Honywood. In the same county Mr Darrel of Calehill was attracting attention as the first Kentish gentleman to undertake drainage operations under the direction of the leading authority, Elkington, reclaiming 70 acres of bog near his mansion.

And so one could go on. But however numerous the examples it is apparent from contemporary accounts that the greater part of the gradual advance in knowledge was achieved by the lengthy work of trial and error carried on by some thousands of little-known minor country gentlemen, substantial owner-occupiers and wealthy tenant farmers. These patient experimenters were not entirely obscure. Acclaimed by Arthur Young in his *Tours*, they were no doubt well known in local circles and in the agricultural societies of the day, but they left little behind them in the way of records, and it is now difficult to find out much about them. One thing is clear, however: they were generally men whose principal business was farming rather than owning land, and this largely explains why it was they, and not the greater gentry and the largest owners, who formed the main body of agricultural advance. The large farmers had most, if not all, of their capital sunk into the production of crops and livestock: consequently they were vitally interested in overcoming practical difficulties of cultivation and in finding means of achieving a better return for their money and effort. The landowners, on the other hand, had their capital sunk largely in land: their interest in improvements was confined in the main to ways and means of improving the value of land as a capital asset. They found that this could best be done by ensuring that it was put to that use in which it was most profitable, and hence their interest lay in enclosure of common fields, consolidation of scattered holdings, reclamation of wastes, revision of tenures, drainage, and other permanent improvements that would enable them to attract and retain the best tenants and maximise their rents. Of course, the lesser squires and country gentlemen, who were both large-scale farmers and the owners of tenanted property, embraced both interests to some degree. Between the larger landowners and the farmers proper, however, the division of interests was clear, and this meant that most of the energy for the improvement of farming techniques, as distinct from the rationalisation of the farming structure and the creation of a favourable environment for efficient farming, came from the farmers rather than from the gentry at large.

The industrial exploitation of estates

A further reason for this division of interests was that the larger proprietors' concern with estate management went considerably beyond the needs of agriculture alone. Many estates offered possibilities of exploitation for industrial purposes, and landowners were aware of such possibilities from very early times. Throughout the centuries numerous enclosures of commons and waste were undertaken with minerals rather than farming in mind. Perhaps the most general estate activity other than farming was the production and sale of timber. Woodlands were cultivated and cut systematically with specific markets in view, large timber for shipbuilding and housebuilding, cordwood for fuel and charcoal burning, small timber for making fencing, barrel staves and hop poles, and bark for the tanners. Where an estate's woodlands were extensive and well managed the produce formed a major item of revenue. Suitable rivers running through a property could also be exploited by leasing sites for watermills and quays, as well as by charging tolls on bridges and on the traffic using the river itself. These activities were seldom very lucrative, however, and frequently led to disputes with neighbouring owners. Use of a river for navigation, for example, often conflicted with its use as a source of water-power, the weirs and dams built to maintain a constant flow of water for the mill wheels offering a serious hazard to river vessels.

Development of mining and manufacturing enterprises also ran into difficulties. The uncertainty of success and the technical problems encountered in mining were good grounds for putting the responsibility for operations in the hands of experienced specialists. Consequently landowners generally preferred to lease out mineral lands for a royalty on the output rather than attempt to assume complete control. Sometimes they participated to the extent of providing buildings, roadways, and horses for the works, but with more cautious owners even the trial digs to find if minerals were present in workable quantities were undertaken by 'adventurers' rather than the proprietor. Sir George Savile's steward was one who advocated prudence in the matter, having, as he said, 'in my time seen so many miscarriages which have arose from the like hopes'. When mines were worked directly, landowners faced the same problems of finding working capital and competent supervision which led them to avoid cultivating their own farmland. In 1740 Sir Robert Grosvenor's steward complained bitterly of the manager of a lead mine on the estate: the manager was so afraid of venturing below to inspect the workings that 'he will not clime down yᵉ Shaft but must be lett Downe by yᵉ Rope, and if yᵉ Rope is a little Worne he has a new rope put to and the other is throwne aside tho' it would have served a quarter of a year longer'[43].

For similar reasons quarries, limekilns, brickworks, ironworks and manufactories for metal goods were commonly leased out rather than worked directly. Before the Civil War the Dorset gentry who attempted to exploit local alum deposits ran into a different problem: conflict with the rights of Crown patentees. Sir William Clavile of Smedmore, for example, 'being ingenious in diverse Faculties, put in tryall the Makeing of Allom, which hee had noe sooner, by much Cost and Travell, brought to a reasonable Perfection, but the Farmers of the Allom Workes seized to the Kings Use; and, being not so skillfull or fortunate as himselfe, were forced with Losses to leave it offe'. Fortunately, Sir William, 'who one Disaster dismayed not', proceeded to erect successful glass and salt works[44]. Sir George Horsey of Horseys Melcombe, who partnered Dud Dudley in his mysterious project for smelting iron with coal, had a scheme for reclaiming the great lagoon of sea formed by the Chesil Bank, but his plans failed and he met his end in a debtors' prison[45]. Much later, in the neighbouring county of Devon, the curiously named Mr Pine-Coffin, squire of East Down near Barnstaple, met a common difficulty when he found his works for producing ochre and umber held up by lack of skilled labour[46].

Begun with high hopes of profit, many of these enterprises of the gentry proved disappointing. Some families became heavily, even fatally, indebted to lawyers and goldsmiths in their search for an industrial El Dorado. It is true that in the Midlands and the north some rose greatly in wealth and status through coal – the Willoughbys of Wollaton near Nottingham, the Dudleys in the Black Country, the Lowthers of Cumberland, and numerous families in Northumberland – but these were exceptional. Before the nineteenth century, profits and royalties from mines, ironworks, and the rest usually contributed only a small part of total landed incomes. The £200 a year received from an iron mill by Andrew Archer of Umbersalde, Warwickshire, in 1693 (about a tenth of his total income) was perhaps not untypical. In some years, however, Archer obtained more from the mill, which he leased and worked himself. His manufacturing profit of £4 on each ton of bar iron sold at £16 10s does not seem to be a meagre one [47].

The inconsiderable character of most industrial revenues reflected the generally small scale of industry itself before the nineteenth century. For example, the two largest of Lord Rockingham's coal mines on his Wentworth estate employed in 1759 only sixteen men and twelve men respectively [48]. Other enterprises were often equally modest; moreover, like the ironworks in the Sussex weald, they were frequently operated on a seasonal basis. Few of the Sussex forges were all-the-year-round concerns, said John Fuller, one of the leading gentleman-ironfounders of the area. His own gun foundry was worked only in the winter months when there was enough water to drive his wheel. In the summer months his men were engaged in moving the guns up and down the infamous wealden roads to the Sussex coast, or to the Medway, for shipment to London, a task that was impossible in the winter when the roads were too muddy. Even the output was highly uncertain, varying at Fuller's forge from as little as eight tons a week to as high as twelve: as Fuller remarked, 'a Furnace is a fickle mistress and must be honoured and her favours not to be depended on . . . the excellency of a Founder is to humour her dispositions, but never to force her inclinations'. He had trouble, too, with his workmen, whose accuracy in the boring of cannon was very approximate: 'Our people no more understand 4 inch 21/100 nor 3 inch 66/100 than they do Algebra' [49].

Where the returns from industrial enterprises were large it was generally because the estate resources were extensive and the landowner was able to find the necessary sums for their development. In 1623 Sir William Slingsby claimed to have spent £700 on his coalmines in Yorkshire, and before 1640 almost the whole of the county's iron industry was in the hands of the landowners. But the process of development was often protracted, and might remain small in scale. James Bankes acquired with his Winstanley estate coal, mills, cutlery and nailing works, but a century later his mines were yielding a revenue of only about £100 a year to his grandson [50].

The successful exploitation of minerals or iron on a substantial scale involved provision of transport facilities as well as the mines or works themselves. Before the 1820s this meant wagon tramways and water transport, and landowners became involved in river navigations, canal companies and harbour works. In north-eastern England disputes and violence over wayleaves and the construction of wagonways were endemic. On the other side of the Pennines, in remote Cumberland, coal could be extensively marketed only by sea and the local mineral owners took the lead in developing the ports. The Curwen family played a major role in the growth of Workington, whence nearly all the Cumberland coal was shipped at the beginning of the seventeenth century. In 1688 Workington probably still had under a thousand people in the town but the first census of 1801 showed a population of 6,440. In addition to being the largest colliery owner at Workington, Henry Curwen was the sole owner of the mines and harbour at nearby Harrington. He laid out this port in 1758, and part of his profits from collieries of some £5,000 a year was invested in shipping there and at Workington. Similarly, the Senhouses of Netherhall founded Maryport in 1749 as an outlet for the coal trade to Ireland, and for imports of timber, flax and iron from the Baltic. In 1780, 298 ships sailed from Maryport laden with over 17,000 wagonloads of coal [51].

Whitehaven, on the same coast, was developed by the Lowther family as a port for shipping Cumberland coal and as a centre of the colonial trade. In 1772 the tonnage of British ships cleared outward from Whitehaven was over twice as large as that cleared from Liverpool. Whitehaven's population quadrupled between 1715 and 1785, and when Arthur Young visited the district he described with admiration the new town being built by Sir James Lowther, an establishment of 300 houses named after himself. The Lowther interest in the area began in 1644 when Sir John Lowther inherited lands once held by the monastery of St Bees. Realising that divided ownership would hinder the making of levels and drainage, Sir John acquired neighbouring mineral lands and rights to the control of shipping at Whitehaven. The scale of his mines, reaching down to 800 feet and galleried out under the sea itself, amazed eighteenth-century visitors. Sir John and his son, Sir James, were said to have invested over half a million pounds in the area before the latter's death in 1755, and the rents and coal profits came to some £16,000 a year [52].

John Christian Curwen, the heir of Henry Curwen, owner of Harrington, shipowner, large-scale producer of coal and ironstone, and agricultural improver of the first order, was a leading example of the squire-merchant-industrialist, the composite entrepreneur who played so great a part in developing such areas as Cumberland and Durham and Northumberland in the eighteenth century. Monthly shipments from his Harrington colliery alone were 14,389 wagonloads in 1785, with a further 5,494 tons sold inland. In the 1780s and 1790s Curwen was busily erecting Boulton and Watt steam engines at his pits for pumping water and winding up the coal. A later engine of 160 horse power and three boilers was described as 'doubtless the greatest power ever erected', capable of drawing 700 gallons a minute. Ironstone had been worked on Curwen's Harrington estate since 1761, and fireclay suitable for making pottery and firebricks was also found nearby, and was shipped to Liverpool. Curwen was a pioneer in the introduction of accident insurance schemes for his colliers and other workers, and he became a recognised authority on Friendly Societies.

In addition, he was a prominent experimental agriculturalist on his farms at Schoose and Moorland Close. His practice of 'soiling' (feeding horses on steamed potatoes and carrots) and his stall-feeding of cattle all the year round on cut grass, cabbages and roots won him a gold medal from the Society of Arts in 1808. He had a great belief in the benefits to the health of children of the regular supply of milk that he promoted, and he achieved remarkable yields from his improved Durham shorthorns, again stall-fed with seven or eight feeds a day. His successes with dairying, breeding, potatoes, and lucerne and other grasses led to wide fame as an improver, a 'Field Marshal in the armies of Agriculture', as he was lyrically described. The famous annual shows of the Workington Agricultural Society were combined with visits to the Schoose farm, where Curwen had in regular employment 80 men and over 130 women. At harvest time some 300 to 450 workers were collected each morning 'by drum and fife', and when the harvest was in they were all regaled in a tent with beef, bread, potatoes and ale. His rural activities were completed by prodigious timber planting – a million trees on the slopes of Windermere – an interest partly inspired by a desire to see barren wastes made productive but influenced also, no doubt, by the high prices of timber during the French wars and the ever-present needs of his own collieries, wagonways and shipping: timber planting was a sphere where his diverse interests were closely joined[53].

In the Midlands, too, industrialist-squires were in evidence. The Tamworth district, convenient for access by canal to Hull, Liverpool, Bristol and London, was being developed by Peel and his partner Wilkes. A little further off, at Measham, Wilkes was also in business on his own. Here, in addition to the Tamworth cotton mill, Wilkes had cotton and corn mills, two steam engines, many weaving-shops, and a number of cottages. He was also building 'a large and handsome inn, which is to be the sign of the tup', wrote Arthur Young, 'for Mr Wilkes is a breeder, and a farmer on no slight scale'. Wilkes was indeed a member of the Leicestershire tup society, hired Bakewell's rams, had over 400 acres under irrigation, and made use of coal wastes to burn over newly ploughed land. 'A few of the old thatched hovels remain to show what this place was; what it will be may easily be conceived', Young enthused. 'But what is done here in ten or a dozen years by one man, who has been at the same time engaged in many other great undertakings, who, in union with Mr Peel, is giving a new face to Fazeley and Tamworth, cannot but make any one from the Continent admire at the wonderful exertions active in this kingdom'[54].

Industrial development was going ahead, too, in the remote fastnesses of seventeenth-century Wales. In the northeast of the principality the Mostyns engaged in lead-smelting, shipping their lead down the Dee. The Wynns of Gwydir sent their lead and copper ores down the river Conway, while the upstart Myddeltons of Chirk employed the fortune derived from Sir Thomas Myddelton, the Denbighshire-born Lord Mayor of London, in overcoming hostility to the mining of the local coal measures[55]. Down in southwest Wales lead and coal mining was widespread if small in scale, and attracted the interest of influential outsiders from neighbouring English shires as well as the native gentry[56]. In the following century Milford Haven dominated the coal trade of Pembrokeshire. The port was established by Sir William Hamilton and his heirs, the Greville family, and its success was based in part on a contract from the Admiralty for building frigates there. From Milford Haven the coal of the gentry's mines was shipped to Ireland, London, Brest and Rotterdam, as well as to ports nearer to hand. The growth of the collieries fostered the local market for timber, and the availability of coal led to the building of iron furnaces and tin works[57].

Economic progress in Wales, with its predominance of rugged mountains and steep valleys, was long hindered by lack of good communications. From an early date the local gentry interested themselves in improving roads and bridges. One Merioneth squire, Sir Robert Vaughan, was so eminent in his roadmaking activities that a neighbour lightly described him as the 'Colossus of Rhodes'. Glamorgan, however, soon reached pre-eminence among Welsh counties for its coal and iron, and Glamorgan gentry were very much involved in the provision of harbours, turnpikes, canals and, eventually, railways. At the beginning of the eighteenth century Sir Humphrey Mackworth was concerned in the early development of Neath, and in the next century George Tennant, a leading mineral owner, built in 1824 the Tennant or Neath and Swansea Junction Canal. Most of the county's few parliamentary enclosures affected commons and waste in the coal-measure districts, and numerous disputes arose over boundaries and the extent of mineral rights. Subsequently, urban development, the building of cottages for the swelling industrial population with its consequent demand for building materials, also affected Glamorgan owners. Landowners in the Rhondda took a close interest in opening up the Valley by railways from the later 1830s. One such family, the Llewellyns, owned 1,800 acres of mineral property, and in 1845 became involved with other owners in projecting a Rhondda Railway which would reach 'immense tracts of Coal and Iron ore' so far unworked through the inadequacy of the parish roads [58].

All over the country there were landowners like the Llewellyns who interested themselves in the transport improvements that were vital if their estate resources, not forgetting their tenants' farm produce, were to be made fully profitable. A Nottinghamshire gentleman, Francis Ferrand Foljambe, writing in 1780, thought himself fortunate because he could convey his coal to the riverside

> without being obliged to anybody, and vessels will be able to load and go away at all times in the driest summers when they are totally set fast at the Rotherham Collieries, besides passing two locks less. I am likewise let in an extensive land sale over my bridge and shut it out from other Collieries. These are advantages that must make it valuable some time or other [59].

Large proprietors built their own private canals, wagon tramroads, and even short lengths of steam railways. Smaller owners joined forces with local merchants and industrialists in the promotion and financing of major projects.

The origin of the turnpike trusts can be traced to a private Act of 1663 by which the local justices obtained powers to turn part of the Great North Road into a toll highway, the costs of maintenance being met out of the tolls. By the beginning of the eighteenth century the idea had been adopted in other places, and turnpikes established by private trusts rather than the justices soon became popular. Members of the nobility and gentry, together with the farmers, were very prominent in the financing of many trusts. In Kent the Charing Trust of 1766 was financed entirely by gentlemen and yeomen, while landowners and farmers were the main subscribers to the Alcester–Wootton, Arrow–Pothooks End, Ipswich–Helmingham, and Little Yarmouth Trusts. A similar enthusiasm applied in the Midlands with the Worksop–Attercliffe, Marple Bridge–Glossop, and Chapel-en-le-Frith–Entreclough Trusts. In 1766 the agent of William Drake's estates at Croft and Holbrook, Lincolnshire, wrote to tell his employer of the proposal to form a Boston–Wainfleet Trust, advising his support. The road, he pointed out, would run within one mile of the Drake estate, and would enable sheep to be sent to Smithfield at all seasons and wool to be sold in both northern and southern markets, 'which can now only be effected in the Summer . . . was the Estate my own I should prefer the Completion of a Turnpike to the Present very uncertain State of the Road on which the Permanence of Business so much depends on Seasons' [60].

Landowners were again to the fore in promoting river improvements and canals. After a period more remarkable for paper schemes than actual achievements, real progress was made with river improvements in the later seventeenth century. Activity was marked in the 1660s, in the late 1690s, and again in the years 1719 to 1721 [61]. In the second half of the eighteenth century canals came much into vogue, and many landowners financed short stretches of private waterway to give access to their mines, or contributed to larger schemes along with local merchants, industrialists, and farmers. What the Duke of Bridgewater did so successfully for his Worsley mines was widely imitated, if not on so large or so remunerative a scale. It has been calculated that landowners provided just under one-third of the shareholding of all eighteenth-century canals in England [62].

It would be misleading to suggest that all landowners welcomed transport improvements. Many put up a strong resistance to them, campaigning against the Bills in Parliament, and using their influence to frustrate them locally. Their objections might be purely aesthetic, as when nineteenth-century owners refused to allow the smoke of railway engines or factory chimneys to sully the view from their windows, and obliged railway lines to go round rather than across their estates. A Yorkshire landowner, Sir George Strickland, told George Hudson, the 'Railway King', that since a projected line near his estate at Boynton 'would be totally destructive of that place which has been the residence of my ancestors and family for five hundred years, I should, therefore, feel it to be my duty to my family and myself to make every exertion in my power' to oppose it [63]. A more material and long-standing objection arose from the fear that a canal, turnpike, or railway might reduce the value of property, for example by breaking a local monopoly held by the estate in the supply of farm produce, coal or building materials, or by damaging the land through causing changes in water levels. Further, numbers of estate tenants were engaged in the business of land carriage, and looked to their landlord to protect their livelihood.

A landowner's attitude towards the transport question was inevitably influenced by the unexploited potential of his property. In such rapidly industrialising areas as the Black Country, Glamorgan and the northern coalfields the landed proprietors were often more closely concerned with problems of industrial production and marketing than with the management of farm land. South Yorkshire landowners were leasing out their forges and slitting mills already in the seventeenth century, and subsequently when ironmasters purchased estates it was partly to get their hands on the timber needed for fuel. Young, in his *Northern Tour* of 1770, reported on numbers of gentry who had established mines, woollen factories, and tanneries: among them Mr Danby of Swinton had enclosed land from the moors to allow his miners to grow corn and keep a few cows, while Mr Dickson of Belford, Northumberland, had improved the roads leading to his works, built an inn, and rebuilt his farmhouses. Near Leeds, Walter Spencer Stanhope, a leading Yorkshire squire and member of Parliament, derived most of his fortune from his father's cloth business and the family interests in coal, iron, bricks, canals, turnpikes and docks.

In the nineteenth century northern landowners joined forces with merchants and industrialists to exploit coal, establish ironworks and promote railways. Many were railway shareholders, and some sat on railway boards of directors. As towns grew and railway communications extended, gentry owners developed their urban property and built new suburbs. The Derbyshire cotton town of Glossop owed its existence to the initiative of Bernard Howard, squire of Old Glossop, who on inheriting the dukedom of Norfolk used his new resources to build a town hall, churches, schools, shops, gasworks and waterworks. A little later Sir Lawrence Palk created the seaside resort of Torquay: and Sir Peter Hesketh-Fleetwood turned Fleetwood into an important port, fishing harbour, and watering place [64].

All this was a far cry from the small country gentleman of the rural counties who saw in the railways a powerful juggernaut destructive of bucolic quiet, or at best a more convenient if intractable means of making visits to distant friends, like the squire of Thrumpton, Nottinghamshire, whose request for a private line to give his carriage access to the Midland Railway was abruptly rejected: his carriage, said the Railway, must be sent round to the station where it would be attached to the train.

The gentry and commerce

As we have seen, the full exploitation of estate resources compelled landowners to seek improved outlets for both agricultural and industrial produce, and hence obliged many of them to take a prominent part in projects for better road, water, and eventually rail transport, as well as harbours and docks. Where ports were developed from small beginnings, and mercantile capital was scarce, landowners were drawn into the financing of shipping and of commerce itself. The Welsh gentry, for example, had long been connected with the droving trade into England, and it was natural that in the maritime counties they should become involved in partnerships to promote shipping ventures in the coastal and overseas trades. In southwest Wales sixty-five of the local merchants trading through the ports between 1550 and 1603 were of gentry status, although the amount of trade they handled was small. Some of the leading gentry, Hugh Owen of Orielton and Sir John Vaughan, for example, participated occasionally with individual shipments of goods [65].

In England, too, the gentry had long-standing connections with commerce. Those of East Anglia were frequently involved in commercial undertakings, and in the fifteenth century Sir John Fastolf was the biggest shipowner among them, shipping agricultural produce abroad as well as to London. Down in Dorset the gentry of the sixteenth and seventeenth centuries had interests in the American trade and the indenturing of emigrants to the colonies; some, like Sir Richard Rogers of Bryanston, were heavily engaged in the rather less reputable activities of piracy and smuggling. So also were many unscrupulous gentry in other seagirt counties whose properties lay convenient to lonely coves and inlets. In eighteenth-century Devon Thomas Benson of Barnstaple forfeited his seat in the Commons when his attempts to recover losses by means of fraudulently sinking his ships were uncovered. Equally unfortunate, but more honest, was John Bridger, whose small estate near Lewes in Sussex was bankrupted by shipping losses incurred in the Seven Years War. Widow Davie, of the great Bideford merchant family of Davie, was reputed to be a witch, and her sailors believed she had her all-seeing eye on them even when they were as far away as Virginia or Newfoundland [66].

In northern England the gentry were heavily involved in the coal trade, as we have seen, and even the lesser country squires sometimes took a flutter in a shipping project. William Blundell of Crosby near Liverpool invested £40 after the harvest of 1666 in 'an adventure to the Barbadoes in the good ship *Antelope* of Liverpool'. William's sister added £5 to the stake, and the ship sailed in September laden with '3332 yards of linen cloth, 61 pairs of men's superbest French falls, 2 hundredweight of candles, 2 barrels of beef, 120 lbs of butter, 20,000 spikes etc., etc.' The *Antelope* returned in the following August with a cargo of sugar, and the voyage 'had so good success as to double our monies with advantage', Blundell wrote in glee [67].

With overseas trade went an interest in colonisation. The foundation of colonies was seen by mercantile gentry as a means of developing new trade connections and of extending old ones; further, it was an admirable means of remedying unemployment and poverty at home. This wide variety of motives influenced William Vaughan of Llangyndeyrn, Carmarthenshire, in his patient attempts to establish Cambriol, a colony of Welshmen on the coast of Newfoundland. But Cambriol, despite personal visits from Vaughan in 1622 and 1628, never flourished to become independent and self-sufficing, and soon after 1630 the little settlement succumbed to the hostile combination of a harsh climate and the depredations of pirates and lawless fishermen [68].

Such individual efforts as those of Vaughan were exceptional. The scale of most overseas commercial and colonising projects, and their expected permanence, made them unsuitable for private enterprise. The necessary fund of capital and expertise could best be raised by forming joint-stock companies. Theodore K. Rabb has estimated that of the 6,336 persons who took part in the various company ventures launched between 1575 and 1630 almost a thousand, nearly 16 per cent, were from the gentry. A few, like the Kentish Sir Edwin Sandys, were deeply involved in the affairs of several companies and kept in touch with their business concerns by frequent visits to London; for the most part, however, the gentry were simple investors rather than entrepreneurs, and the more prudent of them rarely put up more than small sums. Only the rasher spirits staked large amounts from the surplus derived from the rising agricultural rentals of the period or the profits of office, and a handful went so far as to sell land for the purpose. The energy and reputation of the great Devon adventurers – Gilbert, Drake, Davis, Grenville, Raleigh – inspired the modest contributions of the great majority of cautious, stay-at-home squires, and it was the colonising and exploring companies, rather than the more strictly commercial ones, that attracted their main support.

On the whole the enthusiasm of the gentry was aroused rather late in the day, and it was only in 1604 to 1620, towards the end of the great period of company growth, that they took part in large numbers. It may have been that it was only then that the buoyancy of estate revenues gave the majority some surplus funds to risk in such speculative ventures. The motives of the gentry investors, however, were in general more patriotic than commercial, more concerned with England's greater glory, the formation of an empire to rival that of Spain, than with the possibility of lucrative returns. The project most attractive to them was the Virginia Company, England's first successful colonial venture, although its eighteen years of effort were bereft of profit. Religious motives were prominent in the support given to the Massachusetts Bay and Providence Island Companies. Emigrants went to Massachusetts 'some to satisfy their own curiosity in point of conscience, others, which was more general, to transport the Gospel to those heathen that never heard thereof', and as New England grew in the 1630s it became clear that the Massachusetts Company was primarily concerned with establishing a colony where the Church of God would be 'seated in security' [69].

The gentry's role in economic expansion

Adventures in trade and industry brought the gentry into close contact with the world of commerce. Some became, or always were, more merchants than landowners, more concerned with rumours of losses at sea than with the success of the harvest at home. Connections also developed in the opposite direction as merchants proper associated with the landed gentry, seeking social prestige and security for their surplus capital by investing in land. Great fortunes could be made in the inland as well as coastal and overseas trades, in the wholesaling and retailing of foodstuffs and of necessities like cloth and fuel, and imported goods. The famous clothier family, the Springs of Lavenham, had lands, tenements and other interests in 116 different towns and villages of East Anglia. But commercial profits were rarely large enough to buy up whole estates: merchants were more likely to find close association with landowners through marriage, and through loans to proprietors embarrassed by family or political obligations; or through joint ventures for developing the industrial and commercial possibilities of estates [70].

The interconnections between landowners and merchants help to explain why landowners' investments were frequently spread over a number of fields. Landowners took up shares in the joint-stock trading companies, the Bank of England, and later in turnpike trusts and canal companies. They sometimes placed spare funds in government stocks, as these became safer investments from the later seventeenth century; and not infrequently they went further afield, buying Dutch or French securities, and occasionally speculated in lands in America. The great period of overseas investment was the later part of the nineteenth century, and before this the majority of wealthy landowners kept by far the greater part of their money at home, showing a general preference for investments secured on land, principally mortgages, but also the personal bonds offered by other proprietors.

The distinction between the gentry and the business community was generally a clear one. To an overwhelming extent the gentry were primarily concerned with land: even when their industrial or commercial interests were considerable they were more commonly passive investors than active business leaders. As a whole they absorbed more commercial capital through borrowing and intermarriage than they created by their non-agricultural investments. Nevertheless, it is not so much the size of the share of the gentry in industry and trade that makes their role an important one. In London and the home counties, certainly, merchant enterprise and capital far outshadowed those of the gentry, many of whom had recently emerged from a mercantile and professional background. In the provinces the situation was different. Particularly in the more remote regions of the southwest, Wales and the north, the gentry played a vital role in the growth of the local economy. It is true that the country's greatest manufacturing industry, woollen cloth, owed little or nothing to landed enterprise, although cloth created numerous landed families. In the primary industries of timber, coal, iron and building materials, and in the provision of essential transport facilities, the landowners played a crucial part. By modern standards their efforts were minute, but in the context of the backward regions of England before the nineteenth century the gradual accumulation of these tiny increments of capital and enterprise created a novel sense of opportunity and progress which helped bring their undeveloped resources into the mainstream of the national economy.

The greatest efforts of landed enterprise were reserved for agriculture. This does not mean that non-agricultural ventures were thereby neglected, for up to the late eighteenth century most industrial activities were on a very limited scale. We come back to our starting point: before the nineteenth century the economy was basically agricultural, and agriculture employed by far the greater number of the people and produced the greater part of the national wealth. With their controlling position in the country's greatest industry the landowners necessarily directed their main energies to its progress and welfare. And in this task the landowners acquitted themselves well, extending cultivation to moor, marsh and heath, progressively fostering a more productive farm technology, and constantly supervising and bringing up to date the tenurial and physical conditions under which the farmers operated.

The landowners, too, showed flexibility in adapting to changing economic conditions. They were, as we have seen, alive to the needs and opportunities of each changing age. Unlike the more caste-conscious aristocracies of the continent they were, as a whole, never merely selfish guardians of the *status quo*, never concerned solely with placing protection of privileges before the march of progress. This flexibility enabled them to absorb the newcomers to their ranks from the business world, and to work in harmony with the merchants and industrialists with whom they associated in joint ventures. And their range of interests and breadth of outlook made it possible for the business community to acquiesce in the landowners' social and political leadership right down to the latter part of the nineteenth century – until in fact industrialisation itself came to maturity.

Marriage and the family settlement

In the social hierarchy the gentry straddled the middle ground between the dominating heights held by the nobility and the broad lowlands occupied by the yeomen, farmers and husbandmen. Within their ranks the gentry, as we have noted, embraced landowners of very different levels of wealth and status, from the humble country gentlemen and members of learned professions to the titled owners of several thousands of acres. But for all of them a degree of wealth, particularly inherited wealth, conferred respectability and, combined with ancient origins and long connection with one locality, ensured a certain social status and claim to deference. With status went influence, and the greater the wealth the greater the influence.

The preservation of an acquired status and influence thus relied on the preservation of the family's identity and the wealth that maintained it. Hence the constant concern for the continuity of the family and the continuity of its wealth. The older the family, the longer its lineage, the more telling its control of wealth. It was because antiquity mattered that so many gentry interested themselves in their family tree, even if enthusiasm for an extensive lineage occasionally led them into claims that were doubtful or spurious. Old-established families were associated with a particular place – the Verneys of Claydon, the Spencers of Althorp, the Brudenells of Deene, and further back the Cholmondeleys of Cholmondeley, the Okevors of Okevor and the Walpoles of Houghton. Long residence in a particular spot enhanced a family's standing. A centuries-long association with a house gave a family a strong sense of identity and a feeling of permanence. Hence the persistent rounding out of the home estate by purchases of neighbouring property, the expensive creation of impressive grounds or an extensive park, and the constant additions and improvements to the house itself. If financial pressures demanded sales of land then it was the detached or outlying portions of the estate that went, not the main core round the family home. That was preserved to the end. The house's occupants became more than the principal local landowners. Their head was of course the squire of the village, his family 'the squire's people up at the big house', the dominating influence in the neighbourhood, whose views and conduct shaped the social life of the village, and whose affairs provided unbounded scope for speculation and discussion.

Awareness of status necessitated a concern with money. To maintain customary appearances, hospitality, charity and the house itself, a stable, or preferably expanding, income was needed. Income was derived chiefly from the land; hence the estate had to be safeguarded from excessive burdens of debt.

At the same time the continuity of the family had to be secured so far as was possible, and this was no certain matter when a high proportion of even the offspring of the wealthy failed to survive childhood. The marriage of those who did survive was a matter of great import, for clearly a groom or bride of inferior standing reflected on the family's status; a marriage connection with families of superior rank enhanced it. Of course, marriage was important in trade, too, as well as land: it cemented business connections and was a means of acquiring new capital. Among the propertied classes generally the individual's interest in marriage was subordinated to the interest of the family. Not only was marriage important in making political and financial alliances and in protecting status, but in the case of the heir's marriage it was also affected by the need to safeguard the interest in the property of the family at large. From that property the heir's sisters had to be provided with dowries sufficiently ample to get them well married, his brothers with an inheritance, modest in amount but enough to get them started in the world, and his mother with a jointure, as specified in her marriage contract, to maintain her in widowhood. All such provision was a duty imposed by custom as well as by concern for status, and in practice it was ensured by giving members of the family a legal interest in the property.

Thus the maintenance of customary standards of living, the making of socially acceptable marriage contracts, and the protection of the interests of the family all turned on the continuity of the estate and its revenues. Only if the estate remained intact, its revenues safeguarded from excessive debt charges, could the heir carry out his obligations, ensure his sisters an appropriate match and meet the rightful claims of his mother and brothers. The needs of status and family implied continuing control over the estate to see that its revenues were not eroded by extravagance or irresponsibility. Under the care of a prudent heir all might be well, but not all heirs were prudent. Clearly it was essential in the interests of the family at large to establish means of securing the inheritance from the depredations of the heir who turned out an unrestrained builder, a rash speculator, inveterate gambler, over-ambitious politician, or mere incompetent.

Considerations of this kind had always influenced family arrangements. In the Middle Ages there existed various forms of inheritance, including division of estates among heirs (such as the practice of gavelkind in Kent), and 'borough English' where the estate went to the last-born. But although in some areas partible inheritance persisted among the lower ranks of rural society, primogeniture emerged by the late thirteenth century as the predominant, and eventually sole, form of inheritance among the wealthier landowners. And as this occurred the ambition and need to transmit the family property intact led to the early development of family settlements whose main object was the protection of reversions.

The adoption of the strict settlement owed a great deal to the threat to property posed by the civil wars when landowners sought means of protecting estates from forfeitures and fines. After the wars the law courts came to accept the full validity of the strict settlement, not least because the current complexity and uncertain state of the land law made it expedient for judges to respect the practices of the leading conveyancers. In due course the family settlement became a binding legal contract which could certainly be broken only by a private Act of Parliament.

In the strict settlement the interest of the current owner in his estate was merely that of a tenant for life. A proportion, perhaps the greater part, of the estate was "settled", that is, reserved for the payment of dowries, jointure and portions. The life tenant was compelled to devote the income from the settled part of the estate to these specific purposes; he could not sell the land, and was allowed to mortgage it only up to certain amounts and for certain purposes. Sometimes he was not even allowed to develop the land for mining or to exploit it in other ways, and in the eighteenth and nineteenth centuries private estate Acts were obtained to free the life tenant's hands in this respect. Otherwise only the unsettled part of the estate was his to do what he liked with, and then it was often the case that part of the income from the unsettled estates had to be used to supplement the revenue of the settled portion. This was because landowners seem to have been optimistic in overestimating the burdens which the settled part of the estate could bear. But, in addition, the burdens themselves tended to grow as there developed a strong upward trend in dowries, and hence in jointures; for the jointure paid to the life tenant's widow was usually proportional to the dowry she brought her husband as a bride.

By the eighteenth century possibly as much as half the country was held under strict settlement, and the system prevailed through the following century, only somewhat modified by the Settled Land Acts of 1882 and 1890. The desire to preserve intact the family estates, or a large proportion of them, was a matter of prime concern not only to old-established families but also to those who had recently entered the ranks of the landowners and were anxious to see that their hard-won position was not jeopardised by human frailty. Landowners new and old tried to ensure that their property was always in the hands of a life tenant whose powers of disposal and borrowing were severely limited. The system of strict settlement was not, however, quite so cast iron as it might appear. Once in each generation the estate had to be resettled between father and eldest son. Usually this was done on the occasion of the son's marriage, when provision had to be made for future payment of the bride's jointure and the portions of the yet unborn children of the marriage. Before resettling, however, opportunity might be taken to sell land, and this course might be made unavoidable by the pressure of long-accumulated debts.

Normally, the son's marriage brought a handsome dowry into the family, and the prospect of financial improvement it offered might be so rosy as to defer any question of sales of land. To obtain the dowry, however, meant consulting the bride's family on the resettlement of the estates, for her family would consent to the marriage only if they were assured that the bride's interest concerning her jointure, her 'pin money' and the portions of her children to come were adequately secured. All these considerations gave to the marriage of heirs and heiresses a strongly commercial character, with the size of the inheritance or dowry the principal object. The search for a suitable match was often a protracted one, and friends acted as amateur marriage brokers, suggesting possible partners and acting as go-betweens. In a typical example Lord Molyneux suggested a match between George Lucy of Charlecote and the Earl of Cardigan's sister: she was, he told Lucy, 'a very agreeable young lady and an exceedingly good humoured lady and not more prude than what becomes a lady of honour'.

The desire to ensure a good marriage led sometimes to the betrothal of children, a practice that in earlier centuries had been encouraged also by the dangers of wardship. Before 1646 the king exercised a right of wardship over the heirs of tenants-in-chief who succeeded to an estate before reaching their majority. During a minority lands held by the ancient tenure of knight service or grand serjeanty reverted to the Crown, and the king had the right to the profits of the lands as well as that of exercising control over the heir and the heir's marriage. The heir's family had to petition the Court of Wards for custody of the heir and his lands, and this was granted only on payment of a fine that by the years before 1640 had become seriously burdensome. Custody was sometimes granted to a third person, and when this happened the heir's family was occasioned great loss, since the revenues and management of the estate were then taken out of their hands. Wardships formed a valuable property, often sold and resold to courtiers who not only reaped a profit from the estate revenues but also obtained the power of matching the ward in marriage, a valuable instrument in making and reinforcing political alliances. Wardship went the way of the king's other autocratic powers in the Great Rebellion, and the Convention Parliament of 1660 abolished the feudal incidents of military tenures and repealed the legislation on which the Court of Wards based its authority. A cause of much friction and serious grievance was thus finally removed, and thereafter minorities often proved to be beneficial incidents in the history of a family. Guardians, acting under the supervision of the Court of Chancery, took the estate under their wing and used the opportunity to reduce unnecessary expenditure and divert income to estate improvements. However, in the seventeenth century marriages were still sometimes contracted when the girl was only twelve or thirteen; after the wedding night the groom went off to resume his education, the girl back to her mother. The bride and groom were not expected to be in love, and might not even be acquainted before the marriage negotiations began. Affection was supposed to develop because of marriage rather than the other way round. But parents were not so unfeeling as to make matches that were patently unsuitable. The more usual age for marriage was about the early or middle twenties, and this meant that the wishes of the persons most directly concerned had to receive some consideration. Prospective grooms were usually introduced into the girl's home for her inspection, and a period of courtship lasting several months was often permitted. 'They are ancient squires', wrote one young lady of her suitor's family, 'he is very sober and a good scholar, loves poetry and lent me the Dispensery, an extraordinary poem done by Dr Garth, and Dryden's Fables.' And on another occasion her beau was 'upon much nicer airs than ordinary, he had not forgot his scarlet stockings and a tie wig which was powdered to a nicety and he gave me a compliment in verse' [1].

Probably, the further one went down the social scale the more the individual feelings of the young people were respected. Lesser landowners could accept more easily a match which did little for the family's wealth or position, but among the large proprietors the stakes were too great for the irrationalities of the heart to be allowed much weight. Sir John Oglander was one father who gave way to his daughter's wishes. In his notebook he recorded in October 1649

that the match between Sir Robert Eaton's son and my daughter Bridget was never with my approbation or good liking. It was her importunity that induced me to give way unto it, and she was resolved to have him whatsoever became of her, and gave me so much under her own hand before marriage. I confess I never liked Sir Robert or his estate, a swearing, profane man. I beseech God to bless them and to make her happy, which I much doubt. She was both lame and in years, which moved somewhat with me, though most with her.

Nicholas Blundell, a modest Lancashire squire, stated it to be his 'chief Aime to settle my Daughters to their own licking & that they may make choice of a Man they can have, & I'll doe my endeavour to propose such to them whose Serconstances may make them Happy'. He would only admit such suitors 'as I am pretty well assured my daughters may live comfortably with. . . . But to tell me he is a Barronet's son and will have £1500 per annum will not tempt me. I have already refused a Barronet of better estate. I vallew the persun, parts and humours of the man (for that must make a woman happy) more than quality.' In his own youth Blundell had held out for a bride with a dowry of £2,000, an object which at length he achieved. As he told a friend: 'Many Ladys have been proposed with Fiveteen hundered pounds and if formerly that pourtion was thought fit for me, I may now deserve a better, my Father having left me in a very good Serconstance' [2].

Marriage negotiations were often tangled and prolonged. In 1694 Edmund Brydges, a Herefordshire gentleman, wrote of a meeting in a Lincoln's Inn coffee house with a Mr Hobson, whose daughter had been receiving attentions from Brydges's nephew. 'After we had passed a glass or two', Hobson enquired

whether my nephew had acquainted me with the injunction he had laid upon him, not to visit his daughter until he and I had further conferred, which he did for fear his daughter might be entangled in her amours. However, I thought his daughter in no danger for that as I apprehended my kinsman had no greater encouragement from her; neither could he well apprehend that she approved of his address; but I told him I presumed that was a matter consulted between him and his daughter. Why truly, quoth he, 'Giny is a good girl and will be ruled by me; and I have told her that she shall please herself in marriage' [3].

The choice of a wife was restricted by the range of family acquaintance and considerations of status. Particularly in a remote and sparsely populated district, like the Yorkshire moors at the end of the eighteenth century, the choice of brides or grooms was likely to be narrow indeed, as appears clearly in Emily Brontë's *Wuthering Heights*. It was the practice for gentry families to take a bride from their own social stratum and from within the neighbourhood, or at least the county. In the middle seventeenth century two-thirds of the Lancashire gentry married brides of gentry status, and in well over two-thirds of the marriages both partners came from within the county [4]. In making the actual choice the advice of parents was seldom lacking, and was often committed to paper. 'For your WYFE', wrote Sir William Wentworth,

Lett hir be well borne and brought up but not too highlie, of a helthfull bodye, of a good complexion, humble and vertuouse, some

few years younger than your self and nott of a simple wit. A good
portion makes hir the better and manie tymes not the prouder. Take
advice of your wise auncyentt frendes befor yow attempt anie thing
touching that matter [5].

In arranging a marriage the bride's financial prospects were usually the
major consideration, but sometimes the political influence of her connections
might be a more weighty factor. Whatever the case, the details of the marriage
settlement were thrashed out by the lawyers of both families, and the process of
arriving at agreement often stretched over weeks or months. The family of the
bride were of course acutely aware of her market value, for the size of her
dowry automatically placed her in a certain starting position in the marriage
stakes, give or take a little for political influence and social connections. The
groom's family, on the other hand, naturally wanted to see their existing
interests in the estate properly safeguarded, and tried to avoid the creation of
too heavy a burden of future portions. Generally, the size of the children's
portions was related to the size of the dowry, as was the bride's jointure; by the
later seventeenth century the jointure was usually fixed at 10 per cent of the
dowry. In these negotiations the interests of the life tenant himself might be
sacrificed in order to obtain agreement, and he emerged with a severely
circumscribed authority over his estates, a restricted scope for his personal
expenditure, and possibly a limited degree of control over his own children
still to come.

As time went by there was a tendency for dowries, and hence portions
and jointures, to escalate, partly because of the bargaining process involved in
the marriage contract and partly through the ambition of the families to see the
future generation well provided for. It may have been, too, that a fall in the
number of eligible bachelors among landowning families, as a result of deaths
in wars and other factors, raised the scarcity value of those remaining. Moreover, mounting competition in the marriage market was coming from the
handsomely dowried daughters of merchants, contractors and financiers intent
on sealing their financial success with the mark of an estate and title. With
rising demand on the part of the potential brides and a limited, possibly
declining, supply of suitable grooms, the price of a prestigious marriage was
bound to rise. A consequence of the escalation of dowries and portions was that
estate revenues often proved inadequate to meet the burdens placed on them.
Estates became heavily encumbered, and the whole inflationary process might
have been brought to a halt by the ensuing financial stringency had it not been
for the great rise of rents after 1760 and the growing use of the mortgage as a
means of raising money.

These two factors made it possible for landowners to continue on their
path of making increasingly generous family provision while raising their
standards of consumption. After about 1760 estate revenues were fed by rents
which nearly trebled between then and the end of the Napoleonic Wars, the
average rise being of the order of 275 per cent. Buoyant rents were supplemented by increased returns from sales of timber, minerals, and transport
projects as industrialisation gathered pace; and those landowners with properties most favourably situated for taking advantage of the rising demands
for food and raw materials were able to increase their revenues by much more
than the average figure. The new opportunities greatly accelerated enclosure of

common fields, commons and wastes, as they also stimulated mining, and road
and canal building. And all this of course encouraged owners of settled estates
to seek private Acts to give them greater freedom in exploiting their properties.

By the late seventeenth century, as we have noted, borrowing on mortgage had become a safe and cheap form of credit since the courts adopted more
liberal attitudes and accepted the right of the mortgagor to reclaim his land.
Moreover, rates of interest were falling, making borrowing cheaper. By the
middle of the eighteenth century the standard rate of interest on a morgage was
established at 5 per cent, and favoured borrowers might obtain a rate as low as
4 per cent or even less. Gentlemen of reputation could also borrow extensively
on their personal bond on about the same terms, and frequently did so when
short of cash. Landlords would often borrow from their tenants and even from
their servants, and it seems that farmers were willing to leave their money in the
landlord's hands for long periods, in effect using him as a savings bank. A good
deal of land purchase was financed in this way, the seller often being prepared
to leave all or part of the purchase money with the buyer as a loan. The market
in mortgages and bonds was primarily local, but was remarkably extensive in
social terms, stretching down to the lowest levels of the propertied classes. The
great owners, it is true, usually negotiated their loans through their London
lawyers or bankers, but the enormous volume of small-scale borrowing, involving sums of a few score to a few hundred pounds, was essentially local and
personal, arranged between relatives, friends and business associates.

The growing ease and cheapness of borrowing was not without its draw-
backs. In the numerous war years of the eighteenth century heavy government
borrowing reduced the price of government stock, raised its yields, and so made
it a more attractive investment. In these years the money of private investors,
and of the banks and insurance companies, which in peacetime sought an
outlet in mortgages, went instead into the Funds. The difficulty of borrowing
on mortgage in wartime affected the demand for land itself, and heavily pressed
landowners found it unprofitable, or even impossible, to dispose of land when
government borrowing was heavy. At other times the very ease of borrowing
might form a slippery slope down which the reckless slid to eventual collapse.

There were of course many landowners who neglected their affairs and
allowed a passion for sport, politics, building, or simple extravagance, to run
away with an apparently ample income. The majority, however, were wise
enough, or were compelled by their relations, to pause and take stock before it
was too late. In the more extreme cases they surrendered their affairs into the
hands of trustees, a small group of friends and relations who might include their
banker and legal adviser. Such trustees took on the often daunting task of dis-
entangling the confused jumble of mortgages, bonds, annuities and unpaid bills,
and set to work to salvage as much of the estate as possible. During a trustee-
ship, generally a matter of a few years, the family was put on a strict financial
allowance and obliged to retrench drastically. Secondary mansions were put up
for sale or to let; inessential repairs were postponed; servants discharged,
horses sold, hounds disposed of. Active politics were ruled out; the London
season quite out of the question. An accountant was set on the books in order to
ascertain the full extent of the liabilities. Revenue was hastily jacked up by
raising rents, selling timber, and by making inexpensive but advantageous
improvements to the farms: it is remarkable that the most heavily indebted
families often levied the lowest rents, usually for reasons of politics. Any surviv-

ing investments were realised, and if sales of land were unavoidable the least important parts of the estate were put on the market. The most pressing debts were discharged, and the more costly ones of the remaining rearranged at lower rates of interest. All the surplus revenue was devoted to reducing the weight of debt.

It is astonishing how a few years of this kind of medicine would restore an estate tottering on the edge of disaster. In the same way, a minority, when an estate was managed by the heir's relations or by guardians, was often very advantageous for the family finances. Sheer chance undoubtedly played a great part in family history: luck in the marriage market, in the number and sex of the children, in the early death or longevity of parents. Some families, indeed, were able to survive only by the fortunate intervention of one or more minorities which made it possible for expenditure to be retrenched and debts paid off. A jointure, on the other hand, could be a heavy burden on a moderate estate when a widow survived her husband by many years, as sometimes happened.

Marriage, although the most important single factor in the rise of most families, was highly uncertain in its financial consequences. The bride's portion was frequently substantial enough to rectify a difficult situation, and put a family's affairs on a more secure footing; quite often a bride died young, perhaps in childbirth, and the husband was able to remarry and so secure a second dowry. Exceptionally, a family's rise, like that of the Ashburnhams, was founded on a husband's fortune, if that is the word, in running through three brides in quick succession. Unexpected snags often arose, however. The dowry was not always easily extracted from the bride's family: for many years the groom might have to be satisfied with receiving interest on the sum and never see the capital. Again, the eventual payment of the dowry was often dependent on the satisfaction of prior claims on the property supposed to produce it; to obtain payment might involve the groom in protracted and expensive lawsuits. And finally, a childless marriage usually had the effect of preventing the groom's family from obtaining permanent possession of the wife's inheritance.

Further great uncertainties surrounded the fruitfulness of the marriage. A large family, especially if there were many daughters, meant a heavy burden of portions. Indeed, the whole of the bride's inheritance and more might go on providing dowries for her daughters. Sir Philip Monoux was expressing a commonplace view when he wrote: 'Lady Monoux has brought me another child last month. . . . Unluckily it is a female. When a man has so many of that sort more can not be wished for.' Sons were less of a problem for it was usual to give the younger sons no more than some modest help in starting a career and then they were left to their own resources. Where partible inheritance or division of property among the heirs was practised (as in Kent, and fairly widely among lesser owners generally), the estate was bound to be reduced in size if the progeny were at all numerous. Even with partible inheritance, the younger sons and daughters usually received a smaller share of the property, and in practice it was common for the estate to be kept intact by arrangements made among the heirs for selling back or leasing their shares to one of their number. More generally, where property passed to daughters in the absence of male heirs research has shown that the passage of land through the female line was a factor encouraging sales of land. Land was more readily sold in these circumstances, either because the daughter's husband was in trade or a profession and preferred to realise the capital, or because the land was too far from the husband's own estates to be worth keeping. In the early eighteenth century the English aristocracy was failing to produce enough sons to maintain their numbers. This meant that a good deal of land was passing through the female line and was coming on to the market at a time when successful new-comers were seeking estates for themselves. Later in the century there was a higher survival rate of sons and consequently greater stability in the land market [6].

The fortunes of landed families, therefore, were very much at the mercy of birth rates and death rates, and were especially affected by the sex ratios of births and deaths. The limited resources for portions had to be concentrated on daughters, since the chances of making a good match were so greatly influenced by the value of the dowry. Younger sons were provided with a good education and whatever sum had been secured for them in the family settlement. From that beginning they had to make their own way in life. Younger sons of modest gentry families were frequently found in trade in nearby market towns, as mercers, linen-drapers, apothecaries, or even innkeepers and barber-surgeons. The younger brothers of Sir George Sondes, a prominent Kentish landowner of the late seventeenth century, studied the law or travelled abroad on the strength of annuities of £100; one studied medicine at Leyden, another took up soldiering in the Low Countries, two were apprenticed to merchants and one to a London woollen-draper. It is clear that parents often found it difficult to secure for their younger sons a place in society comparable to their own. As the establishments of the great lords were reduced in the later sixteenth and early seventeenth centuries, younger sons found a traditional value to a life of comfort, and perhaps advancement, much restricted. This was occurring at a time when the practice of passing the whole estate to the firstborn son was well established, and younger sons were left to fend for themselves. There is some indication that the resentment of younger sons led them to assume extreme partisan positions in the Civil Wars. Thomas Wilson, writing in 1600, could feel for younger sons for he was one himself.

> Their state [he wrote] is of all stations for gentlemen most miserable, for if our fathers possess 1,000 or 2,000l. yearly at his death, he cannot give a foot of land to his younger children in inheritance, unless it be by lease for 21 years or for 3 lives . . . or else be purchased by himself and not descended. Then he may demise as much as he thinks good to his younger children, but such a fever hectic hath custom brought in and inured amongst fathers, and such fond desire they have to leave a great shew of the stock of their house, though the branches be withered, that they will not do it, but my elder brother forsooth must be my master. He must have all, and all the rest, that which the cat left on the malt heap, perhaps some small annuity during his life or what please our elder brother's worship to bestow upon us if we please him, and my mistress his wife. This I must confess doth us good someways, for it makes us industrious to apply ourselves to letters or to arms, whereby many times we become my master elder brothers' masters, or at least their betters in honour and reputation, while he lives at home like a mome and knows the sound of no other bell but his own.

Fortunately, in the latter part of the seventeenth century and subsequently, the social upgrading of the professions, the better prospect of preferment in the Church, and the growing possibility of a permanent career in the navy as well as the widening prospects of trade and industry greatly eased their situation [7].

One of the side effects of the strict settlement, therefore, was the creation of a class of well-educated gentlemen with a background of country house, public school and university, who generally lacked the means to live in the manner in which they had been brought up. Before the later seventeenth century most of the opportunities open to them were in trade. But once new outlets were available in the Church, the armed services, industry and professions such men formed the hard core of the middle class of modern England. Obliged to work for their living they brought to their professions the devotion, sense of duty and expertise that gave their callings a new and respected status. They provided, for example, much of the driving power behind the reformed and expanding civil service of the nineteenth century, and they produced the expert opinion that informed the growing public concern with child employment, education, and public health. Their attitudes, derived from their social background and education, were generally humane and progressive; and they created a sense of public service in their professions that has so far survived against the pressures of presentday materialism.

The gentry and the community

The proliferation of younger sons in trade and the professions was a factor widening the concerns and connections of the gentry as a social group. Through their family relationships the gentry were obliged to look beyond the confined limits of their estates to the wider world beyond. As we have seen, many had direct interests in business, and in numerous instances the means of establishing a younger son in a business career arose through existing contacts with merchants and tradesmen. The links forged with the commercial and professional classes made the gentry less of an exclusive land-based elite, widened the range of their economic interests, and made their leadership in the spheres of politics and society more generally acceptable.

These wider connections of the gentry, however, consisted essentially of property-owners, even if that property consisted in the main of working capital and stock-in-trade rather than real estate. At bottom the very basis of these connections was a common interest in property in its widest sense, in its better exploitation, and in its protection. Property, it was held, conferred on its owners the right to participation in the process of government; and the eventual extension of the franchise in the nineteenth century was based, quite naturally, on a wider definition of property. The reform of 1832 and the subsequent franchise extensions were limited operations: they made some concessions to the increased importance of the owners of industrial and commercial property, but the reformed electorate remained a minority of the adult population, and the franchise still rested on a claim to property. There was no belief in democracy among property-owners in general. Indeed, it was held that democracy and property must inevitably be in conflict. Wellington expressed this view when he said in 1831: 'A democracy has never been established in any part of the world that has not immediately declared war against property – against the payment of the public debt – and against all the principal objects of the British Constitution, as it now exists. Property and its possessors will become the common enemy.'

Property-owners might present a united front against the pretensions of the propertyless, but this did not prevent them from fighting over property among themselves. The reality of landowners' absolute local power led to their disputes ramifying beyond lawsuits and packed juries into violence; and armed affrays between rival property-owners played a not inconsiderable role in the annals of the gentry. The historian of Tudor Cornwall recounts the details of some fearsome feuds, entailing ambushes, armed raids, robberies and murder, and one such incident involved an illegal seizure of goods on the sabbath by the coroner of the county himself – a nice Sunday occupation for a coroner, as Dr Rowse observes[8]. In the next century, but still in the west country, Benedict Webb, clothier of Kingswood in Wiltshire, came into conflict with Sir Nicholas Pointz, from whom he rented various lands. In March 1603 some of Pointz's men broke into the farm and threatened 'to kill, wound or mischiefe Webb's said servaunts or to cutt off their leggs', and a subsequent hearing of their difference in the Star Chamber failed to bring the hostilities to a close[9]. Many of these quarrels arose over trivial matters, but clashes of personalities and the stubbornness of family pride allowed them to fester into feuds that went on for years, if not generations.

A good deal of the local rivalry arose over politics. The Denbighshire election for Parliament in 1601 brought about a violent clash between Sir John Salisbury and Sir Richard Trefor, involving menaces and the use of mobs. Each of these gentlemen attempted to intimidate the other's supporters by issuing letters of muster and threats of immediate military service in Ireland. On election day Sir John marched into Wrexham at the head of his retainers, preceded by a trumpeter blasing defiance, and his party attempted to seize the church as a base for their operations; Sir Richard countered with a rival force which included eighty of the brawniest Denbighshire coal miners[10]. Everywhere rival political factions employed bribery, force and corruption to gain their ends. It was common in Wales to increase the electorate for the purpose by making temporary grants of land to the value of the forty shillings freeholder's qualification, and throughout the country landowners interested in borough elections bought up urban properties for the sake of an increased command of the votes. Electors were carried to the polls free of charge, royally entertained, and sometimes locked away beforehand to prevent the opposition from getting at them. Sir Henry Slingsby recorded in 1640 that his steward, acting as election agent, was successful in frustrating 'the subtle plots' of his opponents. 'There is an ill custom at this election', he noted, 'to bestow wine in all the town which cost me £16 at the least, and many a man a broken pate'[11].

Prominent county families customarily employed their land stewards as election managers, and campaigns were frequently conducted on an extensive scale with the use of local agents and canvassers. Candidates could count, too, on the support of other owners' stewards to get out the vote. In the Kent elections of 1760 Sir Wyndham Knatchbull-Wyndham, looked for aid to Sir John Evelyn and Lord Abergavenny. Sir John ordered his steward at Deptford to secure his 'whole interest' for Sir Wyndham, while Lord Abergavenny wrote to say that: 'I am this instant returned from my house in Sussex where I went yesterday on purpose to order my steward to go into Kent and inform my tenants and friends there I desire their votes and interest for Sir Wyndham Knatchbull' [12].

It is clear that all those beholden to a particular landlord – tenant farmers, clergy, tradesmen and craftsmen – were expected to vote as he wished, on receiving instructions from his steward or agent. This was not invariably so, however, since some landowners kept aloof from the struggle, or felt it an undue infringement of liberty to demand their tenants' votes. But generally there was an expectation that the landlord's wishes would be made known and respected. Behind this expectation lay the ultimate potential threat of loss of farm, office or profit; but there is little evidence that in fact landowners went so far as evicting tenants for disobedience at election times, or even thought of uttering threats. The landlords' desire for popularity 'in their country' and the wish to avoid unnecessary problems of replacing tenants were countervailing factors of greater weight. Moreover, before the late eighteenth century there was no general belief in democracy as the term is understood today: it was regarded as the natural order of things that the property-owners should be represented in Parliament by other property-owners, and that those dependent on them should lend their support, albeit in return for some favour or inducement. The majority of electors probably regarded the right to vote as a valuable piece of property in itself, to be realised in a low rent for their farms, or at a good price in cash or ale whenever opportunity offered. Feudal traditions died hard in the countryside, and to a considerable extent the old concept of the natural bond of interest existing between the lord and his retainers lingered on well into the nineteenth century. By 1852, when a Northumberland squire, Sir Charles Monck, wrote to his north Lincolnshire tenants, the concept had been some-what modified, though it remained real enough:

> Nothing is more agreeable to the Constitution, and to all ancient usages of the Kingdom, or more advantageous to true liberty, than that landlords should endeavour by all fair means to lead their tenants. . . . I expect of my tenants that they shall not engage their votes before they have communicated with me and come to know my wishes. . . . If it shall after that appear that my wishes and yours are in contrarity there then ought to be the fullest explanation and consideration between us. . . . I promise you that to the opinion of the majority I will submit. But . . . if I am bound to set an example of submission to the majority, the minority must be bound to follow that example, that the estate might not be divided, but act with its full weight for the benefit of all [13].

Down the centuries there echoed the remark of a fifteenth-century landlord: 'The people will go with him that may best sustain and reward them.' The political control exercised by the landowners was not, therefore, so irksome a yoke as might be supposed.

The cost of fighting elections, with bribes to voters running in the eighteenth century at two, four, or more guineas a man, and hundreds or thousands of pounds laid out in entertainment, transport, innkeepers' bills and agents' fees, forced the majority of gentry out of direct participation in contests. Samuel Whitbread in 1802 incurred expenses at his headquarters, the Swan, in Bedford, amounting to £240; the consumption of over 500 bottles of port,

136 gallons of beer and porter, as well as quantities of punch, was accompanied by the breaking of ninety-five glasses, three decanters and a window [14]. The size of the outlays encouraged election pacts, and in some counties an opposed election became uncommon. For active contestants there were permanent hidden costs in 'maintaining an interest': capital laid out in acquisition of urban property, and income lost in the 'good bargains' offered to farm tenants to keep them faithful. For these reasons the parliamentary seats in many counties tended to alternate between a few leading families. The wealthy gentry who kept out of costly parliamentary battles contented themselves with the more modest offices of justice, sheriff or coroner. Primarily they sought these offices for self-aggrandisement, local influence and prestige, rarely for the fees, which were small. In earlier periods an occasional outstanding official might receive a substantial reward in land. A good example is provided by Sir John Holcroft, twice sheriff of Lancashire and twice sheriff of Cheshire, a justice, and *custos rotulorum* from 1547, as well as military officer, charity commissioner, and member of numerous other commissions: in return for his services he received the grant of profitable wardships and was enabled to acquire monastic property [15].

A similar success might be achieved by years spent in the service of a great magnate – in Lancashire, for example, the Earl of Derby. Local work for the Crown, or for a great lord, could well provide an ambitious man with a path to wealth and influence in the age of the Reformation. In the course of the sixteenth century, however, the patronage of the great lords declined in importance. The power of the magnates was broken by the Crown, and already by the 1530s the indentured retaining of gentry by noblemen ceased to be of much significance. Of course it remained valuable to be in good standing with the leading men of the district, if only to have their support in seeking office, or in obtaining an entrée to the Church or civil service for younger sons and other relations.

The leading motive in seeking election to Parliament or a county office was prestige. It is true that a seat in Parliament gave some access to patronage, and might be valuable in furthering public and private objects in the county, such as enclosures of forest and waste, and improvements to roads, rivers or harbours. But many members of Parliament seem to have made little use of these opportunities, were remiss in attending the House, and made little or no mark when they did. Similarly, county offices were valued for their prestige but not for their responsibilities – witness the long lists of inactive justices. County offices however, did carry some limited powers of patronage and, more important, the possibility of conferring favours on friends and servants. Justices could stretch the law to suit their purposes, and there were complaints of the impossibility of obtaining an impartial hearing from the magistrates' Bench. It was particularly difficult to secure any redress against wrongful actions of the justices themselves, and few thought it worth while, or even safe, to bring an action against a justice. As Patrick St Clair of Sustead, Norfolk, wrote in 1736 to his friend, Ashe Windham of Felbrigg, it was a 'dangerous thing' '. . . to complain of a Justice of the Peace, when you have none but Justices upon the Jury'. And a few years earlier St Clair recounted a story about their neighbour, Colonel Harbord, which illustrates well the arbitrary power held by the squires. The Colonel found two men coursing with dogs on Roughton Heath and 'ordered his men to shoot the finder immediately, which was executed, and threatened to send the fellows to Bridwell, and to kill the other dogs, but that one of the fellows fell down on his knees, and begged pardon'[16].

Rigorous in the enforcement of laws that suited them, particularly those protective of property, the justices neglected laws they disliked. For example, the justices in Lancashire, as in some other counties, declined to interfere in the illegal proceedings of their Catholic friends and neighbours. They turned a blind eye also towards the petty peculation of county officials, and did not scruple to exert influence in the appropriate quarter on behalf of tenants and servants. Dudley North, a prominent Suffolk landowner and member of Parliament, received a typical appeal from his bailiff in April, 1748. 'I was nominated at the Quarter Sessions to be Chief Constable for an hundred', wrote the bailiff, 'and I humbly beg the favour of you to speak to Mr Long and Mr Carter to get me off from serving that office, I being if I live to next October sixty-five years of age'[17].

At the same time, the partial wielding of power and influence was associated with an ideal of public service. Many of the gentry had a strong sense of responsibility to the local community, a feeling which inspired the more conscientious of them in their work as justices. Acceptance of social responsibility originated at the domestic and parish level, where the squire slipped naturally into his role of protector of his household, tenants and parishioners. His intervention might be invoked, for example, to preserve some labourers' access to their lands and commons (as occurred in disputes at Sellindge and Brabourne in east Kent in the later years of the sixteenth century)[18]. Or the matter might be more outlandish, as in an incident at Barham, not far away, in 1641. In this incident the squire, Sir Henry Oxinden, was moved to write to his brother-in-law, Robert Bargrave of Bifrons, to ask him to intercede on behalf of a Barham woman accused of being a witch:

Brother Bargrave,
The bearer hereof, by name Goodwife Gilnot, either maliciously or ignorantly, or both maliciously and ignorantly, accused to bee a witch, and having thereby sustained losse of her good name, and by reason thereof being much troubled and perplexed in minde, doth become your humble petitioner that the calumnies layd against her may either be fully proved or the authors of them may receive condigne punishment. I can no way blame the woman for being troubled at the losse of her good name, for all her riches are not to be compared unto it; if she be esteemed such a kind of creature every body will be afraid of her and noe body set her aworke, insomuch as truely shee will be utterly undone.
The allegations against this woman are that she hath bewitched one Brake, who being ill in bed believeth her to bee the cause thereof.
2. The said Brake hath lost divers sheepe and shee is accused to be the cause that they have suffered this sheepwrake.
To answer to the first of these allegations, I say hee is in a consumption, the sayd Brake, and will not follow our advice to be at the charge to go to a physician who by God's help may cure him. To the second I answer, I myselfe have lost divers sheepe and cattell this yeere, and soe have my nighbours likewise, who are not so simple to

believe they were bewitched, nor soe malicious as to accuse anybody for bewitching them.

Thirdy, that she hath a wart or teat upon her body wherewith shee giveth her familier sucke.

I answer to the third, I believe of not a marke uppon her body but what all women have as well as shee, or none injurie if they had it not. She hath a small wart uppon her breast, which you may see and you please, and believe it there is none so familier with her as to receive any sustenance from thence.

But such is the blindness of men in these latter times that, as St Paul preached, they depart from the faith and give heed to spirits of error and doctrines of devills, nay speake lies; and such deep roote hath the fables of witchcraft taken hold in the heart of this and other silly men, now and here, that they will not with patience endure the hand and correction of God, for if any adversity, sickness, losse of corne and cattle, doe happen to their prosperity, they accuse some neighbour or other for a witch' [19].

Many other similar acts of kindness are scattered through the correspondence of country gentlemen across the centuries. They witnessed wills for their tenants, acted as executors and provided sureties; they furnished letters of recommendation and found posts for their parishioners' sons and daughters; at their villagers' request they held sums of money in trust for long periods of time and paid interest to the depositors; and when required they sat on juries and served as churchwardens. Nicholas Blundell lent his tenants greyhounds for coursing hares and nets for fishing. He was not above partaking of the Christmas fare of his cottagers, and he made visits to the sick, offered remedies and paid for a doctor to make calls. When a tenant or servant died his own coach was lent as a hearse. On 29 December 1713 he noted that 'Ann Riding the Widdow gave me £10 to keep for her till she call'd for it, I gave her my Note for it' [20]. Much later in the eighteenth century Sir Joseph Banks was asked by the farmers along the Lincolnshire coast to petition the Admiralty for naval protection against 'smuggling pyratical Vessels which might land merely for Pillage and Plunder'. Sir Joseph proposed that a cutter of eight to ten guns should be provided to cruise between Wainfleet and Saltfleet Haven, asking, 'is it unreasonable for an Extent of Coast of 20 miles to ask from Government such slender Protection?' And in December 1800, during the severe grain scarcity of the Napoleonic Wars, Sir Joseph arranged for a ton of rice to be sent to Boston for distribution 'among the labouring poor of good Characters who do not receive relief from the Parish in Marsham and Revesby'. To overcome the labourers' unfamiliarity with rice he had a number of recipes printed and given out to each family, and he experimented with potatoes to see if they could be made to replace flour. The free rice was to be served out and accounted for by Robin Allowell 'who receives from me a salary of £10 a year for teaching School which he is not able to do well' [21].

The gentry met many calls on their charity, and their purses were expected to be open for the aged or sick, for old tenants who had come to grief, as well as for more public objects. In 1731, for instance, the villagers of Speen, Berkshire, headed by their vicar, appealed to the squire for his help in making repairs to the church:

Honoured Sir,
 We are sensible we need not use many words to a gentleman of
your goodness and generosity; and therefore shall only briefly
represent our case. The tower of our church is fallen down. We have
supported it to our power. Some years ago between fourscore and a
hundred pounds were expended on it and since that we have been at
great charge about it very often. We have a very numerous and
expensive poor; so that we hope you will be so good as to contribute
to the ease of the parishioners [22].

A great deal of letter-writing on the squire's part was occasioned by the
operation of the poor laws. In 1746 Henry Purefoy of Shalstone, Buckinghamshire, was constrained to write to George Denton, the member for Buckingham,
to request his help in a matter causing concern to the ratepayers of the parish:
'One Benjamin Woodcock has run away and left his wife and child to the
parish. I entreat the favour of you to grant our parish officers a warrant to have
him apprehended in any part of the county of Oxon because he dodges about
here from one parish to another.' Five years later the Woodcock case was still
giving trouble, and we find Purefoy trying to establish whether the man had
returned to the neighbourhood as his wife had recently presented the parish
with another child, 'for if we could prove that Woodcock has been in Ireland
during that time we could make the man who she swore the child to, keep
it' [23]. Even the poor who stayed put in their parish could be troublesome. At
Ollerton in Nottinghamshire Sir George Savile was told by his steward in 1731
that the new poor house presently in course of erection had been demolished by
one of the paupers for whom it was intended, 'because he did not like the
situation' [24]. And John Bridger, a Sussex gentleman who had retired to live
in Wimbledon, became involved in a reorganisation of the poor house there.
In 1774 the rising cost of the poor rates prompted the establishment of a
Committee of Ratepayers 'for the better Oeconomy in the management of the
several articles consumed in the Poor House of this Parish, as well as for the
more tender nursing of the sick therein, and particularly for the due instruction
of the younger female part thereof in household work'. The Committee introduced a body of regulations, appointed an elderly couple to see them enforced,
laid down the diet to be provided, and saw that work was given out to the
inmates, including employment in a rope walk. A Committee of Ladies was also
formed to take it in turn to inspect the house and enquire after the children put
out to nurse [25].
 Service as an officer in the militia or as commissioner for the highways
could be troublesome. One such commissioner, Ralph Wood of Gisborough,
had to make frequent rides to Whitby moors in order to supervise road-
building and bridge construction, and a characteristic entry in his journal ran:
'Went to the Highways where we had 8 or 10 carts leading stones and gravel
where we put in a gantree or bridge against Cook's ground in Yarm Lane.
Where I attended the whole day till near 6 without meat and drink, save a little
water. Ye work was done to my satisfaction' [26].
 Sometimes questions of more general concern to the county at large
brought an initiative from the leading gentry. In the later seventeenth century
Sir Edward Dering drafted a memorandum on the causes of an alleged fall in
rents and general decline of the economy of his county of Kent. This alarming

situation he ascribed to a long list of factors, some of which were: 'the extra-ordinary resort to London', and the drain of cash there in payment of taxes (which, he said, were especially burdensome in Kent); 'the want of people by resort to the plantations'; the decline of the cloth trade in the county, and of hop-growing, following the cultivation of hops in Herefordshire; the effects of increased production of wool in Ireland; the neglect of cattle breeding in Kent, so allowing 'the Welsh to carry out every year in ready money many thousand pounds', which could be kept in the county if the cattle were reared and sold in London or to the navy; the increase in cultivation elsewhere arising from draining of the fens and ploughing up of parks, and particularly 'the improve-ment made of the barren and dry parts of some other countries by Clover, St Foin and Trefoile, which is not yet and probably never can be so advan-tageous to this country where the lands are generally not so fit for it'; 'the drinking of brandy grown of a sudden to a very great mischief, it being now sold generally in every village'; and 'the insolence and carelessness of servants requiring more wages and doing less worke here than any county of England'. This account of the causes of Kentish decline was followed by a scheme for recovery: the recruiting of fifty gentlemen of the county, each willing to advance the sum of £200 for five years in order to establish a total fund of £10,000. This fund, it was proposed, should be laid out in purchasing wool, hops, corn and fat cattle during cheap seasons in order to help distressed farmers and graziers, particularly those on the lands of the fifty contributors. It was also to be used in loans or in subsidising house rents for the purpose of attracting into Kent the new cloth trades of Colchester bays, Exeter serges or Norwich stuffs; and the remainder of the fund was to be lent out at interest in London[27]. The document has more than local interest, not least for its coupling of a parochial county outlook with an appreciation of the changes taking place in the country at large. Dering clearly felt the need to speak up for his own 'country' when its traditional occupations were threatened, and it is significant that he looked to other public-spirited gentlemen, rather than government, for help. It was, he saw, a problem for the county to solve, and the responsibility for its solution lay with the county gentry.

Justices of the peace

By the time of Dering's memorandum the key to the administration and welfare of Kent, as of every county, was held by the justices of the peace. From the time of his medieval origins the justice came to assume more and more powers while the other county authorities, the sheriff and the coroner, declined in importance. In the sixteenth century the justice was kept under the watchful eye of the Privy Council and Justices of Assize, but with the Civil War and the breakdown of the central government's authority the justice became much less the local instrument of the monarchy and much more the representative voice of the independent country gentry.

The number of justices appointed in each county rose from three or four in the early fourteenth century to six in 1388, and eight in 1390. By the later fifteenth century the numbers had risen to a score or so in the more heavily populated counties. In Wales the justices were formally introduced by an Act of 1536, but before this local landowners had already assumed some of the justices' functions. The possession of land worth at least £20 a year freehold was the qualification for membership of the Commission of the Peace. This was laid down as far back as 1439, and although the wealth represented by this sum declined with the fall in the value of money in the sixteenth century, it came to be understood that a justice must be a gentleman of some substance. The wages also, settled at four shillings a day in 1388 and 1390, declined sharply in value but remained unchanged; so that by the later sixteenth century and after, those justices who took their duties seriously were badly out of pocket [28].

The medieval justice sat in quarter sessions four times a year, and in large counties moved about from place to place spending one day at each venue. To the original functions of keeping the peace and determining various offences, a succession – Lambarde's 'so many, not loads, but stacks' – of statutes gradually added a host of multifarious administrative duties. Under the Tudors over 170 Acts affected the justices, but their largest areas of activity, other than keeping the peace, were concerned with the regulation of prices, wages and apprenticeship, the supervision of bridges and highways, licensing of alehouses and the operation of the recusancy laws, game laws and poor laws. In 1627 the justices of certain counties were required to arrange lodgings for the queen when she travelled for her health. In addition they were ordered to find 'the most commodious ways and passages . . . through the fields from place to place', so that she might avoid 'the immoderate heat and the dustiness' of the highways. Many of the duties imposed on the justices were of a more routine kind, but were nonetheless onerous. Even the remote and sparsely populated county of Cumberland had in 1574–77 as many as twenty-nine inns, four taverns and 623 alehouses, and William Thomson of Thornfleet, justice and active Sabbatarian, was kept busy fining people for drinking on Sundays, and for swearing, fulling cloth, and 'carding severall Lord's dayes' [29]. In Cornwall the quarter sessions occupied a whole week, beginning at Bodmin on Tuesday and Wednesday, and continuing at Truro on Friday and Saturday, with a day's space for riding between the two towns [30].

The conscientious justice in Elizabethan Norfolk found his hands more than comfortably full: at quarter sessions he helped settle audits of county rates raised for the repair of roads, bridges, and sea defences; he appointed constables who collected the rates, and he also granted licences for alehouses and markets and issued lists of approved wages; he supervised the maintenance of the houses of correction and the raising of purveyance for the royal household; in addition, he assessed pensions of maimed soldiers and authorised relief for those unfortunates who had lost goods through fire. Business became so heavy that, despite the energy exhibited by the full panoply of the Bench at quarter sessions, there was an increased reliance on petty sessions. Here two justices met at frequent intervals for despatching routine matters, especially those in connection with the poor laws. These meetings, too, could be lengthy with a great deal of time taken up by investigation of paupers' settlements and bastardy cases, while any defendants judged to be 'sturdy rogues and vagabonds' (a term which included such doubtful characters as gypsies, petty chapmen, sailors pretending loss of vessels, and students) were consigned to the Bridewell. The schedule of meetings was considerably extended by membership of other bodies and commissions. One Norfolk justice, rejoicing in the name of Bassingbourne Gawdy, was away from home a total of seventeen days during the winter months of January and February 1600. In January he had four meetings at Norwich (involving a ride of twenty-one miles) for quarter sessions (which lasted four days) as well as meetings of the Recusancy Commissioners and Muster Commissioners, and he made another journey to Swaffham for a Bridewell meeting; in February he was off again to quarter sessions and three meetings of the Muster Commissioners, together with a visit to Thetford on militia business [31].

The work was not merely arduous but complex and exacting. The collection of parliamentary and local taxes, for example, was extraordinarily laborious and involved, and was not infrequently subject to neglect or fraud since the business depended on the efforts of a wide variety of bodies and officials. There was no concept of a general tax or general rate, and each new burden was levied on the taxpayer by a separate assessment made by a separate body. The individual taxpayer, for his part, found himself making a variety of sporadic payments to an assortment of officials. These might include such items as purveyance, the mustermaster's wages, repairs to the village pound, maintenance of the house of correction, a constable's rate for catching a prisoner and contributions towards bridge repairs. The justices' regulation of inns and alehouses was sometimes exceedingly detailed. In Northleath, Gloucestershire, for instance, no inns were allowed in specified streets or in the part of the town nearest to Cheltenham 'other than the Antelope only'. The curfew prohibited visitors from leaving a friend's house after nine in the evening, or an inn after ten. No one, other than a child or servant of the house, might enter or leave an inn except by the front door. Tewkesbury innkeepers had to keep their street doors shut during the time of divine service, and were not to allow drinking or gaming indoors.

Strict enforcement of such regulations was likely to make justices highly unpopular. They caused grumbling, too, when they tried to make clothiers keep on their hands in time of slack trade, or prohibited the making of malt or the movement of grain out of the county in periods of scarcity; or when, as in Gloucestershire, they were obliged under government pressure to prohibit the growing of tobacco; indeed attempts at destruction of the tobacco crop gave rise to riots in 1638 and 1639. The mustering of the trained bands called for a certain nicety in fixing the date, if the farmers were not to be aggrieved by the absence of their labourers at a vital season, and if there was to be a true assessment of the military equipment, for the men were known to be in the habit of passing weapons from one to another if musters were not all held on the same day. A justice could not even expect automatic respect for his office. And if insult or defiance betrayed him into rash behaviour he was liable to be hauled up before the Star Chamber: this was the unfortunate sequel of an incident involving Sir John Strafford who, when menaced by a fellow with a pike, dared to go so far as to strike the man with his riding wand [32].

In addition, the county officials were faced by complications arising from vague and overlapping functions. The sheriff, for example, was not concerned merely with the capture and punishment of malefactors and collection of the Crown's revenue; he was further responsible, together with one or two justices, for seeing that the laws were observed 'for the true and sufficient tanning of leather', for the supply of grain to markets, the destination of victuals intended for troops and the provision of armour for the militia. A serious discouragement was the sheer cost of holding office. In Pembrokeshire Sir John Wogan complained that since being deputy-lieutenant he had spent over £1,000, 'which is great for a man of so small a living' [33]. The fees that had to be paid on entering and leaving the office of sheriff were far heavier than the value of the perquisites, and responsibility for the collection of numerous fines hung over the sheriff many years after he had retired to private life. William Dutton, a sheriff of Gloucestershire in the late sixteenth century, was bound, together with his under-sheriff, to remit some £10,000 due to the Crown, but managed to collect only a fraction of this great sum during his term of office. The defaulters were not easily brought to book but, we are told, met all attempts to seize their goods with abuse, 'blows, assaults, hurts, wounds, bloodshed, rescues and threatenings' [34].

It was during the seventeenth century that clerical justices began to take a significant part in the Commission of the Peace. By this time the parish priest had come a very long way from the semiliterate medieval peasant who once looked after the cure of souls. He was now a gentleman, often a younger son of reputable origins, well-read, and boasting a university degree. Gentry of strong religious convictions saw to it that their incumbents were adequately supported, both morally and materially. Many clergy were now socially on a par with the country gentlemen, and partook of their ideas and pleasures. In due course their rise in standing was recognised by admission to the Bench, a promotion generally denied to the humbler men of trade. Indeed, as late as 1833 some county magistrates refused to act with a man who was doubly condemned as a grocer and a Methodist. Their foible was excused as 'genuine patriotism: the spirit of aristocracy in the county magistracy is the salt which alone preserves the whole mass from inevitable corruption' [35].

Two canons of Wells were appointed to the bench in Somerset as early as 1617–18, and the first parochial cleric took his seat in 1623. Legal expertise was also represented on the Somerset bench with fifteen appointments of barristers out of a total of a hundred appointments made between 1625 and 1640. Attendance at quarter sessions in the county was never less than eight, averaged twelve, and occasionally rose to nineteen. A few justices never attended, and others periodically absented themselves, the principal causes – or excuses – being colds, gout, 'extraordinary occasions', and visits to London [36]. Everywhere, however, the number of justices was tending to rise as the powers and popularity of the office grew. In the counties of Kent, Norfolk, Northamptonshire, Somerset, Worcestershire and the North Riding of Yorkshire the Bench nearly doubled in size between 1562 and 1608. In due course more and more responsibilities, such as approval of rules of friendly societies and the fixing of rates for land carriage, expanded the justices' sphere of influence. Even in remote Pembrokeshire the twenty-four justices of 1573–74 (of whom only nine were resident in the county) became thirty-five by 1663, and then doubled by 1727. In 1779 the county boasted a commission 120 strong; in 1790 nearly 200; and by 1836 there were as many as 258. Meanwhile the number of clerical justices rose from three in 1727 to 39 in 1790, a not untypical development [37]. In Hertfordshire the proportion of clergy among the justices rose from only 2 per cent in the period 1635–99 to a quarter between 1752 and 1799 and then to a peak between 1800 and 1833, falling back to 16 per cent in the 1850s, and to only 4 per cent in the 1870s – this process of rise and decline reflecting the secular trends of the clergy's wealth, prestige and political influence [38]. The Act of 1731, which at last raised the medieval property qualification of £20 to a more realistic £100, does not seem to have restricted the appointment of clergymen or the more prominent merchants. In the later eighteenth century the Gloucestershire justices included fifteen clergymen, a dozen clothiers from the Stroud valley, ten Bristol merchants, two barristers, two doctors, a brewer, a mercer and a Cirencester banker and carpet manufacturer [39].

The growing popularity of the Commission of the Peace was connected with its prestige and, one suspects, with the voluntary nature of the duties: in practice most of the work was done by an active minority, usually about a quarter of the whole Bench. The Shrievalty, on the other hand, declined in prestige as the office became associated in many counties with the lower gentry. Unlike the voluntary character of the magistracy, the sheriff's work must perforce be carried out, if principally by unpaid deputies. Further, the office was only for a period of twelve months, and in that space of time it was impossible for even the most reforming of sheriffs to make much impression on his usual inheritance of insubordinate and often dishonest sheriff's officers. Less onerous than the requirement of staying within the boundaries of the county during his term of office, was the sheriff's expensive responsibility for entertaining assize judges and providing the accoutrements for their ceremonial retinue. William Pym, high sheriff of Bedfordshire in 1764, reckoned up his expenses at £144 12s 2d, a sum which included dinners and suppers given during Bedford assizes, fees to the judges' officers, and the provision of livery [40].

The clerical justices rapidly justified their appearance, often becoming the most active and conscientious members of the Commission, and showing a special interest in the reform of the prisons and the relief of the poor. It was a clerical member of the Suffolk Bench who took up the improvement of a local house of correction ten years before the opening of John Howard's prison reform campaign, while in Berkshire the historic Speenhamland decision of 1795 arose from the initiative of a prebendary of Winchester. As many clergymen were presented to their livings by the Crown or by their old colleges, they often came from outside the county and might well bring in new ideas and a fresh approach to local problems. By 1832 clerical justices accounted for about a quarter of the whole, and in several counties they outnumbered lay members at quarter sessions. Often they exhibited a better grasp of law, and were found taking the lead in dealing with criminal cases. Surprisingly, perhaps, they were also active in the pursuit of criminals: in 1813 a friend of the Reverend Christopher Sykes told him of a report of highwaymen having taken flight to Sykes's part of the West Riding, 'and as you constantly attend the Justices' meetings and *are very active* we think it very likely you may hear of them' [41]. There is evidence that the acquisition by clergymen of the powers and status of the Bench was a factor in the growth of rural anticlericalism in the century or so after 1750. The enhanced authority of the parson-justice added to the hostility felt by those who considered the exactions of the tithes to be excessive and unjust, and who believed that the clergy did too well out of enclosures, where the cost of enclosing their glebe and the allotments made in lieu of tithes was met by the other proprietors [42].

Although the energy and reforming zeal of clerical justices made them outstanding figures on the eighteenth-century Bench there were some lay members who could easily bear comparison with them. Not a few expended their leisure hours in a constant press of public business, in meetings of the militia commissioners, charity trustees, inspection of turnpike works, and many similar matters. Dr Moir has written of the impressively named Sir George Onesiphorus Paul, who undertook numerous improvements to the prisons and houses of correction in Gloucestershire [43]. Another example of the conscientious lay justice, concerned to perform his duties well and fairly, may be seen in Sir Wyndham Knatchbull of Kent. Between 1734 and 1745 Sir Wyndham kept a detailed diary of the cases he heard, and he also maintained a Precedents Book in which he noted down the procedures to be observed at quarter sessions, the precise definition of various crimes and their classification, details of the law of master and servant, and the principal statutes referring to the highways and the poor, as well as the rules relating to the appointment of constables, the qualifications of jurors, and many similar matters. Some novel or unusual rulings merited special notice: 'It's a settled point if a Woman having a Settlement before her marriage marries a man who has not a Settlement, after ye death of ye Husband, she and her children gain a Settlement where she was settled before her marriage; but during her marriage her Settlement is suspended.' And again: 'No waggon travelling for hire shall be drawn by more than 6 horses, nor a cart with more than 3. The waggoner shall forfeit all ye horses above 6, and ye Carter above 3 etc: to the use of the person who seizes them' [44].

Despite the evident care for the proper execution of their duties and the humanitarian attitudes of some of their number, the justices seem to have met with greater hostility among the common people as the eighteenth century drew to a close. This was perhaps inevitable in a period of rapid population growth, when villages were becoming industrialised and rural migrants were swelling the new industrial towns. The economic changes were tending to erode traditional attitudes, and the high prices, food shortages and heavy taxation of the French wars after 1793 accentuated the poverty that was widespread in some parts of the country. More people and more poverty meant more petty crime. The justices, it is true, tempered justice with mercy: it became a common practice to value stolen goods at far under their true value in order that the charge of larceny might be classed as 'petty' rather than 'grand', the latter carrying with it the death penalty. The substitution of transportation for the extreme penalty in capital cases was partly due to humanitarian motives. The eighteenth century saw a marked extension of the number of capital offences, so that by 1820 there were as many as 200 offences punishable by death. Increased severity was thought to deter potential offenders in a period when crimes against property were rising, and the state was regarded as having a duty to protect private property. Alternative punishments, such as imprisonment or transportation, were held to be unsatisfactory, prisons operating as centres of corruption and vice, and transportation believed to be not much of a deterrent. The extreme penalty was seen by most people as the only answer when police forces were inadequate in numbers, untrained, and sometimes corrupt. The age was one of great personal insecurity. The prudent waited for the full moon before venturing from their homes at night. Even in London's major thoroughfares highwaymen held up coaches in broad daylight. 'One is forced to travel, even at noon, as if one were going to battle', wrote Horace Walpole in 1752. In practice, the severity of the law was mitigated by the judges' elimination of numerous capital charges and the refusal of juries to convict in many cases brought before them. In the early nineteenth century something like one out of every five or six persons committed for trial was acquitted by the grand jury, and a quarter of the remainder were subsequently acquitted [45].

Nevertheless, in a society where the great gulf between the propertied and the propertyless seemed to be getting wider the justices were inevitably associated with the protection of their own interests. Too many justices believed it wise to apply the full rigour of the law in defence of property. It was one of these who boasted of exacting justice 'with such severity as shall enable any gentleman to hang his watch by the highway with the full confidence of finding it there on his return another day'. The magistracy seemed to embody the forces of tradition and conservatism at a time when ideas of equality and fraternity were freshly in the air. There was indeed a tendency to exclude from the Bench any gentleman of radical sympathies. With the growing fear of revolution, and with events across the Channel in mind, the justices assumed a more unsympathetic, repressive and punitive role at the very time when unrest was intensified by dear food, high postwar unemployment, and the dislocation caused by rapid economic change. The appeals of depressed workers in the hand trades was met by refusal to put the clock back and revive the long-defunct powers of wage regulation and apprenticeship. Nascent trade unions were prosecuted under the new Combination Acts, and where these proved inadequate, under the more effective law of conspiracy. Justices seized and hanged food rioters, and they kept a wary eye open for any sign of sedition or disaffection.

The late eighteenth century and early decades of the nineteenth saw far more widespread and alarming outbreaks of popular unrest than had been known in the more slowly changing, more subservient kind of society that was passing away. Food riots and machine-breaking were commonplace enough in the eighteenth century, but the incidents were generally local and shortlived. However, with the high bread prices and scarcities of the French wars, and the severe unemployment of the postwar depression, unrest assumed much more alarming dimensions, and in various forms persisted for years on end. Attacks on millers and corn merchants, on wagons and barges carrying food, outbreaks of machine-breaking and angry protests at new government measures, became widespread. To these were added some large-scale protest movements: the Luddites, Blanketeers, Swing rioters, anti-Poor Law demonstrators and Chartists, to name the best-known. The threats to life and property, the fear, even, of revolution, called forth countervailing measures of repressive laws, spies, troops, arrests, mass-trials, hangings, transportation and the rest. Faced with eruptions of lawlessness exceeding all experience, many justices cut a poor figure, acting indecisively, failing to agree on the measures to be taken, and omitting to pass on information or coordinate their plans with fellow-magistrates. Worse still, they sometimes lost their nerve, and having little faith in the loyalty or efficiency of the militia, were only too inclined to call in the military on every alarm. Some magistrates showed a degree of sympathy with the Swing rioters of 1830, feeling no doubt that their wages were in truth miserably inadequate. But others were of a different mentality, like James Frampton, who was prominent in curbing the riots in Dorset, and a few years later took the lead in repressing the Tolpuddle labourers' premature attempt to form a trade union [46]. The Frampton kind of magistrate saw not the reality of the grievances and the need to deal with their causes, but only the danger of the symptoms to good order, the authority of the law, and the 'natural subordination' of the labouring classes. It was a period in which only the most level-headed, upright and humane of magistrates could escape the general obloquy, and others less popular with the mob might find their homes set on fire and their persons placed in no little danger.

In this same period there was, furthermore, an increase in the power of the individual justices of dealing with criminal offences. For example, an Act of 1820 gave authority to a single justice to convict persons found guilty of malicious damage to buildings, hedges, fences, trees and woods. A growing number of offences could be heard by one or two justices sitting alone, perhaps in their own parlour, and the power of summary jurisdiction varied from a shilling fine for uttering an oath to seven years' transportation for poaching. Poaching, probably the commonest of rural offences, became an increasingly frequent cause of direct confrontation between justice and labourer. The Game Laws, of course, were not new. As early as 1390 the keeping of dogs for hunting, and the killing of deer, hares and rabbits, were limited to owners of property worth 40s a year. In 1671, after a long series of further laws, the property qualification was set at the level which prevailed until 1831. Freeholders of less than £100 a year, and leaseholders with farms worth less than £150 a year, were prohibited from taking game, and the restrictions extended to deer, pheasants, partridges, hares and rabbits. Under the Act of 1770 anyone who took game at night could be punished by three to six months' imprisonment, and for a second offence by six to twelve months' imprisonment and a public whipping.

Before the nineteenth century, however, there were large expanses of commons and waste land where the small farmer or labourer could enjoy a little sport and supplement his pot without much risk of interference. As Acts of enclosure converted such land into farms and sheepwalks, so the landowners' private game preserves, with their high concentrations of birds and rabbits, came to offer more attractive scope for the plunder of the habitual poacher and the sport of the adventurous village lad. The reaction of the legislature was to protect this special form of landed property with a more harshly deterrent Game Code. It is worth noting, however, that this development formed part of a general tendency to heighten the protection of all forms of property with laws of increased severity: the Game Laws were a particularly vicious example of a general trend towards harsher penalties for common crimes which characterised the first quarter of the nineteenth century. And subsequently, as the reform of the criminal law got under way, so the Game Laws, though remaining harsh enough in all conscience, became a little more moderate and humane. The repressive phase was marked by a new Act of 1800, which empowered a single Justice to punish poachers by imprisonment with hard labour; in 1803 a further Act made armed resistance to arrest punishable by death; and in 1817 armed poachers caught at night were punishable by seven years' transportation. The penalty of transportation under this last Act had the effect of making juries reluctant to convict, and in 1828 this measure was replaced by a new one which reserved transportation for the third offence, while the first and second offences were punishable by terms of three months' and six months' imprisonment respectively.

The heightening of penalties in the early years of the new century followed a period when landlords began to show a greater interest in the preservation of game. With improvements in the effectiveness of firearms, especially with the introduction of the flint-lock gun, shooting came more into vogue, and in the second half of the eighteenth century there is evidence of a growing concern on the part of the landlords to prevent poaching. Proprietors joined in local organisations to protect game, and the subscriptions were devoted to meeting the costs of bringing prosecutions and paying rewards to informers. A national organisation of this kind, the Society of Noblemen and Gentlemen for the Preservation of the Game, was formed as early as 1752. Gamekeepers were authorised to detain suspects and to confiscate their guns, dogs and nets; and further to deter trespassers gamekeeping landlords resorted to such horrifying devices as mantraps and spring-guns.

While these moves were in progress the activities of poachers were encouraged by the growth of the markets for illegal game, especially in London and the provincial cities. Poaching by organised gangs was increasing in the eighteenth century and became widespread in the early years of the new century, only somewhat moderated by the legalising of the sale of game in 1831. This profitable trade encouraged persistent nocturnal warfare between gangs of poachers and gamekeepers in the woodlands of the large proprietors.

> The woods in which Tom Jones fought his great fight with Thwackum and Blifil to cover the flight of Molly Seagrim now echoed on a still and moonless night with the din of a different sort of battle: the noise of gunshots and blows from bludgeons, and broken curses from men who knew that, if they were taken, they would never see the English dawn rise over their homes again: a battle which ended perhaps in the death or wounding of a keeper or poacher, and the hanging or transportation of some of the favourite Don Quixotes of the village [47].

So that country house parties might bag their vast piles of birds (the record for a single day's shooting of 525 pheasants was achieved in 1823) poachers were killed or maimed and, it was stated, between 1827 and 1830 one in seven of all the criminal convictions in the country were convictions under the Game Laws. It is hardly surprising that the justices, so heavyhanded in defence of a species of property so peculiarly their own, should have become associated with class justice in protection of class rights. 'There is not a worse-constituted tribunal on the face of the earth', said Brougham in 1828 '. . . than that at which summary convictions on the Game Laws constantly take place; I mean a bench or a brace of sporting justices.'

The conflict was intensified by the passion for shooting and hunting which in the early decades of the nineteenth century became an obsession with many aristocracy and gentry. Professor F. M. L. Thompson has noted a peak in the number of game licences issued at 51,375 in 1827; a decline in the popularity of shooting followed, associated with some poor seasons for game and the agitation over the Game Laws, to be succeeded by renewed and greater popularity in the second half of the century. Foxhunting,

> a sport eminently suited to the mounted and leisured aristocracy and gentry . . . was an increasingly organised activity, with a growing body of conventions and etiquette, which gave the hunting community a mystique and cohesion of its own . . . most of those who

could command the use of a riding horse found that one of the aims of life was fulfilled in the exhilaration of riding to hounds. It was a fact which, perhaps more than any other, gave vitality, cohesion and stability to county society.

The squires whose estates did not afford facilities for extensive hunts and shoots helped with financial contributions, and they played their part in the preservation of game and foxes, despite the complaints of their tenants [48].

The prohibition on the use of spring-guns in 1827, the reduced penalties on poachers introduced in the Act of 1828, and the legalising of the sale of game in 1831 were indications of a more responsible approach to game preservation in the second quarter of the century. The Game Laws, however, now became more than a target for reformers of the criminal law and a source of friction between landlords and tenants. The ravages of game on corn crops was one of the sticks eagerly seized by the opponents of the Corn Laws for the purpose of belabouring the landed interest. Bright collected evidence of the depredations of game from farmers and in 1845 launched an attack in Parliament, hoping to exploit the farmers' grievance and so drive a wedge between the landlords and their tenants. Grantley Berkeley, a well-known leader of the sporting squires, appeared as the landowners' chief spokesman at the resulting Select Committee. In reply to the attack of Bright he was able to argue, with some justice, that tenants suffering damage from game in fact received compensation from their landlords and enjoyed their farms at beneficially low rents; he also argued, rather less convincingly, that game birds did the farmers much good by keeping down insect pests. In the end the Select Committee reported inconclusively, and the agitation died down with the achievement of the League's grand object, repeal of the Corn Laws. Shooting went on to a new wave of popularity and poaching went on with it, but farmers were not given the right to kill hares and rabbits without the landlord's permission until 1881 [49].

Yet despite all the horror of the Game Laws, and the identification of the justices with class interests, the picture was not all black. As *ex officio* members of Boards of Guardians, many justices were active in local opposition to the harshly deterrent aspect of the New Poor Law, and in practice they considerably moderated the impact of the new union workhouse on the rural poor. In any event, what was the alternative? Suggestions for reform, and particularly the proposal that the justices should be replaced by paid professional magistrates, found support in no quarter. Apart from the expense of such a change it was feared that stipendiaries would be mere tools of the government, 'corrupt jobbers and odious tyrants'. Right down to the 1880s cheap local administration based on parish officials supervised by unpaid justices was still the order of the day. 'It really seems scarcely credible', writes Dr Moir, 'that in the England of the 1880's the surveyors of the highways were still gardeners, bricklayers, broken-down clerks or merely the incompetent relations of prominent parishioners' [50].

For a time the advances in the knowledge and means of dealing with current evils (as in the prevention of epidemic disease) had the effect of stirring the rural justices to greater activity and efficiency. Developments in central government, particularly the introduction of the inspector (as in the poor law and education), acted in a similar way. In meeting their local problems justices could now draw on the knowledge and advice of the experts, and so make decisions with greater wisdom and certainty. In the long run, however, the progress of democracy could not be denied. The extension of the franchise to rural workers made the reform of the Bench inevitable. In 1888 all the administrative and financial functions of the justices, except those relating to the police and the poor law, were transferred to the new elected county councils. The change was a less painful one than might be imagined, for although the justices were shorn of much of their power their estates were also relieved of a considerable part of the burden of taxation, now placed on the shoulders of a wider community. Furthermore, the justices retained some influence in local affairs: in many counties 'the new county Council looked remarkably like the old Quarter Sessions', with magistrates occupying a half or more of the council seats. Public service still demanded men of education and leisure, and so, in its early days at least, the revolution in local government resulted not in the 'abdication of the country gentry' but in their becoming 'constitutional rulers' [51].

To some extent the permanence of the old order was deceptive. By the 1880s merchants and manufacturers were strongly represented at quarter sessions as well as on the new county councils. This penetration of the old citadel of the landed interest was aided by the links which the newcomers made with the ancient gentry through a common public school education, a common outlook on public affairs, and even a common sharing of country sports; and the links were strengthened, too, by common membership of the Volunteer movement, freemasonry, and joint interests in business concerns. When the property qualification for justices was abolished in 1906 the Bench had already become representative of a much broader range of interests than in the past [52]. In relinquishing their ancient monopoly of rural justice and administration the gentry could point with pride to a tradition of centuries of unpaid and arduous effort in the public service. Of course altruism had been subordinated at times to self-interest, just as efficiency had been impaired by ignorance and prejudice. On the whole, however, the Game Laws apart, the gentry could look back on a not uncreditable record: through the years they had maintained the cause of local rights and independence; and given the prevailing ideas of the age, they had held a fair balance between the rival claims of justice, mercy, property and charity. If comparison were made with the corrupt and authoritarian regimes of less favoured countries it might be said that England had not been unfortunate in her ruling class.

The gentry and the Church

The judicial and administrative powers of the justices provided the most obvious agency through which the gentry exercised their social domination of the lower orders. Yet another pervasive channel for their influence, however, lay through the Church. Not infrequently church and manor house lay cheek by jowl, the slender spire of one overshadowed by the bulk of the other, symbolising both the affinity and the relationship of power spiritual and temporal. The association might well be one of blood too, for parson and squire were often related. With the Reformation the gentry acquired wide powers over tithes and the right of presentation to livings. The purchasers of monastic lands became lay rectors, appropriating to themselves the major share of the tithes, leaving to the vicar only the small tithes or a pitiful stipend. The process proved irreversible, and by the early seventeenth century lay impropriations had become 'a vast vested interest which cut right across classes, politics and religion'. It was an interest which proceeded from solid financial advantage when, as often happened, the rectorial tithes amounted to some hundreds of pounds, and the vicarial tithes left to the parson fifty pounds or less [53]. In addition, the Church's practice of leasing out its remaining tithes to land-owners, like the leasing out of Church lands on beneficial terms, further ex-tended the gentry's influence. It is hardly surprising, therefore, that the squire-archy was closely identified with the Church, over whose property it had so much control; or that the old gibe of 'the Tory party at prayer' was levelled at the picture presented by the services of the Church of England.

Nevertheless, Roman Catholicism remained strong among the gentry in some counties, while in others pious Anglicans shaded into the other extreme of Puritanism. Religious radicalism, in fact, seems to have been associated with market towns and certain kinds of rural communities, particularly those in hill areas, forests and pastoral regions. Politics and religion were so closely inter-meshed that an interest in the one necessarily involved a concern with the other. The early seventeenth-century diary of Walter Yonge, a Puritan justice of Colyton in Devon, showed despite his remoteness a strong interest in the activities of both Puritans and Catholics and the influence they had on political questions [54]. Many of the gentry of the sixteenth and seventeenth centuries were almost fanatically devout. The pious Anglican household had its regular round of worship and prayer, its Bible study, and its readings from such works as Fox's *Book of Martyrs*, Bayly's *Practice of Piety*, and Jeremy Taylor's *Holy Living and Holy Dying*. Squire Bruen of Bruen Stapelford in Cheshire was perhaps a rather extreme example. He succeeded to his family estate in 1587, and with a dozen or so children of his own and twelve younger brothers and sisters to educate and launch into the world it may well be that financial circumstances played no small part in his religious inclination towards a devout and economi-cal way of life. He 'regulated his household according to the strict rules of religion', prohibited hunting as the work of the devil, disparked his park, harassed a cousin into giving up piping and dancing on the Sabbath, and burnt the playing cards and backgammon boards that less pious relations brought into the house. He rose at three in summer and five in winter, and after exten-sive private devotions summoned the household for prayers followed by psalms and readings from the Bible, an exercise which was repeated each evening. Two large Bibles stood on lecterns in his hall ready for any member of the household who wished to consult them. Except for two or three servants left to tend the house, the whole establishment proceeded to church in a body on Sundays, singing psalms as they went. To curb profanity in the parish Bruen's servants threw down village maypoles, and about St Andrew's Day distin-guished preachers were brought in to provide a rival attraction to the pipers, fiddlers, bearwards and gamesters [55].

A contemporary of Squire Bruen was Lady Margaret Hoby, the wife of a Yorkshire squire. She had been brought up in the strictly Puritan household of Catherine, Countess of Huntingdon. As a matter of course she readily undertook the many chores of the squire's lady, ordering matters in the granary, weighing out wool, receiving rents and passing the time of day with tenants, mending and sorting linen, and preserving quinces and making gingerbread; but, as her diary shows, she clearly regretted the time taken up by such mundane affairs, and she even deplored spending part of her day in walking with her husband, 'nothing reading nor profiting my selfe or any, the Lord pardon my omissions and commissions, and give mee his spirit to be watchfull to reduce the time'. A typical day in her life, in this instance Thursday, 23 August 1599, was spent as follows:

> In the morning I prayed: then I took order for thinges about the house till I went to breakfast, and soon after I took my Coach and went to Linton where, after I had saluted my mother, I prayed, and then, walking a little and reading of the bible in my Chamber went to supper; after which I heard the Lector and soon after that went to bed [56].

An outstanding example of the old High Church diehard was Hamon L'Estrange of Norfolk. He was one of the High Churchmen who under Charles II tried to hold back the tide of Dissent, and as a prolific producer of savage pamphlets and broadsides and editor of Tory newssheets, he was rewarded by the government with the offices of Surveyor of the Printing Press and Licenser of the Press, and was subsequently knighted by James II. L'Estrange was only a minor figure in this age of religious and political turbulence, but he symbolised the violent antagonisms which divided the ruling class when religious feelings ran so deep as to inspire acts of treason. Eventually, however, the furore created by the Popish plot and by the Roman prejudices of James died down under Protestant William and Mary, and the Church of England's own Queen Anne.

In the eighteenth century religious enthusiasm went out of fashion. The erratic flights of extempore prayer beloved of some Puritan divines – 'Tho' we speak Nonsense, God will pick out the Meaning of it' – was replaced by a more sober tone of discussion. Fanaticism and persecution gave way to moderation and tolerance. The Roman Catholic gentry found life much easier in the calmer atmosphere of the new century. The severe laws against Catholics, Dissenters and Jews remained on the statute book but were not strictly enforced. Penal taxation and the limitation on entry to offices and professions undoubtedly brought down some Catholic gentry, just as recusancy fines in the previous century had laid low men like Sir Thomas Tresham of Rushton. However, in the new century the Catholic families who failed were often those who were already poor and heavily indebted to begin with, and numbers preferred to settle abroad in France and the Low Countries, where they could practise their religion without hindrance and could educate their children in seminaries and convents without breaking the law. Those who stayed managed to maintain good relations with the Anglican gentry and clergy, and like Nicholas Blundell of Crosby, near Liverpool, often dined with the very justices who were responsible for enforcing the laws against Catholics. During the Jacobite scares Catholic gentry came under suspicion: their houses were searched, and their horses commandeered for the army, but they were able to compound before the justices for any breach of the law; and in normal times they could count on the aid of clever lawyers and Protestant friends to get round the restrictions on purchasing land and entering into mortgages.

The revival of fervour among Methodists and Evangelicals in the later part of the eighteenth century affected more the industrial areas of the country. For the most part the countryside remained the stronghold of the established Church, and Dissenting chapels were prominent mainly in the more remote and scattered communities, and in the villages that became semi-industrialised. In forested and upland districts where farming was often only a side employ-ment, and where settlements were spread thinly over very large parishes and were often distant from the parish church, an influx of migrants and the pre-vailing looseness of the social organisation seem to have encouraged the estab-lishment of independent chapels. A connection between these local factors and the growth of Dissent has been established, for example, in the Kentish weald; and other areas where Dissent became strongly entrenched, such as the West Riding dales, east Devon, southeast Lancashire, east Cheshire, north Warwick-shire, west Leicestershire and Rockingham Forest, had similar settlement characteristics [57].

However, through the greater part of the English countryside, the gentry, with their hold on the established Church, continued to maintain a degree of social control over the rural population. Some landowners, such as Sir William Heathcote, would not accept a Dissenter as a tenant. The squire's choice of incumbent was also a matter for care for it could closely affect his authority in the locality as well as his personal relationship with the parson. One who would be willing to keep an eye on game and the tenants, and report defaulters in the squire's absence, was sometimes looked for [58], and generally the squire preferred a local man who shared his views on politics and religion, who was of the appropriate social status, and was connected with his family or estate. Thus an eighteenth-century landowner of the northeast wanted a man

of Northumberland or Durham by birth or one who has so long resided in one of those Counties as to be looked on as a native. . . . Wolfal is an honest man, an excellent scholar but a low and too quiet creature. I would have one not to bring reflection upon myself, one who would be quiet in his office but not so far as to render himself contemptible. . . . Mr Swinburne is a man I should like, barring his determined way of thinking. One of my own principle is undoubtedly a thing to be coveted, as it avoids some shyness which costs trouble to set upon a right footing between people who may be much together and not upon an equal footing. You see, Dear Sir, what I want is a person of our own country, not above residing at a place distant from the busy amusing part of the world, nor one who shall set himself above those he will be to live with, and in principle a Whig [59].

In the squire-dominated parishes a very regular attendance at church was expected. Sir Roger de Coverley was the literary personification of those many squires who got up and looked round the church every Sunday to see if any tenants or servants were missing. John Fullerton of Thrybergh 'was most particular in going to Church mornings and afternoons', and walked there and back, whatever the weather. 'If the servants, but one, were not in Church before the service began, they were told that if they were late again, they should not have the annual treat of going to the Doncaster Race' [60]. The Church was regarded as a moral and restraining influence, a force for stability, and thus a main foundation of the fabric of society. Its authority had to be maintained by regular calls to worship and by what Dr Johnson called 'the salutary influence of example'. The parsons who preached loyalty to the Crown and deference to the squirearchy – and practised what they preached – looked to the squire for support, and usually received it. The links between parson and squire were strengthened by the fact that the former often owed his appointment to the latter, that many incumbents were the younger sons of landowners (although more often of the humbler landowners), and that they shared the same interests in landed property and country sports and perhaps sat side by side on the justices' Bench.

Many parsons, however, took a very restricted view of their duties and saw their living simply as a means to enjoying a gentlemanly country life. Often they were great sportsmen, frequently foxhunters, said Arthur Young, who 'having spent the morning in scampering after hounds, dedicate the evening to the bottle, and reel from inebriety to the pulpit'. Advertisements were known such as: 'Wanted a curacy in a good sporting country, where the duty is light, and the neighbourhood convivial.' There were on the other hand men of conscience, enthusiastic to spread the Gospel and to advance village improvement and look after the poor. When rural poverty was acute in the early decades of the nineteenth century a number of clergy, especially in southern England, took the lead in establishing allotments as a means of helping cottagers to eke out their wages and keep off the parish. A pioneer in this field was the Reverend Stephen Demainbray, rector of Broad Somerford in Wiltshire, who had half-acre allotments attached to the cottages in his parish when it was enclosed in 1806. Clergymen were prominent in the debate which arose over allotment schemes, advising from their own experience what rent should be charged and the terms on which the plots should be let.

Sydney Smith, the celebrated humorist, acted as village doctor in his parish of Foston, where he performed miracles 'with garlic for whooping-cough' and an alternative prescription of 'a pennyworth of salt of tartar'. Scarlet fever he left alone: it 'awes me, and is above my aim. I leave it to the professional and graduated homicides.' Smith was also an enthusiastic preacher and had a habit of pummelling his pulpit cushion to give emphasis to his words. 'When I began to thump the cushion of my pulpit, on first coming to Foston, as is my wont when I preach, the accumulated dust of a hundred and fifty years made such a cloud, that for some minutes I lost sight of my congregation.' A lady who entered the church dressed in crimson velvet was greeted with the words, 'Exactly the colour of my preaching cushion! I really can hardly keep my hands off you.'

Through the parsons, too, education of the lower orders was conducted in conformity with established rules and beliefs. From the ancient grammar schools found in small market towns and some villages down to the parish charity and Sunday schools, the Church maintained its sway through the clergyman's multiple role as chairman of governors, supervisor or teacher. The education was generally of a strictly utilitarian kind and sometimes consisted mainly of an elementary training in crafts designed to ensure that children grew up as useful and industrious members of society. The parson of Eakring in Nottinghamshire was a strong advocate of 'schools of industry', and about 1790 he proposed to start one in his parish. A timber building to hold thirty pupils, he suggested, could be built very cheaply and might be used as a barn if the school failed; and the school's maintenance costs would be very low, only £20 a year for the salaries of two mistresses, with fuel and candles provided for a further £10. His argument was as follows:

> I see here very few signs of Domestick Industry; and when Children cannot be employed in the Field they are either loitering in the street, or lolling over their Books at the little Schools, at a weekly Expence to their Parents for which they learn to read but little better than they might be taught at a Sunday School.
>
> These Considerations have led me earnestly to wish that a working School could be established at Eakring. Such Schools have been instituted in Lincolnshire where the younger children are taught to knit and the elder ones to spin coarse Wool. I procured one of their Books of Reports, by which it appears, that 135 Children between 11 and 12 years old 'earned during the depth of winter Half a Crown per Week' each, A Sum beyond their Maintenance. If only one third of that Sum, or 10 pence per Week, could be earned by Children in general from 8 to 12 years old and Sixpence per week by Knitters from 5 to 8 it would surely be a great Advantage – But *if no profit at all could accrue*, and Children were only employed and taught to acquire Habits of Industry, preserved at a distance from Vice, taught and required to Worship their Maker every Morning and Evening could the Expence of supporting such a School be laid out in any charitable way to a better Advantage? [61]

While easygoing and prosperous clerics like Woodforde spent their days in gourmandising and cards, there were more puritanical clergy and squires who kept a close watch for evidence of moral failings among their parishioners. Tenants who were 'unsteady', given to drink and riotous behaviour, risked notice to quit, and some landowners kept careful notes on their tenants' private lives. In coastal areas there was much concern about smuggling and the demoralising effects of too free a consumption of brandy; indeed, smuggling was so rife that farmers complained of the shortage of farm hands, attracted away from the plough by the high pay given for transporting smuggled spirits. There was, similarly, a general prejudice against village alehouses and the people who frequented them, and some gentlemen held private services in their homes on Sunday evenings as a counterattraction. Where the landowner's control of village property extended to the inn he might oblige the innkeeper to serve hot soup, coffee and tea as alternatives to stronger beverages, as at Lord Wantage's *The Bull* at Ardington, Berkshire, in the late nineteenth century [62].

Quite often the gentry helped to establish friendly societies and provided village halls. At Workington and Harrington J. C. Curwen introduced insurance schemes for his workers with benefits for sickness and accidents, to which he contributed large sums. He became a recognised authority on friendly societies, and his family started a 'manufactory' to provide employment for the poor, and also established a food shop to sell farm produce at cost price during the scarcity prices of the Napoleonic Wars [63]. 'Premiums' or prizes were awarded to labourers who managed to bring up large families without resort to the parish. A similar concern with the poor rates lay behind the various schemes to provide allotments, where labourers might grow vegetables for their cookpot and perhaps keep pigs or a cow. Allotments were a popular nostrum among gentry and rural clergy in the years of high food prices and pauperism during and after the Napoleonic Wars, and a great debate arose over the most appropriate size of the plots and the precise rules under which they should be let. A common provision was that the tenancy ceased if the allotment-holder sought parish relief. There is little doubt that allotments were valuable for labourers, particularly in the low-wage areas of the southern counties. Very often, however, the farmers bitterly opposed them, fearing they would waste the labourers' energy, create a spirit of independence amongst them, and lead them into stealing the farmers' seed.

The country house – 'The theatre of hospitality'; leisure and sport

In providing friendly societies, allotments and village halls, the character of the gentry's influence on village life moved from control towards paternalism. The long arm of the squire's benevolence stretched through various forms of charity from the financial support of the aged to the finding of employment for the workless. Even the modest country gentleman on a few hundred pounds a year was expected to devote part of his income to meeting the needs of his poor neighbours [64]. A fixed sum was allowed for charities in annual budgets, like the £35 that Sir John Bridger set aside from his gross income of just under £2,500 in 1806. Sir John's £35 might be compared with the £150 he allowed for 'strong liquors', or the £30 for 'Gaming', and the £25 allocated to 'Lottery Tickets' in the same budget [65]. Of course the net income of a landowner was very much lower than his gross revenue, often by as much as a third, and it may well be that Sir John Bridger dispensed further sums for charity out of the £300 allowed for 'pocket money and sundries'. Probably a figure near 5 per cent of gross income was not untypical of the wealthy gentry's charitable disbursements.

Many of the more spectacular examples of individual benefactions, such as Thomas Guy's London hospital in the eighteenth century and Owens' College, Manchester, in the nineteenth, derived from financiers, merchants and industrialists, Wealthy landowners certainly lent their names and financial support to important urban charities, but for the most part the benevolence of the gentry was more parochial and on a smaller scale. It tended also to be highly personal, the squire coming to the help of old tenants and servants with reductions in rents or holdings and houses provided free of charge; but individual villagers who had met with misfortunes or come upon sickness and old age could also look to the squire for help. Sir Charles Bunbury's expenditure for 1773–74 included the following items [66]:

	£	s	d
To Mrs Baldwin as usual	2	2	0
To Mrs Gunstone do.	2	2	0
To the Poor on St Thomas's Day 1773 as usual	2	10	0
Widows in the Almshouse	25	0	0
Clothing for do.	5	18	2
Shoes		12	0
1200 Turf for do.	4	16	0

Even casual callers at the kitchen door might expect a little immediate help. Sir Hugh Cholmley fed the 'old people, widows and indigent persons' at his gate, and Lady Margaret Hoby 'dressed a poor boy's leg that was hurt'. Commonly the squire's lady not only provided first aid and nursing but also supervised the preparation of food for the poor, her household accounts frequently recording such outgoings as 'given a poor woman 6d' or 'given a poor Man wt. had losses 6d'. Some squires paid an annual fee to a surgeon or apothecary to care for the sick of the parish. Exceptional circumstances, however, called for exceptional efforts. In calamitous times, like the years of famine prices during the Napoleonic Wars, the poor were not left entirely to the mercy of the parish. In addition to local help, the gentry got up county subscriptions for the purpose of supplying flour to the labouring classes at reduced prices. Some landowners provided allotments and cow-pastures as a cushion against distress, and others took up the possibilities of growing potatoes on waste ground.

The gentry's charity was essentially local in area and practical in character. There was the occasional eccentric, like William Hanbury of Church Langton: impressed by the magical powers of compound interest he planned to give his village an array of religious and cultural institutions by means of the profits made from planting trees. Hanbury's grandiose schemes came to little, but over the country as a whole there gradually accumulated a mass of voluntary benevolence secured as permanent trusts. Most of these charitable trusts were very small, and they were unevenly distributed, but by the eighteenth century they already represented a formidable total of income-producing property. At the time of the Select Committee on Public Charities in the 1830s the land belonging to charities amounted to nearly 450,000 acres (bringing in rents of £874,000), while in addition there were not far short of £6 million invested in mortgages and the Funds. Excluding London, the best endowed counties, the West Riding of Yorkshire, Kent and Surrey, had incomes from charities of some £40,000 or more, while the poorest, Cumberland, Cornwall and Cardigan, were down to less than a tenth of that figure. The great majority of endowments were individually of low value: less than one in sixteen of the nearly 29,000 charities listed yielded more than £100 a year; nearly a half produced less than £5 [67].

Of course, these figures relate only to permanent charities set up as trusts, a form of benevolence emanating principally from the wealthier classes; hence the charitable indigence of the remote and poor counties. The majority of rural benefactors were less well-to-do, and they generally preferred to give small sums for immediate relief of the urgently distressed. Professor W. K. Jordan's studies have shown that in the period 1480 to 1660 there was in total a great volume of charitable effort, and that the gentry made up the largest class of donors: in Buckinghamshire they contributed 44 per cent of charitable benefactions, in Yorkshire nearly a third, and even in the more mercantile Norfolk over a quarter [68]. It is clear that the major developments in national politics and religious questions, as well as purely local circumstances, had considerable influence on donors. Benefactions for religious objects, for example, declined after the Reformation and revived again with the rise of Puritanism; and the attraction of other objects, education, public improvements and relief of the poor, also fluctuated considerably. Over the period studied by Professor Jordan, it is true, the real value of charitable gifts was eroded by the rise in population and the much greater rise in prices. In money terms benefactions rose fivefold, but at the same time population doubled and prices increased sevenfold. Charity, as is commonly the case, did not keep pace with inflation, and the purchasing power of benefactions per head of population fell by some two-thirds.

With the gentry charity usually began at home, in the support of a large household whose numbers were often swelled by the children of friends and by the presence of indigent relations and their chidren. Large households meant large outgoings in food, drink, fuel, candles and servants. The habit of keeping careful household accounts is evidence of the important role, often the major role, that household expenditure played in landowners' budgets. Dependent relations were expected to contribute some money towards their keep, and if they could not afford to do so then they might be required to help in some other way. Sir Henry Slingsby recorded in his diary for 1641 that one of his relations kept in his house an old kinsman 'out of Charity . . . after he had spent his own means; he was forced to give him meat, drink and clothes; and in this poor manner he lived: while he had his sight he was able to keep an account and oversee the servants at their work, and this was the best service he could do' [69].

The gentry's extensive household, and indeed their whole style of living, depended on the cheap labour of servants. Servants were required in the kitchen, laundry and dairy; in the nursery, bedrooms and dining-room; to receive visitors and to fetch and carry and run errands; to feed and groom the horses and drive the carriages; to tend the gardens, park and kennels, and to protect game. Florence Campbell, the wealthy heiress of Robert Campbell of Buscot Park, Berkshire, who achieved a certain notoriety through the mysterious death of her second husband, Charles Bravo, maintained a large staff in her suburban London villa in the 1870s: indoors a butler, footman, lady's maid, two housemaids, cook, kitchenmaid and housekeeper, and outdoors three gardeners, a coachman, groom and stable boy. Even the humbler kind of country gentleman or parson kept a cook, a maid or two and a groom, although the limited numbers of the staff meant less specialisation of function than in the large household. In the eighteenth century the Purefoys' footman was expected to 'work in the garden; lay the Cloath, wait at Table, and go to Cart with Thomas', and their Coachman was to 'drive a Coach well and be used to ploughing and other Husbandry businesse'. A female domestic had to 'milk 3 or 4 cows and understand how to manage the Dairy, and know how to boyll and roast ffowls and butchers' meatt'; she was also to help with the washing, the cleaning of rooms, and scouring of the pewter, 'and when she has done her worke she sits down to spin' [70]. The middling gentry ran to a staff of a dozen or so, and the really wealthy might afford thirty or forty. Wages were low, Dudley North paying his maids and boys only £3 a year about 1735, although housekeepers, cooks, butlers, footmen, grooms and gardeners commanded considerably higher figures. More onerous than the wages of the lower servants were the heavy outlays on food and liveries. All considered, the household staff of a wealthy member of the gentry accounted for several hundred pounds a year.

Unlike the superior servants who might have to be sought for at length and at a distance, the lower kind of domestics were readily recruited in the neighbourhood from the families of tenant farmers and labourers. An ample supply of this raw labour, especially of young girls, could be counted on for there were few alternative occupations. Indeed it might almost be argued that the employment of this surplus and largely unskilled rural labour was a form of charity, as was said in much more recent times of the employment of poor Negroes in white households in the American South. Cheapness and an ample supply seem to have encouraged overstaffing of the larger mansions, resulting in a hierarchy of servants ranked in a complicated range of titles and duties. It was always difficult to find experienced servants who were competent and reliable, and in the late sixteenth century Sir John Harington devised a system of fines to keep his servants in good order: uttering an oath was fined by a penny, and absence from prayers twopence; a penny was the penalty for forgetting to change shirts on Sundays, and for a button missing from a doublet, while the cook was subject to the heavy forfeit of sixpence if the dinner was late. There was usually a very high turnover among the personnel of the servants' hall. Drunkenness, immorality, insolence, theft and incompetence were the common causes of dismissal, and employers required references and made careful enquiries about a prospective employee's antecedents. When Wescomb Emerton, a Nottinghamshire gentleman, went about finding a servant for a friend he was most thorough:

> I have seen the Servant; his Appearance is in his favour – rather tall, but not awkward – lived once with Mr T. Wright, but with Dowager Lady Whichcott as coachman to drive a Pair of Horses – has always waited at Table, can clean Plate and capable of a Service as Butler in a private Family – from every Information I can get is exceedingly sober . . . wishes much to be in a regular Family – desires I would enquire into his Character which he says will bear the strictest scrutiny . . . his Hair is not tied up; but it is growing for that purpose, if you choose to have it so.

And a little later:

> I saw Mrs Thomas Wright and asked some Questions about Wm. Rayner. It is a long time since he lived with them as Postilion; she confirms the Account of his Sobriety, but says he was not of a good Temper, could not bear to be found fault with and behaved very rude and insolent once on that Occasion. When with them he had a Trick of spitting very much about the house, which was very offensive, and his Bedroom was beyond Description so – he said he had a Disorder on him and could not help it [71].

The size of a family's establishment was closely related to its status and the extent of the entertainment given to friends and neighbours. The gentleman's mansion was his 'Theatre of Hospitality', as Sir Henry Wotton called it in his *Elements of Architecture* (1624), and the scale of kitchens and dining hall had to be appropriate to the purpose. At Ingatestone Hall Sir William Petre entertained over twenty guests (including a number of the poor) each day over Christmastide, and when important visitors arrived with their retinues of servants the total numbers to be fed might approach a hundred. The Petre household baked 20,000 loaves a year, and consumed over 2,000 lb of cheese and 2,600 eggs. In 1548 the meat supplies included 55 oxen and calves, 2 cows, 133 sheep and lambs and 11 swine, as well as venison and fowls. The cellars at their peak held nearly 400 gallons of French and Rhenish wine.

Entertainment offered to guests included tumblers, wrestlers, musicians and bands of players; the guests themselves joined in madrigals, and read their parts at sight [72].

Hospitality was an essential function of the manor house, as it was a fundamental element in the landowners' way of life. Your hospitable landlord, according to Sir Thomas Overbury, 'loved three things, an open cellar, a full hall, and a sweating cook: he always provided for three dinners, one for himself, another for his servants, the third for the poor'. Hospitable gentry aimed at earning the kind of epitaph composed for Francis Chaldecot, once Sheriff of Dorset, and his wife: 'liberal constant housekeepers; bountiful relievers of the poor; careful breeders of their children in piety and virtue; diligent and devout comers to the church' [73]. It is true that Overbury held hospitality to be in decline, driven out by 'pride, puritans, coaches and covetousness', but it evidently survived the onslaught of these hostile forces. Hospitality flourished because it went with status and was essential to a family's standing in the community. As a result families fallen on evil times found it difficult to support 'their Credit and Figure in their Countries'. Indeed the burden of keeping up appearances on a reduced income was supposed in the early eighteenth century to be a general factor in the decline of lesser gentry: 'They have Parks and Mansion Houses, and a great Resort of Friends and Neighbours to them; which continually drains their scanty Revenues.' [74] Nevertheless, the honours had to be done, however modestly: when John Allen of Cresselly was away from home on business he instructed his daughter Peggy to 'buy yourself half-a-pound of Hyson Tea, and half-a-pound of good Bohea Tea; with a small loaf of double refined sugar, to treat my Cousin Jordan, yourself, and your friends if they come to see you, both for breakfast, and in the afternoon; if any ladies of fashion come to see you in the afternoon treat 'em with wine, cake, coffy and tea' [75].

A major part of entertaining was occasioned by family events, birthdays, weddings, christenings and funerals. When Sir Walter Calverley married in 1707 he provided gloves for the guests, distributed 'to the servants in the household abt. 16 or 17 guineas', and entertained the local gentry and his tenants on separate occasions [76]. But throughout the year there was always much coming and going of neighbours bearing gifts, helping to solve some problem of transport by lending their carriage or wagon, or offering assistance as amateur nurses and midwives [77]. Many squires provided the parish with summer sports, and perhaps a band and dancing once a year, and joined in themselves [78]. When a team of workmen was engaged for an important task entertainment was always provided on its completion. Squire Blundell engaged men and wagons for the arduous work of marling his fields in the summer of 1712, and when he had his 'Finishing Day' all the 'Marlers, Spreaders, water-balys and carters dined here . . . and had Sword dansing and a Merry Night in ye Hall and in ye Barne' [79].

The rigours and cost of travelling made most entertaining a strictly local affair. Holidays, too, consisted mainly of short journeys to relations or to one of the hundreds of small local spas. Visits to London and the distant watering places were rare events for most of the gentry before the middle of the nineteenth century. Even the turnpiking of the main roads often did little to make them more safe, while the country lanes were dangerously rutted and churned up by farmers' and carriers' wagons, and by drovers' beasts, leaving them 'so full of nastiness and stinking dirt that oft-times many persons who have occasion to come in or go out of town are forced to stop their noses to avoid the ill-smell'. The highly sociable Parson Woodforde seldom ventured so far as Norwich, and the Purefoys were inconveniently kept at home first by breaking an axle of their coach, which 'will hinder our coming to you this moon', then by their coachman's rheumatism, and once again by their coach's breaking an axle and overturning. If it was not broken axles it was smallpox. Henry Purefoy was alarmed to find the dread disease had broken out at Chipping Norton, where 'we must necessarily either bait or lie . . . on our way to Cheltenham. . . . I entreat you will enquire of some of your neighbouring farmers how the smallpox is there, and how long it has been there' [80]. Half-a-century later, in 1789, Wescomb Emerton welcomed to his Nottinghamshire home at Thrumpton a visitor 'driven out of Bedford by the Small-Pox, there being about two thousand persons who have that distemper at this time, either in the natural way or by Inoculation'. As late as 1797 the hazards of winter travel kept gentlemen like Emerton at home:

> Consider the Country in which I live. Roads at any time but indifferent; neighbours at a distance, separated by Rivers as well as bad roads, which makes a visit to Dinner so late in the year almost an impossibility; you are confined, whilst here, within the walls of Thrumpton, without the least society for Mrs. W. and it is not in my power to make it more agreeable to her [81].

Summer travel was a different matter. The wealthier families had long made their annual pilgrimage to Bath, Cheltenham, Tunbridge Wells or Epsom, to take the waters and enjoy a change of scene. There were many spas in the north, too, including Knaresborough and Harrogate, while Buxton was advocated by Sir John Floyer for those suffering from cancer, rheumatism, ulcers, deafness, asthma, hernia, corns, leprosy, gonorrhea, tumours, nephritis and a disordered mind. But the medical qualities of the waters were often less valued than the entertainment offered by company, music, dancing, and card parties. There was the opportunity of mixing with the *beau monde*, seeing the latest fashions, making new acquaintances, marrying off a daughter or two, and obtaining preferment for a younger son. By the eighteenth century some of the advantages of the spas could be obtained also at seaside resorts and county towns where polite society gathered in newly built assembly rooms for dinners and balls, and plays presented by troupes of travelling players.

In time the cult of the spa waned somewhat in favour of the newly fashionable seaside resort. The Long Room at Scarborough was opened for cards, billiards, plays and dances in 1755, and subsequently George III gave tone to Weymouth, as the Prince Regent did to Brighton, and Queen Victoria the Isle of Wight. In 1752 a Dr Russell recommended the drinking of sea water for loosening the bowels, and nearly a century earlier Dr Wittie of Hull advised it for asthma, scurvy, jaundice, gout and leprosy, as well as being 'a most sovereign Remedy against Hypochondriak Melancholy and Windiness' [82]. Wescomb Emerton enquired in 1795 about the amenities of Southend, the nature of its shore for bathing, and whether lodgings were let by the room or the floor. In earlier years he had ventured abroad, finding many English families at

Aix where living was cheaper than in England, the lodgings costing only eight guineas a month. His tour of France was not very successful, however:

> Upon the whole we are not pleased with our Journey but wish ourselves at home again. . . . We have seen but few things hitherto, having met with some very rude behaviour at Amiens, as we were going to see the Cathedral, from a Parcel of Women and Children, who followed us about the Town ridiculing our Dress and shouting 'Voila les Anglais' [83].

In the railway age visits abroad became much more commonplace, as the great number of surviving travel diaries bear witness. At home seaside resorts became more closely identified with a particular class of visitors. Folkestone was one of the later resorts to develop, a creation of the railways which, however, proved attractive to 'carriage society'. Speculators built 'handsome and convenient houses, well adapted for the nobility and gentry' on the West Cliff, while the Marine Parade Building Society set out to build houses worth 1,000 guineas each with a carriage drive 60 feet wide [84].

For those gentry who could afford it the London season occupied two or three months every winter. In London visitors could combine attendance at Parliament and business transactions with shopping and a gay social round of receptions, balls, clubs and theatres. The annual pilgrimage to the capital was an occasion for arranging mortgages with bankers, discussing wills with lawyers, ordering a new coach, refurbishing wardrobes and restocking the wine cellar. The cost of moving family and servants and maintaining a London establishment was no slight strain on even well-lined pockets, as John Taylor commented in verse in 1630:

> To weare a Farm in shoo-strings, edg'd with gold,
> And spangled Garters worth a Coppy-hold;
> A hose and dublet, which a Lordship cost,
> A gawdy cloake (three Manours price almost),
> A beaver Band and Feather for the head,
> Prized at the churches tythe, the poor man's bread.

Sir William Coventry argued that farm rents were adversely affected by 'the nobility and gentry's living so much in London'; demand for produce, he said, was reduced by the absence of the landlords from their mansions, and this in turn discouraged people from taking farms [85]. But there is also evidence that London suffered in turn when the season came to an end. As the aristocracy returned home every spring London became very dull, and depression descended on merchants and shopkeepers:

> The weary Press, at Ease in Safety sleeps.
> No supple Oil the polish'd Iron keeps.
> The Hawkers now we very rarely meet,
> Faction and Treason venting in the Street.
> From *Will's* and *Tom's* the well-dress'd Youths are fled,
> And Silence there with Poppies binds her Head.
> To Country Seats the Men of Sense go down,

And for their rural Joys neglect the Town . . .
The Bankrupt Vintners starve for Want of Trade,
Few Payments now are to the Merchants made.

There were many gentry for whom the attractions of watering places and resorts paled beside the shoot or hunt. London, it is true, was not impossible for sportsmen. There was riding in the parks, and several hunts were established in the capital's environs. A taste for gaming, cock-fighting or pugilism was most easily satisfied by the clubs and alehouses of London. But the majority of sport-loving squires stayed at home. The pleasures of the field, and the hearty eating and drinking that accompanied them, absorbed much of the time of what Macaulay called 'the gross, uneducated, untravelled country gentleman'. With many squires sport was the characteristic and indeed essential feature of country life, a means of dissipating surplus energy, a source of endless interest and pride, and a social occasion that gave point to an otherwise tedious existence. The climax of enthusiasm was reached in the nineteenth century when sport, now more organised and costly, became an obsession for which career, family and estate were all sacrificed. Racing, betting and hunting beggared some very substantial families, and the fanatics had the skeletons of their favourite steeds mounted in their halls, a somewhat grim reminder of former pleasures and lost fortunes.

Many gentry, fortunately, managed to combine a restrained taste for sport and carousing with their more sober role of magistrate, estate manager and social head of the community. Nicholas Assheton's diary for 1617–18 shows a curious mixture of regular church attendance, stag hunts and alehouse tipples. His sideboard groaned under as many as forty dishes, and on occasion he 'tabled all night', and was 'more than merrie' and 'sicke with drink' at the village alehouse [86]. Even the sober Sir John Oglander advised the keeping of 'a small warren for some rabbits when thy friends come', as well as a pigeon-house, a fishpond or two and a spot for breeding pheasants and partridges. Gentlemen of a superior cast of mind sneered, like Lord Chesterfield, at such 'rustick, illiberal sports of guns, dogs and horse' as he said characterised the 'English Bumpkin County Gentlemen', while *The Tatler* specifically excluded diversions of the field from the 'entertainments of a Rational Creature'. Sports-men, nevertheless, spurned such animadversions. Sir George Savile, for one, was not afraid to admit to being 'one of the Rank of men called Country Squires and can not deny but that I have a Passion for my Doggs' [87]. Sir Thomas Parkyns of Bunny, near Nottingham, so far defied convention as to practice wrestling with the young men of the village on his own hearthrug. He composed a treatise on the art, entitled *The Cornish Hug*, and in his will left money for prizes to be awarded to the best local practitioners. Four years before his death he vaingloriously erected a monument in the church depicting him-self in a wrestling pose, but he was also shown more modestly as prostrate on the ground with Time brandishing his scythe over him [88].

A number of popular sports, boxing, cricket and cockfighting, owed much to the enthusiasm of country gentlemen who provided prizes and the added interest of large wagers. Horse racing was very much the creation of the aristoc-racy, and again it was they who offered the prizes, established the rules and encouraged the placing of heavy stakes. They supported the sport, too, by going in for racing stables, complete with trainers and jockeys, and many gentlemen acquired a reputation as expert horse breeders. When the opposition to blood sports got under way in the later eighteenth century some more sensitive gentry gave it active encouragement. Denys Rolle, of an ancient Devonshire family, wrote a pamphlet attacking cruel amusements, and as a magistrate took steps to suppress ill-famed alehouses, cockfighting and bull-baiting at Torrington, the village near his seat. But while gentlemen might advocate the prohibition of popular blood sports such as bull-baiting and cockfighting, and spoke up in favour of the protection of animals Bill, they were usually silent on the subject of the gentry's more exclusive diversion of hunting. Keen foxhunters like Lord Dudley Stuart claimed that their amusement involved little or no cruelty. Hunting was in any case more private, less exposed to public view, more aristocratic and formalised, and so more easily divorced from the arguments applied to the plebeian sports associated with the disreputable and the rabble [89].

Houses, gardens and parks

If he were unambitious in politics, unremarkable in local office and uninterested in estate management, the wealthier landowner might still achieve some distinction by his association with the family mansion. One way in which he could leave an enduring monument to subsequent generations was by undertaking a complete rebuilding of the family home, though he might well be content with the more modest achievement of adding a wing, rebuilding the stables or extending and beautifying the park. Another channel for expression of his interests and personality lay in the decoration and furnishing of the house, the introduction of pictures, sculptures and *objets d'art*, specially commissioned, or more likely picked up at sales or abroad on the grand tour.

A good deal of new country-house building was carried out at the time of the Reformation when Church lands and properties fell into lay hands. Abbeys, bartons and granges were replaced, or sometimes converted into private residences. A detailed examination of a sample of country houses in Hertfordshire shows that in the sixteenth century the houses, including those built on monastic sites, were usually placed near or on the edge of the villages, with their grounds stretching away behind them. In 1596 there were only twenty houses standing in their own deer parks. By the eighteenth century the old manor houses in the villages were increasingly being left to the minor parish gentry and the larger proprietors were obtaining privacy by establishing themselves in parks isolated from the community by high walls, lodge-keepers, long driveways and belts of trees. By 1800 there were eighty parks in the county, and the number continued to increase in the course of the nineteenth century. Over half of the houses in this Hertfordshire sample were originally built in the sixteenth century, the middle decades being particularly active for new houses, a reflection of the wealth of the gentry at this time and the advent of brick as a new and cheaper material for construction. In 1740 over half of the houses still maintained their pre-1660 appearance, and nearly a third had a pre-1600 appearance. By 1820, however, many of the Tudor and older houses had been pulled down and rebuilt so that, together with the completely new houses, over half now presented a style of the past eighty years, and only just over a tenth still maintained a pre-1660 appearance [90].

It is probable that the general style of many of the large houses, not only in Hertfordshire but throughout the countryside, remained Tudor until well into the eighteenth century. The great activity in housebuilding which marked the middle and late Tudor period dominated country houses for almost the next two centuries. As a building medium brick increased rapidly in popularity during the reign of Henry VIII, replacing stone and the old timber framework filled in with wattle and daub. Compton Wynyates in Warwickshire is one of the most famous of the new brick style of Tudor domestic house. Greater height, and hence a more impressive façade, also became a characteristic feature of even the more moderate-sized houses of the Tudor period. In Elizabeth's time the quadrangular design, where the main hall and its wings completed a square, sometimes with a gateway tower built over the entrance range, became less fashionable. The entrance range was abandoned, leaving the quadrangle open at the front, and the next stage was to draw back the two side wings to form the typical E-shaped house of this era. This design was easily modified or enlarged by changes to the wings. These could be drawn back or extended beyond the hall block as cross-wings, making a more compact and convenient H-shape, as at Montacute House in Somerset. The long gallery, often occupying the entire length of an upper floor, was an important addition to Elizabethan houses, providing space for the display of pictures and sculpture, and offering scope for a promenade in bad weather and possible use as a ballroom. Externally the houses became more symmetrical, with windows and ornamentation corresponding on each side of a centrally placed porch. Internally the houses often grew exceedingly elaborate with carved staircases and panelled walls, enormous fireplaces replete with heraldic devices and fantastic carvings, and intricately moulded ceilings.

It was at the close of the Tudor period that Sir Henry Wotton wrote his *Elements of Architecture*, based on a study of Palladio and other continental sources. He argued the need for careful planning and design, an informed choice of materials and deliberate choice of site. The house should be remote from foggy fens or marshes, and not lack exposure to sun and wind; thought should be given to avoid 'malign influences' which might cause 'earthquakes, contagions, prodigious births'. Views that were 'vast and indefinite' were not in favour, nor was it wise to 'build too near a great neighbour as it will mean living on Earth as Mercury is in the Heavens . . . ever in obscurity under brighter beams than his own'. In the seventeenth century the classical influences deriving from Italy spread beyond Wotton and his readers. The Palladian style, named after Andrea Palladio of Vicenza, became dominant in most important new building. Palladio had erected numerous buildings which were seen and admired by English visitors on the grand tour, and his treatise on classical design became a standard source of reference. In its English adaptation the hall of the Palladian house became merely an anteroom or entrance and lost its former importance in the older vernacular tradition. The doorway to it was in the middle of the entrance wall, approached by a flight of steps and covered by an impressive portico or pillared loggia. From the hall doors opened on to the groundfloor rooms, and a broad staircase rose to the principal suite of rooms above. Externally mullioned windows were replaced by sash windows with pediments, the whole appearance being plain and strictly symmetrical. External ornament was eschewed or very much restrained, and relief was provided by the use of stone dressings to frame areas of red brick.

This severe classical style dominated English country-house building from the Restoration to the end of the eighteenth century, though smaller Palladian houses were something of a rarity and the more modest country house continued to be built in the tradition of Wren with simple brick or stone façades, in the style of Groombridge Place, Sussex, The Moot at Downton in Wiltshire, or the grander Belton House in Lincolnshire [91]. The typical smaller Georgian country house was a square building of three storeys, with a basement below and attics above, usually in red brick and often stuccoed. A pediment rising before the attic gave the front a heavier and more impressive air, and the steps and portico of the main entrance also added dignity. Internally the rooms were large and lofty, and well lit by large windows. The squareness of the rooms was relieved by attractive plasterwork and elegant fireplaces, paintings, sculptures and hangings. But servants were often condemned to work in damp, ill-lit basements and to sleep in dark and cold attics. Sanitation showed some progress: bathrooms were beginning to come in during the eighteenth century, as well as rather sparse and primitive indoor toilet closets.

Many minor gentry, particularly in Wales and the more remote parts of England, continued to live in what were originally the principal houses of the neighbourhood, but which by later standards were regarded more as old-fashioned and inconvenient farmhouses. Their furnishings, too, were generally simple and ancient. There might be a considerable array of armour, some silver vessels and cutlery, one or two Turkey carpets and wall hangings; but most of the furniture would be of plain wood, serviceable but lacking in comfort and colour, and the linen might be flaxen and coarse. In such houses the way of life, too, was old-fashioned and simple. Households rose at six in winter and four in summer and retired at eight or nine. The servants, both domestic and farm, dined with the family, and the fare was abundant but homely. In the later eighteenth and nineteenth centuries, in periods when farming was prosperous, many of the old-fashioned country gentlemen rebuilt their houses or moved into larger ones built on a more luxurious scale; they furnished with the latest fashions, banished the servants to the kitchen, and generally brought their way of life more into line with their wealthier and more sophisticated neighbours. If they could afford it they followed the Gothic revival which gathered force in the nineteenth century. Wyatt and his better-known nephew Wyattville, Barry, Pugin, Scott, Street and Waterhouse developed the new fashion of soaring spires and crenellated towers which dominated the new houses of the period.

The wealthy nobility and gentry had long used their money and their wider appreciation of the arts to fill their houses with paintings, antiques, sculptures and stylised furniture. Many of the paintings, it is true, were merely copies of old masters rather than originals by living artists; English artists, indeed, only slowly struggled towards recognition, and many had to eke out their commissions by copying, and by painting coaches and even inn signs. The antiques, too, might be spurious, heads and busts specially manufactured in Rome for the indiscriminate appetites of English visitors. There was a considerable interest in sculpture, and the new monuments in Westminster Abbey drew large crowds of country visitors to London in the middle of the eighteenth century. Wealthy gentry commissioned sculptures for their homes or used them to ornament family tombs and chapels in country churches. A taste developed, too, for the exotic. *Chinoiserie* became a vogue, and Chinese screens, cabinets, summerhouses and pavilions never failed to draw the attention of visitors.

However, relatively few of the gentry could afford the grand tour or could contemplate the acquisition of expensive *objets d'art*. When they built a new house or remodelled an old one they drew up their own plans and personally supervised the works. They might be fortunate in engaging a master mason or carpenter-builder who was fully capable of realising their ideas or could copy from another model in the neighbourhood. It is remarkable that the combination of amateur gentleman architect and obscure provincial craftsman so often succeeded in producing houses of fine proportions and good taste, with much skilful detail in the woodwork and plasterwork of the interior.

With a move to a classical taste in houses went a sea-change in garden design. The formal Italian, Dutch or French garden with its terraces, flights of shallow steps, gravel walks arranged in a rectangular pattern or radiating from a central point, orderly rows of statuary, elaborate topiary work and geometrical beds of carefully cultivated plants, held sway in the seventeenth century, much influenced by the work of André le Nôtre, who was responsible for the layout of the grounds at Versailles. The formal garden with its artificial, highly regulated appearance, often contrasted oddly with the wild uncultivated woods and hillsides which stretched beyond its boundary walls. With the growing fashion of surrounding the house with extensive parks and woodlands, the formal garden came to be regarded as too stiff and artificial by the early years of the eighteenth century. The new vogue was for informality, an irregular though still carefully planned design of garden that would merge naturally into the parks that landowners were creating.

The new landscape gardening involved the creation of naturalness by artificial means, and was much influenced by the fashionable landscape painting of wild, romantic scenery which came from the brushes of Salvator Rosa, Claude Lorraine and Gaspard Poussin. The new garden was made to slope down towards a rippling rivulet or rock-girt lake, and waterfalls and cascades added charm to the scene. A gothic or Chinese bridge, a delicate Chinese pagoda or summerhouse, partly shaded by trees, served as focal points for the eye, and as one turned to gaze further afield openings in the trees provided a view of a distant spire, temple or ruin. The work involved in creating the necessary slopes, diverting streams, building rocky cascades and grottoes, dredging out lakes, planting woodlands and erecting temples and ruins was prodigious. Sometimes a handy Cromwellian ruin might serve the purpose if it were battered a little more to create a suitable classical appearance, and occasionally a conveniently situated church would offer a vista of tower or steeple. Hundreds of trees were planted to shade the approach to the mansion, to soften the lines of the house itself, and to provide a romantic backdrop. Stretches of grass were broken up by carefully sited clumps of trees, to give an impression of a rolling parkland running away to the horizon. The trees chosen were mainly of oak, beech and ash, the ones most profitable to sell when it came time for thinning, and the full effect might take two or three generations to be realised.

The most famous landscape garden of the early eighteenth century was Lord Cobham's at Stowe in Buckinghamshire, though a close rival, less encumbered by temples and other contrived introductions, was the garden created at Stourhead by Henry Hoare, the banker, who bought the estate in 1714. The waters from six springs forming the source of the river Stour were brought together and carried underground, to pour from a grotto into a specially constructed lake surrounded by beech trees and rhododendrons. The great gardens, like the great houses, attracted visitors by the score, and the touring of famous houses became quite a regular diversion of the travellers of the time. John Byng visited many a country house that lay in his path, and his journals recorded the few occasions when, to his indignation, he was refused admittance. Arthur Young, also, thought it necessary to embellish his early farming tours of the 1770s with accounts of houses, gardens and paintings interspersed among the more serious business of turnips, lucerne, ploughs and seed-drills. Housekeepers were usually ready to take strangers round in return for a small remembrance, though Young complained bitterly of the exorbitant fees extracted by the gatekeepers at Blenheim.

Vanbrugh and Bridgeman were the first designers to move away from the highly formal garden towards the new landscape effect, but William Kent, Lancelot 'Capability' Brown and Humphry Repton, who between them almost spanned the whole eighteenth century, were the chief exponents of the new style. Kent, originally a painter, took to creating his landscapes on the ground. He used the 'ha-ha', a sunken fence or fosse, to avoid an explicit distinction between garden and park, and in effect made both one harmonious whole. Kent, said Horace Walpole in his *Essay* on modern gardening,

> leaped the fence, and saw that all nature was a garden. He felt the delicious contrast of hill and valley changing imperceptibly into each other, tasted the beauty of the gentle swell, or concave swoop, and remarked how loose groves crowned an easy eminence with happy ornament, and while they called in the distant view between their graceful stems, removed and extended the perspective by delusive comparison. . . . The great principles on which he worked were perspective, and light and shade. Groups of trees broke too uniform or too extensive a lawn; evergreens and woods were opposed to the glare of the champain, and where the view was less fortunate, or so much exposed as to be beheld at once, he blotted out some parts by thick shades, to divide it into variety, or to make the richest scene more enchanting by reserving it to a further advance of the spectator's step. Thus . . . he realized the compositions of the greatest masters in painting.

Capability Brown, who saw in some 180 major gardens 'great capability for improvement', began as an under-gardener at Stowe under Kent's supervision. Among his creations were the gardens at Blenheim, Chatsworth, Luton Hoo and Audley End. Brown developed certain repetitions in his style, particularly his practice of planting a copse on the crown of a bare hill, and in time his gardens came to be considered rather too elegant and insufficiently wild to suit the demand for the ruggedly picturesque. Repton, who in his turn transformed some 220 gardens, tried to meet this criticism by moving away from the rather studied naturalness of Brown. He also restored the flower garden to the front of the house, and opened the way for gardening to become the consuming interest of numerous country gentlemen and their ladies[92]. New types of ornamental and flowering trees and shrubs, together with roses, wisterias and many other varieties of flowers were introduced from abroad, and the growing interest in gardens can be seen in the expanding stock lists of nurserymen from the early eighteenth century onwards[93].

It is remarkable how many English landowners were willing to find the very considerable sums needed to undertake one of Brown or Repton's designs, especially when the full effect achieved by the mature trees would not be seen in their own lifetime. The transformation of country houses and parks had also some interesting social effects. Large sums were invested by landowners in buying out small freeholders and copyholders in order to extend their ring-fence and provide the necessary space for the classical effect. The land acquired was often of poor quality for farming purposes, and as sales were made voluntarily (though no doubt under some degree of pressure) little conflict seems to have arisen between the large owner and local occupiers. Sometimes, indeed, they were willing to leave part of the purchase money with the landowners at interest as an investment. There were, however, instances of illegal encroachments by large owners on forests and common land, and sometimes hamlets were forcibly removed to make way for the park, though quite commonly the villagers were rehoused in a new model village a mile or two away. This arrogant exercise of local power did not usually extend to the removal of churches, and in Brown's day an inconvenient spire was obscured by carefully sited trees.

The expanded parks and belts of woodland also served to isolate the larger proprietors from the local community, and tended to emphasise their political and social separateness, just as the huge sums devoted to building of mansions and landscaping of parks emphasised differences in wealth. On the other hand, the work created by building and gardening was very significant, given the limited size of the local community, and such employment was spread over long periods of years. The indulgence of a taste for the classical and romantic helped incidentally in relieving the poverty which came to be a more serious feature of the countryside in the later eighteenth century. Moreover, the landowners' isolation was not complete: their houses were open to any respectable visitors and to tenants calling on estate business, and villagers were allowed in the grounds on special occasions for a fête or celebration. Nevertheless, until the age of the National Trust and noble showmen, the costly beauty of the country house and its environs was available to relatively few, and the greater exclusiveness of landowners, their creation of stately homes and magnificent surroundings, formed an anomalous contrast to the spreading wastes of factories, slagheaps and slums fomented by the industrial revolution.

Culture and education

Through the influence of novelists like Fielding and of historians like Macaulay it is the Squire Western type of country gentleman who has come to typify the gentry at large. But how typical, in fact, was the rumbustious, carousing, cursing foxhunter of literary and historical fiction? Even Macaulay was forced to water down a little his picture of the country bumpkin squire, admitting that 'unlettered as he was and unpolished, he was still in some most important points a gentleman' [94]. Defoe was one of those contemporaries who argued the gentry's contempt for education, picturing them as buying their books by the yard for the sake of filling up their shelves, and preferring to live 'not like men of learning but like gentlemen. They enjoy their estates and their pleasures, and envy nobody.' Yet, rather contradictorily, he went on to argue that what made the upstarts from business acceptable in the circles of old-established gentry was the education they could afford to provide for their sons: so that the newcomer's son who 'was sent early to school, has good parts and has improved them by learning, travel, conversation and reading, and above all with a modest courteous gentleman-like behaviour: despise him as you will, he will be a gentleman in spite of all the distinctions we can make'[95].

Though the Squire Western type existed, refinement of speech and person and the cultivation of good manners had long been considered the mark of a gentleman. Since the Middle Ages the gentry had placed their sons in an aristocratic household as a kind of finishing school. Daughters cultivated the polite arts of music, singing, languages and deportment under the guidance of a private tutor or in a ladies seminary. The concept of a gentleman was analysed and discussed, and treatises on courtesy and manners were available from late medieval times. Refinement, however, was limited to a very select group of families in any one neighbourhood, and it was not until the eighteenth century or later that some ordinary country gentlemen gave up their habits of licentious carousing, brawling and swearing. The Leicestershire gentry, said John Evelyn in 1654, were 'great drinkers', and the description was no doubt capable of much wider application. But there was a gradual transformation of manners as the result of education, travel and the breaking-down of provincial isolation. Journals such as the *Tatler* and *Spectator*, and novelists and play-wrights, held rustic ignorance and bumpkin boorishness up to ridicule. The polite society of spas and resorts instilled approved standards of behaviour and decorum. Contemporaries remarked on the change: Dr Johnson could remember 'when all the decent people in Lichfield got drunk every night, and were not the worse thought of', and Arthur Young compared table manners in France with those of England, noting that in France napkins were *de rigueur*, diners refrained from drinking out of another's glass, and the French were cleaner in their persons. In his book on Ireland Young had observed that the class of Irish country gentleman had characteristics similar to those found among their English counterparts a generation or so before,

> men among whom drinking, wrangling, quarreling, fighting, ravishing, &c. &c. &c. are found as in their native soil . . . they are growing better, but even now, one or two of them got by accident (where they have no business) into better company are sufficient very much to derange the pleasures that result from a liberal conversation.

Fortunately,

> a new spirit; new fashions; new modes of politeness exhibited by the higher ranks are imitated by the lower, which will, it is to be hoped, put an end to this race of beings; and either drive their sons and cousins into the army or navy, or sink them into plain farmers like those we have in England, where it is common to see men with much greater property without pretending to be gentlemen[96].

By the end of the eighteenth century the cultivation of manners marked the gentry off from all but the wealthiest of farmers and tradesmen. Jane Austen's snobbish Emma would have no truck with such people:

> The yeomanry are precisely the order of people with whom I can have nothing to do. A degree or two lower, and a creditable appearance might interest me; I might hope to be useful to their families in some way or other. But a farmer can need none of my help, and is therefore in one sense as much above my notice as in every other he is below it.

Emma goes on to dismiss her friend Harriet's beau, a farmer, as

> very plain, undoubtedly – remarkably plain: but that is nothing compared with his entire want of gentility. I had no right to expect much, and I did not expect much; but I had no idea that he could be so very clownish, so totally without air. I had imagined him, I confess, a degree or two nearer gentility.

In practice the great majority of gentry had, of necessity, to be men of some education and learning. Only thus could they oversee their estates, take their place on the Bench, and join in polite conversation with the dignitaries of county, Church and state who came their way. They were in truth an *élite*, performing essential administrative, judicial and social functions in a society by no means illiterate; and in order to play their part as governors and keep the respect of the governed they had to exhibit a superiority of wisdom and culture. A great amount of direct evidence supports this view. We need not be too impressed, perhaps, by the considerable proportions of country-house libraries and the wide range of titles on the shelves. We do not know, for instance, whether Roger North of Glemham Hall, Suffolk, ever opened the copies of Hobbes's *Leviathan*, Bacon's *Henry VIII*, Ricaut's *History of the Turkish Empire*, or Hakluyt's *Voyages* which he possessed in 1719, nor whether his catalogue of music means that the works by Corelli, Albinoni, Vivaldi and Lully were ever performed. But we do know that many country squires ordered new books from their London booksellers as soon as they heard of them, and like Henry Purefoy became more than a little irate if the wrong title arrived, a mistake which he said put him 'in mind of the Confusion of Languages at Babell, when one asked for an Hammer they gave him a Trowell' [97]. Among the squires' ladies books of sermons and devotional works were popular. In 1625 Lady Isham lent Anne Washington ten such works, as well as a book about the French garden. Other well studied works included Sidney's *Arcadia*, *God's Revenge aginst Murther*, and Artemidorus's *Interpretation of Dreams*. However, it was not generally thought that 'women were born to read authors or censure the learned'. More suitable for them were such seventeenth-century works as *The Accomplisht Lady's Delight in Preserving, Physic, Beautifying and Cookery* or *The Gentlewoman's Companion*. The intellectual capacity of women was believed to be limited. Swift thought that books on anything but devotion or domesticity were likely to turn a woman's brain, while in 1774 Dr Gregory advised his daughters: 'If you happen to have any learning, keep it a profound secret, especially from the men, who generally look with a jealous and malignant eye on a woman of great parts and a cultivated understanding' [98].

Life in the country evidently did not deaden intellectual curiosity, and indeed a retired situation made it possible for a leisured gentleman to pursue systematically some branch of learning. Gentry were prominent in the Society of Antiquaries, founded in 1572, and distinguished antiquarian works flowed from the pens of such men as Camden, Stow, Spelman and Lambarde. Sir Henry Spelman, who died in 1641, was a Norfolk proprietor and noted historian as well as antiquary. His son, Sir John, published a *Life of King Alfred the Great*. Dr Rowse has written enthusiastically of Carew's *Survey of Cornwall* (1602). Carew, he says, though merely a plain country gentleman, was well versed in the chronicles, and he knew and read French and Italian, in addition to Spanish and German. Moreover, Carew was not alone among the Cornish gentry of the time. There were also the young poet Charles Fitzgeoffrey, and William Carnsew, whose diary reveals a close interest in medical matters and a knowledge of a wide range of literature, including works on medicine, religion, history and current affairs. Neighbouring Devonshire provided a musical patron in the shape of Richard Champernowne of Modbury Castle, near Plymouth. Champernowne maintained a private choir and, it was reported, 'being naturally and often oppressed with melancholy more than he could wish, he has – though to his own charge – brought such as he has found whose voices contented him' [99].

Dorset, too, had its poets, such as George Turberville of Bere Regis, who published some of his poems in 1567 and produced a number of later works. In Wales the Elizabethan and early Stuart gentry helped, like their English counterparts, in founding local grammar schools, and spent their spare time in genealogical research and in producing volumes on geography, religion and the history of Ireland. Welsh gentlemen supported bards and minstrels as regular members of the household; at St Donat's Sir Edward Stradling was particularly active in fostering Welsh culture, acting as patron of the bards, financing the publication of a Welsh grammar and accumulating a library of books and manuscripts relating to the principality. At Carew Castle Sir John Perrot could boast of a library that included works in French and Spanish, and his music room housed examples of all the known instruments of the time, together with a collection of music. Nor was this cultural activity shortlived. The patronage of literature remained a preoccupation of many Welsh gentry down to more recent times, and some contributed works of their own composition [100].

A remarkable band of scholars flourished in seventeenth-century Kent. The Digges family had already reared eminent mathematicians during Elizabeth's time and went on to produce Leonard Digges, poet and translator, and Sir Dudley Digges and his son Dudley, authors of consequence. Sir Robert Filmer was well known for his *Patriarcha*, a defence of Charles I's use of the royal prerogative, while somewhat less controversial was the work of George Wyatt, son of the rebellious Sir Thomas, who wrote principally on military science and history and left behind him an uncompleted *magnum opus* on Anne Boleyn. Sir Thomas Hawkins of Nash Court was a poet and translator, while at Surrenden Dering Sir Edward Dering assembled one of the greatest accumulations of manuscripts and made 'the ultimate antiquarian's discovery' of an original copy of Magna Carta. His contemporary, Sir Norton Knatchbull, was a respected critic, especially in Greek and Hebrew, while at Whornes Place, Cuxton, Sir John Marsham acquired an international reputation as a collector of coins and medallions and published a major history of the ancient world in

1672. Robert Plot of Borden is regarded as the father of county natural historians, his *Natural History of Oxfordshire* appearing in 1677, followed by a number of other works. Finally we have Sir Roger Twysden, who with Selden and Spelman is regarded as one of the three big figures in the historical scholarship of the period. His father, Sir William, built up a collection of books and manuscripts, and was a student of Hebrew as well as of palmistry, physiognomy, and astrology. Sir Roger conducted historical investigations amongst the collections of Sir Robert Cotton, the antiquary, as well as those of Canterbury and Rochester Cathedrals and Bodley's library in Oxford. His *Historicall Vindication* dealt with the English Reformation, and he published numerous treatises and pamphlets on government and political questions [101].

Not all counties could boast of comparable intellectual activity, but certainly there were throughout the land many similar instances of serious if amateur scholarship among the gentry. Northamptonshire could boast Sir Justinian Isham, the second baronet, who laid the foundations of the library at Lamport Hall. Warwickshire produced Sir Francis Willoughby F.R.S., a distinguished naturalist of the seventeenth century. With John Ray, the Cambridge naturalist, he toured England and the continent, and after Willoughby's early death Ray published their joint work under his friend's name. A century later Hampshire housed the well-known parish naturalist, Gilbert White of Selborne. He inherited the family property in the parish he made famous, and lived there as its parson most of his life. In Bedfordshire Sir John Osborn treasured his library of rare volumes, and the county also had Edmund Wingate of Harlington, the mathematician, Edmund Castell of Higham Gobion, the orientalist, and Edmund Wyld of Houghton Conquest, described as 'a would-be scientist'. Others who could boast of a remarkable library were the naturalists Sir Thomas and Edward Knyvat of Ashwellthorpe in Norfolk. John Evelyn, the diarist, had a strong interest in scientific matters, and in November 1651 made a visit to Sir Kenelm Digby to discuss chemistry; he came to the conclusion, however, that 'Sir Kenelm was an arrant mountebank'. And Lady Cheney of Toddington, Bedfordshire, had as steward an amateur musician, Henry Lichfield, to whose midnight compositions she lent a 'gentle ear', the more so as they were presented by the voices and instruments of her own family [102].

On a rather different plane the eighteenth century saw a remarkable growth of cultural life based on assembly rooms, theatres and circulating libraries. Music flourished in a number of cathedrals and provincial towns. Circulating libraries, supported by the subscriptions of market-town residents and country gentry, appeared in such remote resorts as Tenby and Haverfordwest, and there was evidently a growing readership for works on religion, politics, history, agriculture and political arithmetic, as well as for the more obviously acceptable novels, essays, poetry and books of travels. The circulating library at Southampton had 7,000 volumes at the end of the century, and the extent of book purchases may be gauged by the existence of 150 booksellers in provincial towns, and an even greater number in the capital. Authors of the day frequently relied on the private subscriptions of nobility and gentry to get their works into print, and libraries were an important element in the publishers' market. In country towns and expanding industrial areas like Birmingham, taverns and coffee houses, together with book clubs and debating societies, developed into centres of political discussion. They were perhaps not so specialised in their clientele as were the London clubs and coffee houses, but they still played an important role in forming public opinion [103]. The growing interest in the wider world of affairs was exemplified also by the early appearance in London and many provincial towns of newspapers. The Norwich paper first appeared in 1701, that at Bristol in the following year, Exeter in 1707, Worcester 1709, Newcastle 1710, Nottingham 1710, Liverpool 1712 and Stamford 1712, followed by many more. Country gentlemen in the home counties were able to get the London newspapers, and the evening papers were produced at about four or five o'clock in order to catch the country deliveries. Henry Purefoy, who in the 1730s lived at Shalstone in Buckinghamshire, complained bitterly when his newsagent sent him some unwelcome substitute for his favourite evening paper.

Many lesser gentry, the principal country patrons of circulating libraries, had received only a local grammar-school education, in company with the sons of farmers and tradesmen. Nevertheless, there appeared from this background some of the best-known writers of the day, such as Arthur Young, F.R.S., the internationally famous agriculturist; both Young and his friend Thomas Ruggles, the authority on the Poor Law, were products of Lavenham Grammar School. The classical education, though imbibed through a country grammar school, evidently laid a sound foundation for those capable of building on it. In their daily correspondence and diaries, in their liking for the apt phrase and classical tag, country gentlemen showed an easy command of literary style. Good, vigorous English was very evident in men like Young and Cobbett, writers of limited formal education.

Education also had its strictly practical aspect. For younger sons a good education was often their only stock-in-trade, their means to a genteel if modest livelihood in the professions, the Church, government service, or the establishment of a great lord. 'For good husbandry in thy children', urged Sir John Oglander, 'be sure to bring them all up in a vocation, so that they have no cause to complain against their father as not being in a way wherin they may walk and do themselves good. Send some of them as scholars to Winchester College, some to London to be merchants: Let none be idle. Make them but scholars and they are fitted for any employment, Divines, Civil or Common Lawyers, Physicians or secretary to some great man, etc.' [104] For a younger son law, after classical languages, was the most generally useful branch of knowledge. But the heirs to estates also thought it useful to base their career as landowner and magistrate on a smattering of the law. 'A man who owns a house must needs own a houseful of evidences', it was remarked, and hence one explanation of the popularity of the Inns of Court among gentry families in the sixteenth and early seventeenth centuries. Many gentry, however, went first to university, and it has been argued that the sixteenth century saw something of a 'cultural revolution', with the gentry adopting a new ideal of the learned responsible gentleman, devoting himself to the tasks of government and social leadership. Before 1640 the proportion of justices with a university or Inns of Court background, or both, was rising, although most of the men with this kind of education came from the wealthier ranks of the gentry. There were regional patterns too. A remarkably large number of Welsh squires followed a well beaten path from local grammar school to Oxford or, rather less likely, Cambridge. Some then proceeded to the Inns of Court, leading John Lewis of Glasgrug to exclaim 'praise be to God we have ... as able and knowing gentry as ever' [105].

It was a matter for pride that William Wynn, the squire of Glyn in Merioneth, was able to place his son 'in Oxenford, a famous University', urging the lad to 'speak no Welsh to any that can speak English . . . and thereby you may . . . freely speak English tongue perfectly. I had rather that you should keep company with studious honest Englishmen than with any of your own countrymen, who are more prone to be idle and riotous than the English' [106].

It is arguable how far the education obtained at university or the Inns was really very valuable in Elizabethan and Stuart times, or even in later periods for that matter. By 1600 the number of students entering Oxford and Cambridge had risen from some 150 to between 400 and 500 in each university. Royal colleges, Christ Church and Trinity, had been founded, and the regius professorships established. Between 1530 and 1570 the number of gentry entrants was large, the universities being seen as providing an education for an *élite*, offering status, entry to government office, or admission to the clergy, whose standing had risen with the Reformation. Nevertheless, the average age of admission was only fifteen in the sixteenth century, and sixteen in the century following. Some students entered as young as ten or twelve. Degrees could be purchased without fulfilling residence requirements, and many undergraduates stayed only for a year or so. It is true that the average age of admission was tending to rise, that the tutorial system was developing in the colleges, and that the curriculum eventually broadened to embrace modern languages and modern writers as well as the classics. On the other hand, while the proportion of the increased total of undergraduates who came from the gentry was rising, the average period of attendance remained brief, and this together with the neglect of lecturing on the part of the academics meant that for many of the wealthier students university performed little more than the function of a finishing school, an alternative to residence in the household of a great lord. Teaching was still in the hands of clergy, and essentially universities remained seminaries for clergy. Such conservatism and ineffectiveness caused many to prefer the alternative of the Inns of Court or the private tutor, the latter advocated by Locke as providing teaching 'of most and frequentest use'.

Dissatisfaction with the education provided by the English universities expressed itself in the formulation of alternative schemes of higher education, schemes which often originated with those responsible for the upbringing of wards from the upper levels of society. Effective and wide-ranging reform was long postponed however, indeed until the middle nineteenth century, and those concerned with obtaining a good grounding in some particular branch of knowledge favoured universities abroad. Leyden, for example, was noted for mathematics and the sciences, and Padua was preferred by those interested in medicine [107]. Nevertheless the two English universities retained a high reputation in literature and philosophy, and the general decline in standards was not marked until after 1760. Even then all was not somnolent: there were some brilliant scholars and teachers, and tentative moves towards reform were made in the later eighteenth century.

At the Inns of Court, as in the universities, teaching was neglected and the conduct of the wealthier students, at least, left much to be desired. Youths of assured fortune took little interest in their studies, perhaps believing with the Marquis of Argyle that only history and mathematics were proper subjects for persons of quality, the remainder being fit only 'for schoolmen and people that must live by their learning' [108]. The Inns rose in standing when the

Reformation reduced the significance of canon law, while the growth of the financial and business world, as well as the expansion of transactions in land, provided greater openings for a career in the common law. Already in the fifteenth century the four chief Inns – Lincoln's Inn, Gray's Inn, the Inner Temple and the Middle Temple – each held some 200 students. The first professional schools for laymen, their popularity was increased by their location in London, offering opportunities for entering the capital's society and its commercial milieu. The attractiveness of the Inns was further enhanced by their provision of a general education as well as law, including history, scripture, music, fencing and dancing. When about 1550 the Inns' reputation became firmly established, there was a big influx of students, with a rising proportion coming from the landed aristocracy. Unlike the universities there were no scholarships, so the fees and the expense of living in London restricted entry to the fairly well-to-do. In the period 1590 to 1639 probably as high a proportion as three-quarters of the entrants came from the nobility and gentry, a much higher proportion than in the universities. Geographically, the Inns drew support mainly from the home counties, East Anglia and the southwest. The majority of these students gave most of their attention to their non-legal studies and the pleasures of social life, spending their time in versifying and wit, drinking, gaming and womanising. The status of common lawyers was not as yet very high, and the students tended to divide into the socially superior who gave little attention to their books, and the socially inferior who were more career-oriented [109].

Many students attended principally for the social advantages to be gained from a stay in London, not remaining long enough or applying themselves sufficiently to obtain more than an elementary knowledge of law. Though it was obviously advantageous for a gentleman to have some acquaintance with the law in this highly litigious age, a thorough knowledge of specialised branches of the subject could be acquired only by a combination of private study of the manuals, attendance at court and participation in the aural learning exercises – the case-puttings, moots, and readings – supposed to be provided by the Inns. Probably few landed gentlemen left with much more than a nodding familiarity with legal terminology, forms and procedures, and for practical purposes they had to rely on professional advice and on the printed works which were produced specially for laymen. The significance, therefore, of the increased numbers of gentry attending the universities and Inns resided not so much in any academic advantages they might acquire during their brief and negligent periods of study, but rather, as Professor Barnes has remarked, in the 'broadening experience largely denied their predecessors' which 'enabled them to undertake more successfully those duties of county government which most of them entered upon at a very early age and pursued without cease till they died' [110].

In the later seventeenth century the Inns' function as a finishing school for wealthy gentlemen declined and the organisations reverted more to their original professional purpose. The proportion of aristocratic entrants declined and that of students from mercantile and professional families rose. For a general education the wealthy landowners now preferred the grand tour or private tutors. Furthermore, it was realised that a smattering of legal knowledge was of little practical use, and might even be dangerous. For matters of any consequence it was necessary to consult an expert, and trained lawyers of reputation were increasingly available. Moreover, the acquisition of adequate legal knowledge was a painful and tedious process, and most landowners could well afford to consult lawyers or rely on estate administrators who often had a legal training [111].

For their practical day-to-day purposes gentry could obtain more useful knowledge from books. Justices' manuals were specially compiled for their use, and from the sixteenth century onwards numerous and reliable works gradually accumulated on such relevant subjects as agriculture, estate management and land surveying. The seventeenth century saw suggestions for providing formal training in agriculture, and such old standbys as Fitzherbert's *Boke of Surveying* and *Boke of Husbandry* (1523), and Thomas Tusser's *Five Hundred Good Points of Husbandrie* (1573) were supplemented by the works of Barnaby Googe, John Norden, Gervase Markham, Gabriel Plattes, Walter Blith and many subsequent writers. Though many of the books contained a good deal of error, vagueness and shameless borrowing from earlier works, the landed gentleman and his steward were increasingly able to secure from them the best available advice on how to run their estates and cope with the practical problems of farming [112].

The children of the lesser gentry generally left home from the age of six upwards, some to go to boarding schools, some to be brought up in the homes of friends or relations, and others to be apprenticed. Girls seem to have gone to school a little after the age of seven or eight that was common for boys, but girls were often educated in private households by tutors. The education of girls was always a less serious matter, for as one late seventeenth-century writer argued, females had the lesser share of reason, making their sex 'the better prepared for the compliance that is necessary for the better performance of those duties which seem to most properly assigned to it'. Grace Sherrington, daughter of Sir Henry Sherrington of Lacock Abbey, Wiltshire, recorded in her journal typical details of the daily routine she followed under the watchful eye of a relation:

> When she did see me idly disposed she would set me to cypher with the pen and to cast up and prove great sums and accounts and sometimes set me to write a supposed letter to this or that body, concerning such and such things, and other times let me read in Dr. Turner's *Herball* and Bartholomew Vigoe, and other times set me to sing psalms, and other times set me to some curious work, for she was an excellent workman in all kinds of needlework [113].

In the more modest households the squire or his wife did duty for the professional tutors engaged by the wealthy gentry. William Blundell, for example, tried his hand at tutoring, 'up to the ears in Plutarch, in a hot dispute whether Alexander the Great or Caesar was the braver man. . . . We are here so far from speaking good Latin that our English is almost barbarous.' Parents were sufficiently in command of the classics to dispute the competence of tutors and schoolmasters, and they often held strong views on what should be taught, and how. In 1640, for example, Sir Henry Slingsby picked up from Montaigne's *Essays* the notion of having his son taught Latin 'without Rule or Grammar' [114]. The curriculum, both at school and at home, was based on Latin, with the addition of arithmetic, geometry, astronomy, history, geography, modern languages and music. Weight was placed on accomplishments such as dancing and fencing, and particular emphasis was laid on the cultivation of good style in writing, and literary forms and imagery.

For the sons of the wealthy, foreign travel was the ultimate finishing process to be added to private tutor, grammar school and university. Relatively few families could afford the expense of a protracted tour abroad, when the boy's entourage might include three or four tutors and servants. In these circumstances even prominent families restricted the full tour to their eldest son, leaving the younger sons with only a foreshortened version, or none at all. In the sixteenth and seventeenth centuries the aim of foreign travel was to acquire a practical knowledge of foreign countries and languages, particularly of France, and an understanding of the peoples, their habits and outlook, together with some knowledge of their economies. While these objects remained of importance, the later and more elaborate grand tours of the eighteenth century became more markedly cultural, and included a study of French and Italian art, sculpture and architecture.

The majority of gentry, however, could not begin to envisage an extended foreign tour, although sometimes it might prove convenient to send their sons to relatives holding diplomatic or commercial posts abroad. Lacking such connections they contented themselves with a good grammar school. In the course of the sixteenth century newly founded or revived grammar schools acquired a high reputation for their teaching. Particularly noted were Eton, Shrewsbury, St Paul's and Repton, together with Tonbridge, Sedbergh, Bury, Norwich, Thame and Blandford, to mention only a few. Numerous grammar schools attached to religious establishments had been lost at the time of the Reformation but the effects were not so serious as has been supposed; by 1530 there were still 300 of them, and by 1575 the number had risen to some 360. Girls were not admitted; boys attended from the age of seven or eight to fourteen or fifteen. In addition to the usual Latin, logic, rhetoric and mathematics, the better schools concentrated on correct use of English, and in the later sixteenth century began to introduce history, music and modern languages into the curriculum. Lower down the social scale the sons of minor gentry attended their local grammar schools, where they rubbed shoulders with the sons of professional men, farmers, merchants and tradesmen. For obvious reasons the Catholic gentry preferred to employ tutors privately at home, but for the rest the grammar school was chosen as generally efficient, cheaper, and more suited to their station in life [115].

Indeed, in the sixteenth and seventeenth centuries, as later, education was seen as a means of keeping people in their place. It was designed to fit them for particular functions within a certain rank in society. With the growing specialisation of knowledge and the expansion of the professions, a non-specialised 'liberal' education became the hallmark of gentility. A wealthy gentleman's son loitered his way through university, where his only serious study might be one of arms and pedigrees; his last wish was to be mistaken for a scholar, and when he went on to the Inns of Court he studied 'to forget what he learned before' [116]. As education became directed towards preserving rank and function, wealthier families began to favour a more segregated form of schooling, electing to send their sons to what had become more socially exclusive schools, such as Eton, Westminster, Shrewsbury, St Paul's or Winchester, though some parents lacked faith in even the most reputable of schools and chose to keep a close eye on their sons through the medium of private tuition at home. The minor grammar schools became more markedly the resort of the lesser gentry, while the gathering of nobility and wealthy gentry in selected public schools created among them a sense of common identity and natural superiority [117]. The educational fissures separating the higher levels of the ruling class from the lower gentry grew wider in successive centuries as the 'public schools' – in effect the superior grammar schools of national reputation – became more clearly marked off from the local grammar schools, and as the universities, and for a period the Inns of Court, tended also to become the preserve of the wealthy. A direct link between certain well-known public schools and certain Oxford and Cambridge colleges was early established, creating further distinctions even within those attending university. At the same time the growth of charity schools in the country towns and villages defined a fairly clear social cleavage at a lower level between the lesser gentry, substantial farmers and prosperous tradesmen, and the subordinate ranks of small farmers, petty tradesmen and artisans.

English education thus developed along increasingly distinct social and functional lines. So far as the gentry were concerned the grammar schools, and for a wealthy minority, public schools, universities, the Inns and perhaps foreign travel prepared them for a prospective role among the ruling class, a role that might be significant in the national sense or might be obscurely parochial. The differing degrees of prestige attaching to particular schools and forms of education created a greater awareness of social distinctions, and also fostered resentments, especially in families where elder sons went up to university and younger sons left the local grammar school for an apprenticeship. On the whole, however, the common base in the liberal education maintained the sense of a common culture permeating all ranks of the ruling class and enabled the meanest squire to communicate almost on even terms with the powerful magnate. Among the gentry education remained on the whole more a cohesive than a divisive influence, cementing common membership of a culturally homogeneous if hierarchical *élite*. There was not among the gentry that great and dangerous gulf between well educated and badly educated which remains so marked a feature of modern society.

'Noblesse oblige'

Education in a variety of forms, but with a common foundation in the classics, fitted the gentry to their place in society. It set them apart as a cultured *élite*, just as their incomes from landed property and investments set them apart from those obliged to spend their days in earning a living. With their superiority of birth, wealth, leisure and education the gentry were able to fulfil their role as keepers of the peace, unpaid civil administrators, promoters of the public good and benefactors of the poor and unfortunate. They fulfilled, too, a role of social leadership, setting standards of taste and encouraging a liberal attitude towards social change. In Wales, for example, as David Jenkins remarks, the gentry 'did constitute a linkage whereby alternative standards, some higher than and some different from those commonly accepted were presented to other members of the local society . . . the mansions were, too, centres for the diffusion of the English language as English was the language of every gentry family' [118].

It is true that the gentry's belief in their inherent superiority and natural right to regulate the 'lower orders' led sometimes to overbearing pride and misuse of the extensive powers they commanded. Inevitably they also expected an unceasing tribute of deference from the inferiors whose lives they influenced at every turn. Their sensitive sense of status exhibited itself even in disputes over the ranking of private family pews in the most prominent part of the church. Nevertheless, it is remarkable that the English gentry in general showed a strong sense of public duty and of social obligation towards their subordinates. Characteristically they wanted to be held in popular esteem, to be thought of as generous landlords, humane administrators, honest magistrates and trustworthy bulwarks against misfortune. Deference was more to be earned by sincere respect than demanded by feudal right. Arthur Young might well complain that landlords sacrificed farming efficiency for the sake of personal popularity, but it might be countered that lenient rents, undisturbed tenants and conservative estate management produced in the end more social benefit than any gained from heavier crops and fatter beasts. And despite the general conservatism of the gentry, they shared, as we have seen, a willingness to move with the times and an interest in developing the resources of 'their country' for a wider advantage than their own revenues.

Undoubtedly the gentry saw themselves as the major pillar of stability in a world which, bereft of their influence and control, would dissolve into uncertainty, lawlessness, and chaos. Without their support of Church and constitution, their enforcement of the rule of law, their moral leadership and social example, civilised life would collapse. It was part of their social function, moreover, to sweeten and improve the quality of that civilisation which they upheld, by doing all within their power to safeguard prosperity and employment, by improving public facilities such as transport by road and river, and by providing hospitality and entertainment for the neighbourhood. It would be foolish to argue that the mythical 'Merrie England' really existed under the squirearchy, though indeed the black side of rural life – the poverty, landlessness and hopelessness of the labourers – has been so overdrawn by some historians as to produce an equally unbalanced picture. Rural life in reality presented a mixture of hues, and although at certain periods the greyer tones seem to predominate we should not be too hasty in blaming the gentry for the adverse effects of forces which they neither understood nor controlled. They could not prevent population from rising to excessive levels nor harvest failures from causing famines. But where the gentry's influence could be effective, in the day-to-day life of the villages, it seems likely that it was far more a force for good than for evil.

6 The closing phase

In the nineteenth century, as we have seen, the old pre-eminence of the landed interest was eroded by the rise of the industrial state, and its parallel, the coming of democracy. The balance of the economy shifted from agriculture to industry and trade. The typical Englishman was no longer a countryman but a town-dweller. Farming, which had once maintained the bulk of the population, was by the beginning of the twentieth century only on a par with other major employers such as the building and transport industries. But though eclipsed, agriculture remained a significant element in the life of the country: over a million workers still relied on farming for a living in the early decades of the present century.

As the old economic supremacy of the land declined and disappeared, so too did its weight in politics. The forty-shilling freeholder and the pocket borough were relegated to political limbo. Aristocratic management of the electorate finally came to an end with universal education, the secret ballot and the Corrupt Practices Act. For some considerable time, however, the political influence of the landowning aristocracy outlasted the destruction of their electoral base. Down to the 1880s rural counties like Lincolnshire still chose their members of Parliament from among the greater gentry, and in the country generally farmer M.P.s were rarities [1]. Peers still played a major role in governments: the inferior status of the House of Lords was formally established only by the great budget crisis of 1909–11; there were still seven peers in the cabinet of sixteen formed by Bonar Law in 1922, and six in Baldwin's national cabinet of twenty-two formed in 1935, though some were new creations from outside the old landed interest; and it was only in 1923, when Baldwin was chosen to head the Conservatives instead of Curzon, that it was realised that the day of noble prime ministers was over.

The landowners and industrialisation

It would be wrong to see the industrialisation of Britain as something entirely alien to the landowners or as a trend that they all bitterly opposed. A good deal has been made of the hostility shown by owners to river and canal improvements in the eighteenth century, and to the spread of railways and factories in the nineteenth. So far as the individual proprietor was concerned there was always a balance to be drawn between economic advantage and aesthetic considerations. The arrival of a canal, railway line or industrial community might open a prospect of enhanced values for land required as track or factory sites, as also opening a possibility of higher farm rents and lower poor rates. Against these gains had to be balanced noise, smoke, depredations wrought to game preserves, and a probable drain of country labour out of traditional employments. It is not entirely surprising that landowners wished to protect the beauty of houses and parks on which much care and many thousands of pounds had been lavished, insisting consequently on canals or railways being routed at a distance and intrusive chimney stacks shortened or disguised as gothic towers. Even in purely economic terms transport improvements were not necessarily advantageous. They might disturb the local advantage enjoyed by an owner's farms, brickworks, limekilns, coal mines or iron works. In the eighteenth century turnpiked roads or improvements to river navigation might be at the expense of the farmers' local markets, the landowner's mills on the river banks, or the drainage of the neighbouring fields. Subsequently the appearance of canals or railways, bringing coal from a distance, might reduce the value of woodlands. The mere breaking up of the country by canals, railways, factory villages, even enclosures, might ruin it for sport.

But those landowners who sought to protect their way of life from industrial encroachments were counterbalanced to a considerable degree by those who supported or initiated them. English landowners, as we have noted, were generally eager to exploit the industrial potential of their properties, and had been doing so ever since the Middle Ages. Agriculture was far from providing the only legitimate outlet for landed property. There were profits also in timber production, in quarrying and brickmaking, lime-burning, mining, iron furnaces, and the watermills used for a variety of purposes in the textile, leather, iron, paper and many other industries. Numbers of landed families, in the Midlands and north especially, owed their rise more to coal and iron than to corn and sheep. The Willoughbys of Wollaton, the Roses of the Sussex wealden iron industry, the Lowthers, Senhouses and Curwens of Cumberland, the Dudleys of the Black Country, are only a sample of the more prominent. Ventures in the field of transport were the foundation of the wealth of such great families as the Egertons and Leveson-Gowers. Landowners were frequently the initiators and principal financiers of river navigation and turnpikes, and went on to help pioneer the railways. The Dudleys built canals and stretches of private railway line, in addition to fostering transport developments in the Black Country generally. In 1797 Lord Dudley constructed the first railway in the area having iron-edge track, and in 1829 a line employing both a steam locomotive and winding engines was opened between his Shut End coalfield and a loading basin connecting with the Staffordshire and Worcestershire Canal [2].

Other landowners were remarkable in developing ports as outlets for their minerals and farm products. The Cumberland coal ports owed much to the local gentry, as did those of southwest and south Wales. As the demand for minerals grew in the eighteenth and nineteenth centuries, their exploitation proved a valuable source of income for proprietors fortunate in possessing coal measures or accessible deposits of lead and ironstone. In the northeast coal created the fortune of the Ridleys of Heaton and Blagdon, who received a baronetcy in 1756 and a viscountcy in 1900, becoming owners of some 10,000 acres. Others similarly, if not equally, enhanced were the Cooksons of Neasham

House and Meldon Park, Cuthberts of Beaufront Castle, Strakers of Stagshaw House, Taylors of Chipchase Castle and Joiceys of Newton Hall and Ford Castle. In the West Riding there were the Charlesworths of Chapelthorpe Hall, and the heavily indebted Ralph Sneyd, whose Staffordshire royalties bid fair to prove his salvation. Lead-mining produced substantial incomes for proprietors in the Pennines, Cleveland, northwest Yorkshire, the Midlands, and Cardiganshire. Some had been working their lead for a long time, like the Blacketts in Allendale and Weardale, whose property passed to the Beaumonts, owners of pits and mills on their Durham and Northumberland estate around Bywell Hall. Prominent ironmasters, such as the Baldwins, Guests, Walkers and Crawshays, established themselves as landed gentry[3]. It is hardly surprising that an analysis of the gentry heads of families who sat in the Parliament of 1841–47 shows a sixth as primarily businessmen, and over two-fifths as connected with some form of business[4].

The industrial involvement of so many members of the landed interest necessarily influenced their attitudes towards the declining status of agriculture. Some great landowners had been the principal movers in the development of mining, transport and iron production in the vicinity of their estates; numbers were closely interested as partners, directors and shareholders in the various ventures. As ports, industrial towns and residential areas expanded with the growth of the urban population, so urban estate revenues became of mounting importance, more obviously to such as the Grosvenors, with their London West End and Pimlico empire, or the Butes with their new coal port of Cardiff; less obviously to such as the Faunces, owners of ground rents in Newington and Kennington, Sir Thomas Maryon Wilson, who drew a large income from ground rents in Hampstead and Blackheath, the Gilberts of Truro, the Scarisbricks of Stockport, and Sir George Tapps Gervis, benevolent provider of 'the invigorating repose and that commixture of fashion and retirement' that attracted the 'superior class of seaside visitors' to his new resort of Bournemouth. Some of the more genteel, it is true, were tending to withdraw from business investments, like the Bests of Boxley. They had made their money out of the sailors who quaffed the products of their Chatham brewery. In the nineteenth century the Bests saw fit first to lease out their brewery, and finally, in 1894, to dispose of it outright, together with eighty public houses in the Medway towns, for the sum of £150,000[5].

For those who remained involved, the rise of industry and its accompanying urban conglomerations helped handsomely in supplementing what after 1815 proved to be a rather inelastic revenue from farm land. By 1844 the Senhouses' farm income of £2,000 came to be equalled by the revenues from coal royalties, ground rents, quays, yards, market place and ropewalks which went with their creation of Maryport[6]. However, many of the lesser gentry, in particular, as distinct from the wealthier elements within the landed interest, had little or nothing of such revenues. Their estates were limited to a few farms and woodland, with nothing more industrial than perhaps a chalk quarry, gravel pit or malthouse. Even those landowners who possessed minerals or ironworks found that the revenues tended to fall off in the later nineteenth century as pits became exhausted and industrial locations changed. The Beaumonts' colliery revenues from their property near Wakefield rose to a peak of over £9,000 in 1874 but then fell away to only £3,500 within the next twenty years[7]. Only that minority of owners who had substantial interests in urban ground rents, warehouses, wharves and the like managed to maintain or improve their non-agricultural incomes in the late nineteenth and twentieth centuries. Some had been sufficiently longsighted to appreciate that their coal, lead or ironstone would not last for ever, and had diverted resources into other types of investment. To some extent diversification was a process they could hardly avoid when the proper exploitation of their estates often obliged them to help finance turnpikes, canals, docks and railways. But this kind of diversification often yielded meagre results in the long run. Many turnpike trusts were in a bad financial condition by the early nineteenth century, and from the mid-1830s the competition of railways had a devastating effect on their toll revenues. The incomes of most canal companies also collapsed once railway competition became really severe – the Bridgewater Canal was an outstanding but rather rare exception. Harbour facilities often ceased to be profitable when coastal shipping declined and the trade that fed them ran down – and most of them were concerned mainly with coal, like the havens created by the Cumberland gentry. Even railway stocks proved disappointing, the majority of them producing returns only a little better than did Consols. Better yields might be obtained abroad, but then the risks were greater; and not all railway promoters were honest, as the activities of the real-life Hudson and the fictional Melmotte serve to remind us. There remained the safe government stocks and municipal undertakings, banks and insurance companies, but these produced little more than land did, and without land's social advantages and amenities.

The fortunes of farming: the break-up of landed estates

Diversification of assets, therefore, was not a sure solution to meeting the challenge of the industrial age. And, in any event, many of the lesser squires had little means or opportunity for diversifying. Their surplus income was small or non-existent, and their estates too small or too encumbered for them to contemplate parting with land. They remained, like many more wealthy gentry, heavily dependent on rents. Fortunately, for a great deal of the nineteenth century rents did not let them down. Farm rents almost doubled during the Napoleonic Wars, fell somewhat in some areas after the wars with spasmodic and scattered depression among the farmers, and then recovered. The level of rents reached by 1815 proved generally to be that which held for the next sixty years. The repeal of the Corn Laws in 1846 did not bring the dire results which were forecast. Wheat prices fell at first, levelled out, and then fell only very slightly over the next twenty-five years, while the prices of livestock products rose substantially. This development probably widened the existing margin between the rents obtained in the arable south and east and the higher levels achieved in the more pastoral north and west. But all rents edged upwards by an average of some twenty per cent between the 1850s and the 1870s, though the main increases occurred in profitable dairying and fattening districts, and where landowners invested heavily in new field drainage schemes, provided improved farm buildings to house the superior kinds of stock now carried on the better farms, and built cottages for estate workers and farm labourers. It is not known with accuracy how many millions of acres were drained in the new era of machine-produced pipe and tile – some of the work, certainly, was badly done and had to be done again – nor how many millions of pounds were borrowed or diverted from other purposes by landowners to finance drainage and new buildings. At £5 an acre, and sometimes twice as much, drainage was not a cheap improvement. It was as costly as enclosure had been at its most expensive, but it produced far from comparable returns. In the majority of enclosures a return on investment of at least 10 per cent, more commonly 20 per cent, was realised. The drainage projects of the middle of the nineteenth century were nothing like so remunerative, nor in general were they expected to be. Influenced by the 'high farming' ideas advocated by agricultural experts and agents of the leading estates, landowners saw drainage, new buildings and cottages as the means of making farming more efficient, flexible and productive, more able to withstand the greater competition which was expected to follow the repeal of the Corn Laws. It was, as Professor F. M. L. Thompson has remarked, 'a rescue operation' – 'a last, expensive, homage to king corn' – and not the more effective for being directed mainly towards the succour of the arable producers. As a rescue operation it failed either to rescue or to pay.

True, many of the landowners were fulfilling their traditional obligation of providing their tenants with the means of more efficient farming, though not all possessed the will or the resources to involve themselves in the necessary expenditure. Those that did followed the long-established practice of making the tenants contribute by adding 5 per cent of the outlay on drainage to the rents, though less frequently was anything added for the essential accompanying expenditure on farm buildings, and rarely for the sums expended on cottages and farm roads. The recovery of the drainage investment depended, however, on a sufficiently long-term rise in rent levels, and this failed to materialise. Even those owners who, like Sir James Graham, had started early on the process of land improvement experienced disappointing results. Sir James spent £93,000 on his Netherby estate over twenty-six years from 1819 and received a return of barely 4 per cent on money which he had to raise at $3\frac{1}{2}$ per cent. Those large owners who started later when high farming was all the vogue – and most of them did not begin until about the time of repeal – found that returns were more of the order of a mere 2 or $2\frac{1}{2}$ per cent; and this at a time when interest rates varied between $3\frac{1}{2}$ and $4\frac{1}{2}$ per cent, and returns in the commercial world were expected to be about 8 or 9 per cent. It seems likely that the majority of gentry owners were more cautious or more niggardly than the great proprietors. They probably tended to go in less wholeheartedly for drainage and associated works, though when they did so they may have obtained a better return. Most of the gentry did not have the large mineral or other non-agricultural sources of income to allow them to launch costly schemes of improvement[8]. They were not in a position to follow the lead of great landowners, like the Sutherlands in the west Midlands and the Butes in Glamorgan, who were following a deliberate policy of subsidising agriculture from their other sources of revenue. Few of the gentry had the resources to take so magnanimous a course, even if they wished to.

From 1879 rents yielded before the storm of cheap grain imports coming from America, Russia and further afield. The railways and advances in steam shipping struck sharply at the natural protection that distance had offered English farmers, and before long cheap corn was joined by cheap frozen meat, while imports of dairy produce, fruit and vegetables from the continent had already affected the farmers' home markets for some years. Worst hit were the arable areas of the south and east, where much of the heavy expenditure on drainage had been only too literally sunk. There rents fell heavily, by some two-fifths on average, but more in individual cases. The more pastoral regions of the north and west of the country saw much lower rent reductions. In favoured dairying areas like Cheshire the fall averaged only a little over 10 per cent, and since prices were also falling there was in real terms no effective fall in rent levels. Much depended on local conditions of soil, access to markets, and the adaptability of the farmers. In both arable and pasture areas the reductions in rent failed to save tenants who had been severely hit by the extraordinarily bad seasons marking the opening years of the depression. The harvest of 1879 was the worst of the century, and the early 1880s were also remarkable for sopping cornfields and destructive outbreaks of disease among the livestock. Farmers whose working capital was depleted by these disasters were in no shape to meet the more lasting effects of increased foreign competition. Landlords eventually cut back their estate expenditure in line with the fall in their rentals, and in the arable areas, especially, expensive improvements came to a halt. In the thirty years after 1880 economy was the watchword. Tenants were helped by abatements and subsequently by permanent reductions in rents, but most landlords could do little more for them. In badly hit counties like Essex not a few farmers decided to emigrate, to Canada or New Zealand for example; those who remained to stick it out eventually bankrupted, and were replaced by Scots or West Country men who tried their hands at dairying on the former arable farms.

From the 1880s it gradually became clear that the repeal of 1846 had at last produced its cheap food, and with it the collapse of high farming and the old agricultural system. Many estate owners came to the conclusion that the old principles of landownership and management were no longer applicable, that land as an investment was finished. In previous depressions they had approached the problem with self-confidence and a justified belief in the survival power of land as the most permanent of all assets. When prices fell they responded not merely with rent reductions, but with more positive encouragement to keep the tenants on the farms. They bolstered up threatened farmers with various forms of help, taking the local rates off their shoulders, providing seed, giving compensation for diseased livestock. They expressed their confidence in ultimate prosperity by rebuilding farmhouses, adding new barns and undertaking costly improvements such as drainage. But the 'great depression' of the 1880s and early 1890s seemed to mark the end of an era. Landlordism itself was under attack, especially in Ireland, but also at home with the new legislation on settled estates, game and tenant right. The collapse of arable farming came as the culmination of two generations of political and economic decline, and for many landowners it seemed that the time had come to recognise the changed circumstances of land in the industry state.

Some, perhaps, would have done more for the farmers had their means permitted. They found, however, that though prices in general were falling, the expenses of running a country house and keeping up customary standards did not fall very much, certainly not as much as did many rentals. Grassing-down of arable land and provision of field water supplies, vital for livestock farming, was expensive and did not always produce worthwhile returns when the land was re-let. It happened, too, that those owners in the arable south and east who experienced the heaviest decline in agricultural incomes, were those who generally had little or no income from industrial sources to help them out. Some estates on the poorest land were let out for shooting, the residence often going with the land. In the breckland of Norfolk shooting became the most prominent activity in the countryside, and partridges were said to have been 'the salvation of Norfolk farming'. Other areas of poor soils, heaths and moors were appropriated as sites for reservoirs to supply the growing cities, or for military barracks and training grounds[9]. Parsons who relied on their glebe for income found themselves in straitened circumstances, as did the fellows of Oxford and Cambridge colleges whose estate revenue fell off sharply. Perhaps the country squires of limited agricultural estates felt the impact most. Rider Haggard, the novelist, was one of those who in the 1880s found a small estate insufficient to support a house and family. He let it, and moved to London to practise at the Bar. His country background, knowledge of practical farming and ability in writing led him to undertake a protracted tour of investigation, in conscious imitation of Arthur Young more than a century before. And his method of going about it was very similar to that of Young. He advertised his intended visit to a county and accepted those invitations, often from complete strangers, to visit farms and estates which offered a good geographical sample of the various kinds of farming. This, 'the heaviest labour of all my laborious life', resulted in *Rural England*, published at the beginning of the new century, a detailed, and generally depressing, account of contemporary conditions in the English countryside[10].

Haggard's picture of rural England in decline provided gloomy confirmation, if it were needed, of rundown estates, discouraged farmers and a labour force moving from the land. Conditions were better in pasture areas where rents and profits had fallen much less, but even there falling prices and increased competition had wrought their effects. Some landowners were selling out, and probably many more would have done so had not the land market been dominated by conditions of rapidly falling prices and a lack of purchasers. By the mid-1890s land was selling at least a third lower than before 1879, and the average fall was 65 per cent – but cheapness had not produced many eager buyers. Those in the market were mainly industrialists, manufacturers, brewers, bankers and contractors. They included J. Colman, the monopolist of mustard, members of the Wills family, the great tobacco and cigarette manufacturers of Bristol, J. Robinson, brewer of Nottingham, John Wood, a cotton spinner from Glossop, and Henry Brassey, of the celebrated family of contractors, who bought Lord Westmorland's Apethorpe in Northamptonshire[11]. The new men had made their money in the London money market, in the export trade, in textiles or in building, or in satisfying the wants of the urban millions. Some rose to wealth and gentility within a generation, paralleling the sudden rise of merchants, financiers, lawyers and officeholders in the sixteenth century. During Lord Salisbury's administration of 1886–92 a third of the new peers came from business. They included merchants, brewers, wool-combers, an engineering and armament tycoon like Armstrong, and a bookseller like W. H. Smith. Of the 246 new titles conferred between 1886 and 1914 only a quarter fell to heads of old-established landed families, those who had formerly furnished the majority of new peers; though it is true that some industrialist peers had already acquired land, and a proportion of the new peers recruited from among the diplomats and colonial governors were younger sons of noble and gentry families [12].

This new leavening of the aristocracy did not create a serious fissure, at least not immediately. Some of the *nouveaux riches* bought estates from old families anxious to sell. Others went only as far as renting a country residence or some acres of shooting. The old landed circles adjusted to the circumstances as they had often done before. To some extent, though by no means entirely, the newcomers were absorbed. Old-established aristocrats married into new wealth, as they had always done; and for heiresses they looked further afield, across the Atlantic in fact which was more novel. Respect for money and ability, on the one hand, met with a corresponding respect for lineage and social distinction. There was a certain adulation of the great industrial empire-builders and selfmade millionaires. The men of new wealth joined in country pursuits and interests, and the men of ancient title graciously accepted invitations to join boards of directors. By 1896 a quarter of the peerage held director-ships [13]. A *Punch* cartoon of 1908 caught the new style of aristocratic society: a blue-blooded duke and his consort are visiting 'the Goldbergs' little place in Dumpshire', and seeing a group on the palatial terrace her Grace exclaims: 'Good heavens! D'you see who've just arrived? The Talbot de Vere-Howard-Montgomeries! And talking to company promoters and soap-kings and I don't know what as if they'd been born to it! I'd no idea they were getting into such good society!'

In the later 1890s prices and rents levelled out, though they did not recover much lost ground. As conditions in the countryside slowly improved, many old owners concluded that the time was opportune to think of selling. The spectre of heavier death duties and taxes on property, raised first by Harcourt in 1894 and subsequently by Lloyd George in 1909, was as yet insubstantial; but it was sufficient to provide a new pretext for parting with ancestral acres. The controversy over taxes on land seemed a portent of the shape of things to come, while many owners had more immediate pressures at hand in the shape of heavy burdens of mortgages and interest charges. Many farms, it was true, were now under-rented, but they needed money spending on them and there was a reluctance to raise rents substantially. New strength in the land market, with a firmer demand and higher prices, proved the clincher. Between 1910 and 1913 several hundred thousand acres of land changed hands [14].

Immediately after the 1914–18 War the sales resumed and for much the same reasons. Even urban possessions found their way to the estate agents and were broken up among property companies. Some owners were forced into selling by the pressure of accumulated debts; and there was the need to meet death duties, a need which the recent carnage in France had intensified. But these owners appeared to be in the minority. More were taking the opportunity of the continuing good conditions in the land market to get out of land into more remunerative forms of investment. Something near a quarter of England changed hands between 1918 and 1921 [15].

From the landowners' point of view, redistribution of assets was a means of escaping from a debilitating burden of interest charges and at the same time of improving the return obtained from remaining investments. Rented farm land rarely produced a net return of more than about 3 per cent, which was substantially less than the interest payable on mortgages, and markedly below the 7 or 8 per cent obtainable from trustee securities. When selling it was the usual practice to give the tenants first refusal, and this was convenient to owners for tenants would buy farms as whole units. Many tenants were eager to purchase, especially when they could have the bulk of the purchase money left as a mortgage in the old owner's hands at a moderate 5 per cent. For the former owners 5 per cent free of all the trouble and expense of estate management was a good deal more attractive than the meagre return offered by rents, especially when land had lost its former advantages of power and influence.

For the former tenants who now became mortgaged owner-occupiers the solution proved less happy. From the low point reached in the later nineteenth century, when owner-occupiers held only about a seventh of the land, a remarkable transformation occurred between 1910 and the early 1920s. The proportion of the land in the hands of owners rose to over a third; and with renewed prosperity in agriculture since the Second World War this share has risen further until over a half of the country is now owned by its occupiers. Between 1921 and 1939, however, renewed agricultural depression fell with especial severity on those farmers who were buying their land. For them there was no longer a landlord to interpose himself between the farmers and market forces. Fixed interest charges did not have the flexibility of rents, and there was no estate office to help out with repairs to buildings or the cost of changing to new modes of cultivation. In the 1930s, *The Times* claimed, half Norfolk was virtually owned by the banks. The state had to come in to establish new sources of long-term farm finance, regulate markets and raise prices. Even where landlords remained in being they could often do little to help. Rents raised soon after the Great War fell back again when prices collapsed in 1921. By 1936 rents reached their lowest point for at least sixty years, perhaps for more than a century. Even in the years immediately following the Second World War rents were still below the level of the 1870s. By that time the surviving landowners could look back over seventy years of depressed estate revenues; and for fifty of those years they had been obliged to meet heavier outgoings in taxation, wages, maintenance costs and living expenses generally. Unless they had been more than usually fortunate in marriage, in business activities, or in discovering other sources of revenue, they could no longer play the part in agriculture that had been theirs for centuries past [16].

The landed interest in eclipse

The decades of the great depression and the succeeding era of radical readjustment saw the landed interest in decline, and eventual eclipse. Looking back to times before the depression it seemed that the fortunate generations of those halcyon days had shown an almost feckless disregard of the clearly signalled storm warnings; instead of husbanding their resources in preparation for the blow they had squandered them in careless pursuit of luxury and extravagant diversion. In its entirety such a view could hardly be sustained by an impartial survey of the landed interest as a whole, but there was enough truth in it to lend it credence. For many landowners there occurred in the nineteenth century a certain withdrawal from participation in affairs. Numbers of the lesser gentry, especially, had long dropped all but a passive peripheral interest in politics as elections, already expensive in the eighteenth century, became even more so in the nineteenth. Sums like the £14,000 spent on the

South Durham contest of 1841 were enough to deter even the great landowners, and after all there were a great many other things to spend money on [17]. To part with one's thousands and still be defeated filled the cup to overflowing, and an experience of this kind – in their home county of Staffordshire too – was enough to make the enormously wealthy Leveson-Gowers decide to have no more to do with 'the broiling and political quarrels' of county elections [18]. It seemed, too, as if politics had become more problematical and less rewarding as the franchise was widened, as questions of reform split the landed interest, and as even the farmers sometimes broke away from aristocratic leadership. Farmer-M.P.s were highly unusual, but the protection, cattle-plague and malt-tax issues brought three gentleman-farmers to Westminster in the 1850s and 1860s.

The withdrawal of many owners from active politics may help to explain why the 'Chandos clause' of the 1832 Reform Act had so little effect on the security of tenure of tenant farmers. The clause gave the vote to all those tenants paying £50 or more in rent, and was thought to result in a direct encouragement for landowners to substitute annual tenures for long leases so that they could keep the political whiphand over the farmers. In fact, the evidence suggests that other influences were more important. Long leases had declined in popularity since the severe price fluctuations of the Napoleonic Wars and their aftermath had shown how unwise it was for either landlords or tenants to commit themselves to a fixed rent for long periods. In the following decades leases were desired by neither side. Landlords and tenants preferred the flexibility which the absence of a lease offered for adjusting rents to changing circumstances, as well as for allowing a shifting of the balance between arable and pasture, and for making associated changes in the size of farm units. For most small farms leases had long been exceptional, and their tenants felt little insecurity. Many went on for generations on the same farm on the basis of merely annual agreements, while leases of twenty-one years aroused in tenants the expectation of a revision of terms and a probable change of occupier at the termination of the lease [19]. A recent study of Lincolnshire politics in the mid-nineteenth century suggests that a combination of prudence, gratitude for past indulgence and hope for future favours was influential among tenants who customarily followed the landlord's political wishes. In the countryside there was a long tradition of deference in this matter, but many of the large farmers in the county were highly prosperous, commanded large resources of capital and sometimes owned estates in their own right. 'These men were not likely to quail before an overbearing agent, or go in fear of reprisals if they spoke their minds' [20].

In the affairs of the counties, as in national politics, the gentry found their traditional functions increasingly under attack from the 1830s, as Poor Law and police reforms created new organisations on wider territorial bases, and new policies and new professional standards followed. The process continued in succeeding years when Whitehall intervened more persistently, though the gentry clung to their control of county administration until a remarkably late period. County councils, after all, became a fact only in 1888, and after that date much of the leadership in local affairs was still assumed by those members of landed families who kept their place in the county and retained their old sense of public duty. Some squires continued to play the traditional role, like Rider Haggard's father, the squire of Bradenham Hall in west Norfolk, who combined a somewhat outdated local paternalism with the chairmanship of quarter sessions. A latterday Sir Roger de Coverley, the older Haggard allowed no one to leave church on Sunday till he had stationed himself in the porch to count the congregation as it left[21].

Until the twentieth century relatively few gentry found in farming compensation for a reduced role in politics and county government. There was a select band of agricultural pioneers, like the celebrated Philip Pusey, editor of the Royal Agricultural Society's *Journal*; the pioneer agricultural chemist, Sir John Bennet Lawes of Rothamsted; and the London patent razor strap manufacturer, turned experimental farmer in Essex, J. J. Mechi of Tiptree Hall. Numbers of squires attended the county shows and supported with their subscriptions the activities of the Royal Agricultural, Bath and West of England, and less eminent societies. But such country gentlemen were surprisingly few. The Bath and West scarcely exceeded a thousand members throughout the nineteenth century, and the typical agricultural society relied mainly for support on interested amateurs, clergymen, doctors and academics. The societies' main objectives were to encourage invention in farming techniques and to spread innovation among the farmers. The farmers, however, were notoriously resistant to 'tiresome professional and scientific details'. The readers of the scientific articles in the leading journals were a small coterie. In 1853 the Bath and West sent only 473 copies of its *Journal* to members, and sold a mere twenty-one copies to the public. Aristocratic proprietors and leading gentry were willing to lend the societies the dignity of their names as patrons, vice-patrons, presidents, vice-presidents and members of governing bodies. No doubt they sincerely felt the public and private advantage of agricultural improvement, but few were willing to take on an active role. There were exceptions, such as Thomas Dyke Acland who, like Sir John Bennet Lawes, had a special interest in chemistry; Acland was prepared to deliver lectures on the subject to rural audiences. But none of the forty-eight council members of the Bath and West, the people who did the work of running the Society, possessed a title[22].

The interest of the gentry turned more often to their homes, their parks and gardens, than to farming. They spent money on adding gun-rooms, billiard-rooms and conservatories. They rebuilt stables, kennels and carriage-houses. Plumbing and drainage were modernised, kitchens remodelled and, eventually, electricity installed. Parks were planted, gardens beautified and drives and walks laid out afresh. The Norwich firm of Boulton and Paul was one of the manufacturers specialising in iron buildings and furniture for the grounds of the gentry and wealthier middle classes in the towns. Their comprehensive catalogue included a range of items from rollers, mowers, garden seats and ornamental gates, to 'fishing temples', elaborate hunting establishments, shooting boxes, foxhound kennels, aviaries, summerhouses and pavilions. Quite a number of squires and their ladies took a keen interest in gardening and supported the work of local garden societies. Park-making and the taste for horticulture had encouraged the growth of specialist nurserymen in London and elsewhere from as early as the beginning of the eighteenth century. Catalogues of the varieties stocked by the leading firms were circulated to lists of regular customers, and already in the eighteenth century there was a big demand for novelties from abroad. By the early decades of the following century wistaria and the tea rose had been imported from the Far East, together with dahlias, petunias, lupins, ornamental trees like the Douglas fir from America, and many others. Already in 1804 the growth of interest in gardening had led to the formation of the Royal Horticultural Society. Contemporaries spoke at this time of the delicious 'rural paradises which now surround our country houses'. Coach passengers passing Colonel Howard's residence at Leven's Bridge in Westmorland descended in order to view the Elizabethan house and fine topiary work, the fountains, statues and lawns [23]. Few landowners, perhaps, exceeded the delight which John Thomas Brooks of Flitwick Manor showed in his deer park and gardens. He had a separate garden for each of the four seasons, as well as an American garden, rose garden, summer bulb garden, botanic garden, exotic flower garden, a labyrinth, and of course kitchen gardens, in which he took a close practical interest [24].

The squires' ladies, when not taken up with running the house and supervising work in the gardens, were absorbed in reading, letter-writing, drawing, and painting, music and fancy needlework. Fine afternoons were devoted to walking, boating, archery, croquet and tennis. Many were fine horsewomen and might ride to hounds, though their presence on the hunting field was not generally welcomed. Evenings were spent in music, cards and conversation. The great majority, probably, had abandoned any very active part in running the estate, helping in the kitchen or cooking for the poor, as had been common in previous centuries. Their main function, after childbearing, was to entertain and be decorative. However, many still kept up the useful social function of visiting the poor of the village, taking an interest in the school and village affairs generally, and providing clothing, fuel and other help for the aged and distressed. In the absence of a doctor the squire's wife often offered the sick first aid and the traditional remedies, and the mansion, like the vicarage, not infrequently served as village dispensary.

The running of a country house became more troublesome as standards of entertaining rose and the drain of country people away to the towns reduced the supply of servants. Servants' wages tended to rise in the later nineteenth century with the growth of alternative employments, and the whole way of life of a country house was founded on cheap labour. The numerous rooms to be kept clean, large quantities of food to be prepared, meals to be served, laundry washed, fires laid and mended, and errands to be run – to say nothing of grounds to be maintained, horses groomed, carriages cleaned, dogs fed and exercised – all rested on the services of a small army of servants. The growing cost and increasing scarcity of servants were factors which, combined with reduced incomes, caused many gentry families to move to a smaller house, go to live abroad or set up home in some English watering place.

The tendency of lesser gentry to centre their lives on their homes and estates, as long as they could keep them, was partially offset by the growing ease of travel. To go far afield in one's own coach, with coachmen, footmen and horses, was expensive, prohibitively so. Before the railways journeys could be done most cheaply by mail or stage coaches, if one were prepared to suffer the discomfort of cramped quarters and the lack of privacy. This left for the majority of the more well-to-do the hiring of post-chaises and horses, which was still fairly expensive if the journey were a long one and servants had to be taken along in addition to the family. Fresh horses had to be hired at each ten- or twelve-mile stage, and a post-chaise carried at most two passengers and two servants, and required two horses (four if speed was important) and a postboy to take the horses back at the end of each stage. A pair of horses and a postboy cost from 1s 3d to 1s 9d a mile, to which had to be added meals en route [25]. An annual visit to the sea, for only a small family and a couple of servants might well cost between £30 and £50 in travelling expenses alone. The railways changed all this. The enormous trade in the horses required for stage coaches and posting rapidly fell off, the great rambling coaching inns, some with stabling for hundreds of horses, declined into somnolence and decay. Where all the coachmen and ostlers went was a mystery. 'Is old Weller alive or dead?' asked Thackeray. 'Alas! We shall never hear the horn ring at midnight, or see the pike-gates fly open any more.'

The railways meant a far greater freedom and cheapness of movement for the gentry as for the urban middle class. They could afford to visit London more frequently and go further afield on holiday. The nearer watering places, Scarborough, Buxton, Weymouth, Brighton and Sidmouth, lost their charm as the railways opened them up for middle-class manufacturers and their artisans. Even in the coaching era the popular watering places were likely to be full 'of the middle class of people, such as farmers, tradesmen &c.' as a somewhat snobbish visitor to Freeston Shore in Lincolnshire wrote in 1805; 'sometimes one upstart country squire who has just transformed himself by little gold from a village peasant, or now and then a lordly innkeeper, who has sprung up from a post boy, ostler, waiter, or even boots'. Later in the nineteenth century, however, the wealthier gentry could contemplate shooting expeditions in Scotland or think of sending their sons on enlarged versions of the traditional grand tour. The shortening of voyages achieved by the steamships, together with lower long-distance fares, now made a visit to America or the Colonies a serious possibility. In the middle years of the century some hardy spirits went off buffalo shooting on the Great Plains of North America, or later embarked on big-game hunting in Africa or India. Mountain climbing in the Alps came in, and Lucerne, Interlaken, and Wengen became familiar names among the *cognascente*. The more staid or valetudinarian went for protracted stays at the noted European spas, the traditional Spa in Belgium or Baden Baden, Kissingen in Bavaria, Rhinefelden in Switzerland, or Ischel in Austria. The motor-car, when it appeared, reinforced the trend, making carriages and coachmen super-fluous, and providing even greater flexibility of movement. The general effect was to loosen the gentry's roots in the soil, further to reduce his interest in local affairs, and to encourage him to become more of an absentee. A larger number of landowners took to living more or less permanently in London or abroad. They found in their Pall Mall clubs the company and convenience which offered good substitutes for the former habits of visiting in the neighbourhood and entertaining at home from the resources of their own kitchens and cellars. Visits to the country became confined to excursions for a little hunting or making up a shooting party. Even these might prove too expensive and bother-some. The old house was shut up and its game preserves let to a wealthy businessman. The household was dispersed and the tenants became a mere list of names on a rent account. As the agent increasingly replaced the resident owner, some of the effects ascribed by Cobbett to absenteeism appeared more widely: a gentry

foreign in their manners, distant and haughty in their behavior,
looking to the soil only for its rents, viewing it as a mere object of

speculation, unacquainted with its cultivators, despising them and their pursuits, and relying, for influence, not upon the good will of the vicinage, but upon the dread of their power.

The sporting gentry

It would be wrong to overemphasise the new mobility of the gentry. True, the attractions of living in London or abroad may help account for the very substantial turnover which Professor Thompson has found in gentry estates in the middle decades of the century. In the early 1870s 10 per cent of the greater gentry, and 15 per cent of the squires, were newcomers who had arrived since the 1840s [26]. Other and older factors were at work, however: extravagance in all its various forms, misfortune and the dying out of old families. Some of those who disappeared had accumulated vast debts in following sport and in gambling. Sir St Vincent Hynde Cotton of Madingley Hall, Cambridge, lost his estate through play, and was sufficiently eccentric to take up a career as coachman on the Brighton Road under the name of Sir Vincent Twist, and another who took up the calling of the older Weller was the unfortunate 'Mad Windham', who was obliged to part with his Felbrigg inheritance. For too many of the gentry betting, like sport, became an obsession. Gambling on the turf and cards predominated, but wagers were laid on all kinds of trivial matches and casual events. The London gaming rooms thrived, and the feats performed for wagers – a walk of a thousand miles in a thousand hours, or eating twenty fried eggs in less than five minutes – were both prolific and puerile. 'Squire' George Osbaldeston played whist for £100 a trick and £1,000 a rubber, and once lost £4,000 on a trotting match. With such recklessness ruin was inevitable. The bankrupts gathered at the nearest point of the continent, Boulogne, to be out of reach of their creditors, and they seldom dared to return [27].

Leading examples of the great sporting characters were Sir Tatton Sykes, Grantley Berkeley, and George Osbaldeston. Sir Tatton, of the Sledmere family, was the owner of 34,000 Yorkshire acres. During a long life which began in 1772 he was said to have seen the St Leger seventy-four times, and he sold his brother's priceless Elizabethan library, medals, coins and pictures to pay for his hounds. One of his legendary feats of stamina was to ride from Yorkshire to Aberdeen for the purpose of winning a race for Lord Huntly, covering 740 miles in five days. Down to his death in the 1860s he remained an eccentric who insisted on wearing the long high-collared coat, chokers and frills of the Regency. Beloved by his tenants and detested by his family, he imposed on his household a spartan regime of rising at dawn, washing in cold water, and other unnecessary discomforts, together with frequent application of the parental whip [28]. Grantley Berkeley, the second legitimate son of the fifth Earl of Berkeley, was more typical of the hunting and shooting set of London bucks. His career included a visit to the great plains of North America to hunt buffalo, an undistinguished period in Parliament, and a defence of game preservation before a Select Committee of the 1840s. He had some pretensions to literary powers, and when his three-volume historical romance of Berkeley Castle was severely reviewed in the press he fought a duel with one of the critics, and horsewhipped the editor of *Fraser's Magazine*. The third of this remarkable trio was the celebrated 'Squire' Osbaldeston, 'Squire of all England'. A great follower of the hounds and of racing, he excelled at every branch of sport. On one occasion he brought down 100 pheasants with 100 shots, and on another he bagged 97 grouse with 97 shots; he could put ten bullets from a duelling pistol through the ace of diamonds at 30 feet; at forty-five, after a crippling accident in the hunting field, he rode 200 miles across country in nine hours for a wager; he was a fine oarsman and brilliant tennis player, and at cricket he ranked among the six best amateurs in England. At sixty-eight he rode his own horse at Goodwood and lost by a neck. Racing was his downfall and throughout his life he could never resist a wager: in advanced age he once sat in his chair for twenty-four hours without moving in order to win a sovereign [29].

Among those incorrigible sportsmen and gamblers who became sadly reduced, if not quite to the Boulogne level, were Squire Osbaldeston and Henry Chaplin. The 'Squire' declined into relative penury through continual borrowing to satisfy his passion for the turf. He admitted to losing nearly £200,000 by betting and keeping racehorses: even as a student at Oxford he kept two horses and hunted three days a week. By the 1840s his rentals were almost entirely absorbed by interest on mortgage debts amounting to over £100,000. Ever optimistic he carried on, looking always for the killing that never came, and hoping against all the evidence that a providential discovery of coal on his land would come to his rescue. In the end he was obliged to sell up for £190,000, and after settling with his creditors had just enough left over to live modestly in a succession of country villas, his evening wagers at the Portland Club limited to a mere guinea an evening. He was sportsman enough to recognise his own failings. Looking back on the ruin of his estate he admitted: 'I am an example of the adage that "A fool and his money are soon parted" ' [30]. Chaplin's case was very similar. On his Lincolnshire estate he dispensed hospitality with magnificent prodigality to guests from the Prince of Wales downwards, kept four packs of hounds and hunted six days a week, almost entirely at his own expense, and in addition maintained an extensive deer forest in Scotland. When by an extraordinary chance of freak weather conditions he won the 1867 Derby with an outsider, he presented his trainer with a cheque for £5,000 and his jockey with another for £1,000 [31].

Albeit the occasion of debts, and sometimes ruin, country sport was one of the main attractions keeping the gentry at home on their estates. Not all great sportsmen were inveterate gamblers of the Osbaldeston or Chaplin breed. Some, like Ralph Lambton, were long-established members of Parliament and well-loved landowners; Tom Smith, master of the Craven and the Pytchley, was a progressive agriculturist and engineer; Thomas Assheton Smith, a master of hounds for fifty-nine years, was a master of the classics, man of science, and a member of Parliament [32]. The immortal John Peel, who died in 1854 at the age of seventy-eight, was huntsman for Sir Frederic Fletcher Vane at Arrowthwaite, Cumberland. Peel's grey coat was woven from the local wool, and he regularly hunted twice a week, frequently covering fifty miles of country in one outing. But too often the love of sport became a craze, an excuse for extravagance and neglect of family affairs and estate, and was often associated with a dissolute taste for excessive gambling and drinking.

Sport, too, had its direct effects on social relations in the countryside. Of the village sports, cricket, and sometimes bowling, brought squire and village together. Many a young local lad acquired valuable patronage, and perhaps the entry to a good career, through making his mark in the squire's eleven. Shooting was a different story. It set the squire and his grand friends apart from the village. By law, as we have seen, shooting was restricted to the superior landowning classes. The farmers disliked game preservation because the pheasants, partridges, hares and rabbits stripped their fields, and they were not allowed to shoot the marauders, though on some estates they might be permitted to shoot ground game if it became a very severe nuisance. The ordinary villagers were under suspicion as actual or potential poachers. They were frightened into keeping out of game reserves by harsh penalties, though not with complete success. Occasionally, however, there was a local tradition that anyone might shoot game freely on a certain day of the year, sometimes Boxing Day or the fifth of November. As early as the 1770s it was being argued that farmers should be allowed to kill game in order to keep down the depredations on their crops. Touring Suffolk in 1784 Arthur Young noted that at Mr Gross's 'great farm of 2700 acres' at Capel St Andrews the carrots had been

> so eaten up by the innumerable number of hares which his landlord, Lord Archibald Hamilton, preserved, that he has determined to sow no more. In these cases the tenant doubtless has his recompense in the rent, but the public has none. The profusion of game in this and another of his lordship's farms, Butley Abbey, Mr Chandler's, which are together above 5000 acres, puts a barrier to good husbandry, and prevents one of the best articles of culture in the kingdom from spreading. It is not only the hares that do this mischief, but their preservation nurses up a breed of rabbits which add to the evil. The reflection I have added is my own, and not the farmer's, who seemed very well inclined to second his landlord's wishes.

As Young pointed out, farmers affected by game preserves did have the compensation of low rents and were not altogether dissatisfied, but they often took matters into their own hands more than they would admit to the landlord's agent. There were not many farmers, said one observer, who could not produce from the pantry a hare, or two or three brace of birds; and some farmers turned a blind eye to the activities of poachers in return for a hare or brace to send to a friend in town [33].

In the early nineteenth century the Game Laws rose to a crescendo of fierceness in protection of landowners' preserves. And, for all that, ineffectively; the trade in game increased rather than diminished. Quite often the keepers themselves were in league with the poaching gangs and the whole network of coachmen, guards and inn ostlers that saw the prey safely conveyed to its destination at Leadenhall Market, the fashionable watering places or industrial cities, and so to the poulterers' shops. Some of the gentry were themselves notorious poachers, like Peter Hunter, who regularly raided the woods of his neighbours' properties in Hampshire [34]. Some owners of shooting land did more than present their bags to their friends. In defiance of the law they sent their own venison, hares, pheasants and partridges to London poulterers with whom they had an understanding. And the poaching, after all, would never have reached the scale it did without the remunerative outlet presented by the tables of the wealthy townsmen.

As the penalties became harsher and the keepers' measures more brutal, so the poachers took to working in large gangs for mutual protection. The use of spring guns and mantraps, until they were prohibited in 1827, only embittered the poachers and made them less careful of keepers' lives. Cobbett, riding near Canterbury in 1823, saw the notice: 'Paradise Place. Spring guns and steel traps are set here.' 'A pretty idea it must give us of Paradise,' he growled, 'to know that spring guns and steel traps are set in it.' He went on in characteristic vein:

> This is doubtless some stock-jobber's place; for, in the first place, the name is likely to have been selected by one of that crew; and, in the next place, whenever any of them go to the country, they look upon it that they are to begin a sort of warfare against everything around them. They invariably look upon the labourer as a thief.

The ineffectiveness of the law in preventing poaching brought about a revulsion of public opinion, which was heightened by the severity with which offences were punished. Two cases of 1821, involving such prominent landowners as Lord Palmerston and Thomas Assheton Smith, attracted great attention. Two men, both in their late twenties, were executed, one for assisting in killing a gamekeeper, the other for shooting at a keeper. Of sixteen prisoners condemned to death at that particular Winchester assizes these were the only ones to hang, and both men had been recommended to mercy by the jurors. The judge, Cobbett reported, stated that it was necessary to deter others, 'as resistance to gamekeepers had now arrived at an alarming height, and many lives had been lost' [35].

Within ten years the Game Act of 1831 removed much of the evil arising from game preservation. Its sale was legalised, and any landowner and his sons could shoot game on their own land, while tenant farmers could do so by permission of their landlords. But game remained a grievance among the farmers for many years to come. Hares travelled miles to get at turnips or carrots, and rabbits made enormous inroads into cornfields near their burrows. It was not until 1881 that a new law permitted tenants to destroy hares and rabbits on their farms without the landlord's permission. After 1831 shooting was no longer legally restricted to a small privileged class, and the penalties on poaching were moderated. In practice, it remained an aristocratic sport, largely confined to country-house parties of the well-to-do, and there was something artificial and unhealthy in the elaborate management of hatcheries and winter feed for birds destined for wholesale slaughter – all to enable a few gentlemen to boast of having shot so many birds in a day, their scores solemnly recorded in game books. The methodical destruction of deliberately fattened and carefully protected birds, the *grande battue*, became in the early years of the century a feature of great estates, noble proprietors gathered with leading gentry to establish new records of slaughter.

Foxhunting, unlike shooting, did not cause such social friction in the countryside. There was a streak of cruelty in it, but as the reactionary John Byng remarked:

> From our cradle there is a love of field sports handed down to us
> from Nimrod; and confirmed by the Norman Conquest, as a right of
> gentry: Nor do I hope to live to see the San Culottes of this land

laying all distinction waste – and in defiance of law, and submission proclaiming what they call the rights of man.

In the sport's early days the wholesale destruction of lambs was a factor in encouraging men like Squire Draper of Berwick Hall in Yorkshire, and William Somerville of Warwickshire, to go to the expense of keeping a pack of fox-hounds. In a later phase, hunting was approved of by many for its bringing money into the country. Farmers, however, complained of gates left open, hedges broken down and crops trampled on, but again they had the compensation of low rents. In addition, as hunting grew, it became a common practice to pay tenants' claims for poultry destroyed by foxes, though there were suspicions that such claims were often artificially inflated. In some areas damage done to farmers by game and foxes was assessed by two disinterested persons, one nominated by the farmer and the other by the landlord, with a third as umpire. The gentry recognised such compensation as part of the cost of the sport. 'How can you expect to have foxes,' asked Ralph Lambton, a noted master, 'if you don't pay for the mischief they do?' [36] Also important in mollifying the farmers was an invitation to take part in the hunt. Some tenants indeed, like those of Lord Yarborough, were expected to take part, not merely by feeding and exercising the puppies boarded out on their farms, but by turning out to the meets suitably appointed and on a good horse. Trollope maintained that a great many farmers hunted regularly, and that without the farmers' support the sport would have been impracticable. Farmers would otherwise refuse to cooperate with the squire's huntsmen, could easily destroy litters of fox cubs, and might even lay down poison for the hounds. Without the farmers 'any attempt to maintain the institution of hunting would be a long warfare in which the opposing farmer would certainly be the ultimate conqueror'.

Hunting, too, brought a touch of colour and excitement to a dull winter scene. 'A fine field of hunters in their scarlet coats, rushing over forest, heath, fence or stream, on noble steeds, and with a pack of beautiful dogs in full cry, is a very picturesque and animating spectacle', observed an early nineteenth-century enthusiast. Hunting called for some degree of horsemanship, hardiness and courage. The thrill of taking fences made the recently enclosed grasslands of the Midland counties attractive hunting country, though many experienced hunters declined ever to jump fence or hedge and made it a practice always to go round by the gate. There were many cold bleak days without a fox, when hunters and dogs returned dispirited, and in time a shortage of foxes made the substitute of the bag fox a necessity. But a true wild fox leading a long, exacting chase was something that all countrymen could enjoy, an excitement which Surtees conveyed so well:

> The hounds gain upon him, and there is nothing left but a bold
> venture up the middle, so, taking the bed of the brook, he endeavours
> to baffle his followers by the water. Now they splash after him, the
> echoing banks and yew-studded cliffs resounding to their cry. The
> dell narrows towards the west, and Mr Jorrocks rides forward to view
> him away. A countryman yoking his plough is before him, and with
> hat high in the air, 'TALLIHO's' till he's hoarse. Pigg's horn on one
> side, and Jorrocks's on the other, get the hounds out in a crack; the
> countryman mounts one of his carters, the other runs away with the

plough, and three sportsmen are as near mad as anything can possibly be. It's ding, dong, hey away pop with them all!

The fallows carry a little, but there's a rare scent, and for two miles of ill-enclosed land Reynard is scarcely a field before the hounds. Now Pigg views him! Now Jorrocks! Now Charlie! Now Pigg again! Thirty couple of hounds lengthen as they go, but there is no Pomponius Ego to tell. The fox falls back at a wall, and the hounds are in the same field. He tries again – now he's over! The hounds follow, and dash forward, but the fox has turned short up the inside of the wall, and gains a momentary respite. Now they are on him again! They view him through the gateway beyond: he rolls as he goes! Another moment, and they pull him down in the middle of a large grass field!

'Hooray! Horray! Hooray!' exclaims Mr Jorrocks, rolling off his horse, and diving into the middle of the pack, and snatching the fox, which old Thunderer resents by seizing him behind and tearing his white cords halfway down his legs. 'Hooray!' repeats he, kicking out behind, and holding the fox over his head, his linen flying out, and his enthusiastic old face all beaming with joy. (*Handley Cross*, 1854.)

When in the eighteenth century the fox supplanted the hare in hunting men's affections, the faster quarry and longer chase – sometimes extending to twenty miles or more – called for speedy thoroughbred horses and faster hounds. The first master to attempt to breed hounds specially for foxhunting was Hugo Meynell of Quorndon Hall, who in the second half of the century, hunted what later came to be called the Quorn country. A wily prey, fast riding and the hazards of fences added to the attractions of the sport. The heart of the Midlands, Leicestershire, Rutland and Northamptonshire, in par-ticular, provided the ideal conditions of rolling fields and limited areas of woodland. Hunting, with its demands on horses and time, was not a poor man's sport, and only the wealthier landowners, like the Dukes of Beaufort, Earls of Berkeley, and Thomas Assheton Smith, could afford to maintain packs of hounds and organise hunts at their own expense. When the Quorn was run privately by Sir Harry Goodricke it cost him as much as £6,000 a year – more than many gentry had as their total income. Packs of hounds might change hands for as much as £2,000, though usually less, and there was a great outlay on hunt servants and the protection of the coverts[37]. From an early date masters of foxhounds found it necessary to defray the expenses by inviting subscriptions. The first such pack was the Cheshire County Subscription Hounds established in 1746 by Sir Peter Warburton. In the nineteenth century many members of subscription hunts resided at a considerable distance, in London or the cities of the Midlands and north, and came down by train, chancing whether the weather would prove suitable to go out. Trollope held that £500 a day was about the sum a master should demand for hunting an average country, £2,000 a year if the hunt was required to go out four days a week. Even then he could expect to be out of pocket: 'To a master of foxhounds is given a place of great influence, and into his hands is confided an authority the possession of which among his fellow-sportsmen is very pleasant to him. For this he is expected to pay, and he does pay for it'[38].

With some gentry hunting, like shooting, became a predominant part of their lives. They hunted as children, hunted while at university, went down to hunts when in London, and at home were in the saddle up to six days a week. The correspondence of Francis Ferrand Foljambe illustrates the life of the sporting gentry. He hardly had time to write to friends for 'Sunday is the only writing day for gentlemen here unless it is very bad weather indeed. . . . I have shot all day and danced or played at commerce all night. . . . I had yesterday a most excellent day's hunting with Lord Darlington.' Surtees tells of a foxhunter who borrowed the first volume of one of Scott's novels, and after he had kept it a long time declined the offer of the second volume, remarking, 'By the time I get to the end, I've forgot the beginning, so I just begin over again, and it serves my purpose quite as well as a new one'[39]. Among their most regular companions were to be found the local parsons, and sometimes the master himself was a cleric. One hunting parson, when asked if Lent made any different to his sport replied: 'Certainly. Always hunt in black.' Trollope commented, 'the hunting parson generally rides hard. Unless he loved hunting much he would not be there.' When hunting ran into a deficiency of foxes, masters rented additional woodlands for coverts, and planted gorse to protect the foxes from fox-stealers. Even the celebrated lawsuit of Essex v. Capel, in which Lord Essex successfully prosecuted the Hon. and Rev. William Capel, vicar of Watford, master of the Old Berkeley Hunt, for entering and damaging his property in April 1809, gave little check to the enthusiasts. After the case a few opponents of foxhunting came forward, such as Sir William Manners who warned the Belvoir hunt off his Belvoir estate, but they were exceptional[40].

A common justification of hunting was its effect in linking landowners with townspeople, and what was called the 'democracy of the hunting field'. Incidentally it got rid of foxes, though this object was deemed insufficient to warrant the destruction of other people's property, as Essex v. Capel showed. To join in the sport, it was argued by one of the counsel in that case, 'clergymen are descending from their pulpits; bankers neglecting their counting houses; brewers running away from their breweries; tradesmen, clerks, and a variety of description of persons are all flocking from London'. In further support of the equalitarian nature of hunting, Trollope argued that on the hunting field would be found not merely country gentlemen and farmers, but 'attorneys, country bankers, doctors, apothecaries, maltsters, millers, butchers, bakers, innkeepers, auctioneers, graziers, builders . . . stockbrokers, newspaper editors, artists and sailors'[41]. But sportsmen of the old county families regarded themselves as superior to these new recruits: when a hunt caused damage to people's hedges or private grounds they tended to blame the 'damned stockbrokers', who, they said, could not control their horses. Nevertheless, remarked F. E. Green, the lust of sport had inspired a certain arrogance among the country gentry, and he quoted the example of a notice board placed on the roadside near a village school: 'Please drive cautiously. Hound puppies are at walk in Greywell village'[42].

Squire and villagers

Fortunately for the strength of good feeling in the countryside not all the squire's money went in guns and cartridges, thoroughbred hunters and subscriptions to foxhounds. Many owners kept up the tradition of annual feasts for the tenants on the squire's birthday, when his son came of age, and other special occasions. The practice was often extended to the workers at collieries, iron-works and other enterprises which were part of the estate. Frequently the squire modernised cottages, helped establish a school and encouraged village friendly societies. Sometimes he presented the village with a football ground or cricket field and organised the matches. In the village of South Rauceby, Lincolnshire, the Willson family, whose property dominated the village from the 1840s on, were mainly responsible for providing the school. They also built a waterworks, provided a reading room, supported the Sunday school, and held social func-tions in their grounds in support of the church [43]. It is interesting that in 1861 predominantly agricultural counties, such as Wiltshire, Westmorland, Oxford-shire, Rutland, Essex and Dorset, had the highest proportion of registered school children, while the industrialised and urbanised counties were amongst those with the lowest figures. Of course, the population of the latter had grown much more rapidly, but it seems that in rural counties there was a greater voluntary effort to meet the need for more schools, with the greater gentry rather than the aristocracy or small squires taking the lead. The greatest burden of providing village education, however, fell on the poorly paid parents who met the weekly fees for their children's attendance, and on the local clergyman who usually acted as the school's manager, treasurer and super-numerary schoolmaster [44]. Parsons, especially when they were large pro-prietors, often did much for the village. Prebendary Stephenson, for example, rector and principal owner at Lympston, Somerset, from 1844 to 1901, rebuilt the village in neo-Gothic style. At North Tuddenham in Norfolk the rector spent over £5,000 of his money on the church, rectory and parish schools. If they did not do more it was often because their view of the provision necessary for the working classes was a limited one. There would have been wide agree-ment with the sentiment expressed by an inscription on a school at Shalbourne in Wiltshire: 'A.D. 1843 – This school was built for the purpose of giving a bible education to the Children of the Poor' [45].

Generally the sums spent by the gentry on improving village life were small in relation to the amounts allocated to private entertaining, travel and sport. In the later nineteenth century, when rents were falling, a great many country gentlemen had to draw in their horns in all directions. Not only did the village suffer, but their town houses and sometimes, a greater blow, the family home, had to go. The labour on which such houses were so heavily dependent became more costly, especially so after 1914 when labour costs rose by more than half in twenty years. Professor Thompson's investigations indicate that between the great depression and the mid-twentieth century only a third of the gentry families in Essex, Oxford and Shropshire remained in possession of their country seats. Another quarter had sold their seats and moved to smaller homes, to London, or to the colonies [46]. Some of these vacant country houses were bought by new gentry families. Others, too decrepit or costly to attract a purchaser, were eventually demolished. A number came finally into the hands of the National Trust. The remainder were turned into private schools, nursing homes, centres for the handicapped, government research and training establishments, offices and flats. Where the gentry survived with their home intact it was often through judicious redistribution of assets, new non-agricultural sources of income, or success in commercial farming. Not a few estates came to be run strictly as businesses, taking full advantage of advances in scientific farming, the benefits of markets regulated by marketing boards, and the support of subsidies provided by the state. Some such gentry have become leading figures in the growth of large-scale specialised farming and cooperative marketing organisations which have characterised the English rural scene in recent decades.

Nevertheless, many have still found time to play their part in affairs through county and rural district councils, hospital boards, university councils, school governors, preservation societies and a variety of other organisations. Their children have entered widely into the arts, as well as into the expanded professions, public administration and enterprises in the Commonwealth. As a reviewer of the eighteenth edition of *Burke's Landed Gentry* recently remarked, the impression conveyed 'is certainly not one of ineffective or worn-out stock. At one end of the scale (from a twelfth-century family) is the chairman of the Atomic Energy Authority, at the other, the current Miss United Kingdom.'

'The peaceful surrender of power'

In relation to the industrialisation of this country a distinguished historian has remarked:

An economic transformation on this scale could not fail to have profound repercussions on the balance of social and political forces, and the fact that this readjustment was carried through peacefully and, indeed, under the direction of the leaders of a social class now entering upon its decline, is one of the most remarkable political phenomena of the age[47].

The phenomenon to which he drew attention was indeed remarkable. In the mid-nineteenth century, with the industrialisation and urbanisation of the country in full spate, the landed interest still held on to the political reins, though the economic power that sustained their grasp was crumbling. The aims of the reform of 1832 were essentially conservative: to abolish irresponsible pocket boroughs and enhance the 'legitimate influence' of the landowners in their counties. The Act was not intended to bring about a revolution, but to adjust the old forms of political power to new circumstances. And no revolution was required to transform the country into the democracy of 1883 and after. The steps, though not imperceptible, were gradual and progressive. The measured retreat of the landed interest owed something, no doubt, to the lack of a centrally controlled police and the smallness of the standing army. Political leaders, as Professor Thompson has commented, 'were sensible enough to realise that they could not risk a head-on collision with the new forces, whether of the middle class or of the democracy, if only because in the last resort the established order did not dispose of sufficient physical force to resist determined and united attacks'[48]. He goes on to point out that the quality of political leadership was one important reason for the peaceful passing of landed power, while the existence of a reform wing within the landed interest was another. Further, the ability of landed society to absorb members of other classes 'must be accounted a prime reason for the failure of the cleavage between capitalists and land-owners to become so deep as to be unbridgeable'. As right of property ceased to justify the landowners' control of power, their influence rested increasingly on voluntary deference, on recognition that England's landed class was 'essentially liberal-minded' [49]. At the same time the middle-class attack on the landed interest, which after Corn Law repeal took the form of demanding 'free trade in land', could not be pressed home. For one thing, aristocratic control of land was less restrictive than was supposed; for another, an attack on landed property, as distinct from the duties which protected landed incomes, had dangerous implications when a propertyless class was in course of obtaining the franchise.

So, the historian of these changes concludes, the most important service of the landed interest has been 'the peaceful surrender of power' [50]. In the preceding centuries the landed classes had been privileged to enjoy both great power and great wealth. On occasion both were misused in seeking selfish and shortsighted ends. But over the long span of time it is clear that the landed class, of whom the gentry formed the core, provided the country with leadership that in general was enlightened and progressive. It is highly significant that the first industrial revolution occurred in a country ruled by this landed class, a class which had long considered land as an agent of production and not merely as a source of feudal power and social prestige. And the growth of industry itself owed not a little to their energy and enterprise. Modern England developed not in spite of the landowners, but with them, and through them.

7 Conclusion

The historical importance of the gentry is not related to their numbers, which always made up but a tiny proportion of the total population, even in the countryside; nor is it related to their social eminence, for less than one in ten bore any kind of title, while that titled minority enjoyed no special privileges of rank. The great majority of gentry were indeed undistinguished people, living out an obscure career within a severely circumscribed environment. The gentry's importance derived essentially from their ownership of land, the principal form of wealth and greatest source of political power until very recent times. From the sixteenth century the gentry acquired a hold on about half the territory of England, leaving the Crown, the Church, the great owners and the yeoman freeholders to share the other half between them. The great factor in the gentry's dominating position was their success in finding advantage in the major turning points and trends of modern history – the Reformation, the economic and political decline of the Crown, the gradual expansion of the economy, and even the early stages of the machine age. With this success they achieved economic and political independence of the Crown and great lords, while the position of the gentry as the dominating middle element in the hierarchy of landowners conferred on them the real power in county government. It is true that after the Restoration it was the great landowners who came to control Westminster and the central administration, and who acquired an enduring hold on the sources of patronage. Nevertheless, secure in their provincial base of the county, the gentry remained a force to be reckoned with, and an indispensable arm of justice and government.

It is misleading to write as if the gentry formed a homogeneous and uniform social group. Indeed, elaborate historical theses have been founded on the opposite assumption – that they were hopelessly divided into conflicting elements: 'rising' and 'declining' gentry; 'court' and 'mere' gentry. It seems more realistic to emphasise the common bond of interests forged by ownership of landed property and an appreciation of its advantages and responsibilities and to observe the powerful influence of a common educational background in establishing a pervasive cultural link between the various levels of landed society. Thus in matters concerning rents and farming, the security of property and the stability of the country, enjoyment of country life and a care for the distressed and poor, the greatest of dukes and the most modest of country gentlemen generally thought and spoke in almost identical terms. Naturally, the great differences in wealth and influence that existed within the ranks of landowners made for an acute awareness of status within the hierarchy: deference was necessarily shown to social superiors, but it was a deference rendered freely, and only rarely grudged or tinged with servility. The small country gentleman had as much pride in his own lineage and his status 'in his country', and perhaps more, than had the duke in his. When he described himself as 'a plain country squire' he meant to convey in a phrase the idea of a certain style of living and an assured social position, not mere modesty. Such a 'plain country squire' once welcomed a visit from Lord Berkeley and other important figures by asking 'Pray let me have a day or two before that I may be ready to give you the best reception (I mean without ceremony) I am able' – a request that smacks more of pride than humility[1].

The independence of the country gentleman sprang in part from the independence of his means. He was no official looking to his salary nor a tradesman concerned for his custom. His estate might be modest and his income much reduced by family settlements, and the protection of his property might well involve him in disputes and lawsuits with more powerful neighbours. But in so far as his land was unencumbered and his title clear, it was his to use as he wished. Secure in his own private property the squire enjoyed as much independence as did the greatest lord. Further, within his own more limited 'country' he was nearly as influential. He was a member of the propertied class and hence of the ruling class. He participated therefore, if only in some very minor degree, in that comprehensive apparatus of political, legal, religious and cultural control which has been discussed in earlier pages. The regulatory and paternalistic powers of the landowners long survived the decay of feudalism – indeed at this very time the representatives of the agricultural workers complain of the survival of 'feudal relationships' in the countryside.

What is often meant here is the prevalence of tied cottages, the face-to-face relationship of employer and employee instead of the impersonal character of the factory, and the social division between the farmer and farmworker, a division which has been emphasised by the middle-class invasion of many villages. But generally little remains of the paternalism which marked landowners' efforts to improve village housing and amenities in the later nineteenth century. Too often these efforts were accompanied by an excessive concern for the villagers' morality and sobriety. Landlords' estate villages usually avoided the worst evils of unhealthy overcrowding, disrepair, damp, and the degrading 'bucket system' of sanitation. Estate housing was customarily well built and well maintained, and the village might boast a meeting room or hall, as well as street lighting and a school. But, as Seebohm Rowntree remarked, although

> from a material point of view the labourer directly or indirectly under the sway of some paternal if autocratic landed proprietor is better off than the labourer in some 'independent' village . . . [there is] the danger that the individual himself may become part of the estate. And this danger is often realised keenly. We repeatedly found villages in which the farms were poor, the work was precarious, and everything had a forlorn and 'out-at-elbows' aspect, glorying in their superiority over some adjacent village who inhabitants were better housed and better fed but 'couldn't call their souls their own'[2].

Not long after Rowntree wrote these words, however, the great majority of paternal landlords were obliged by economic circumstances finally to abandon their role of village improvers and mentors. The village was left to the farmers, their labourers, the new middle-class residents, and the paternalism of White-hall and the county councils. With migration of labourers from the countryside and growing scarcity of farm labour their lot has improved, but they remain labourers and not landholders. The old idea among them that the land was 'sent for the poor to live off' – was 'God's land, not the farmers' ' – seems to have disappeared with the acceptance of an unashamedly capitalist society in the countryside.

The relationships which existed between squire and farmer down to the nineteenth century were indeed feudal in one sense, since unrevised farm leases continued to specify the tenant's responsibility for performing carriage and other services for the landlord, gifts of capons at Christmas, eggs at Easter, and so forth. But by the eighteenth century these survivals, more often than not, had been commuted into cash payments. Numbers of manorial courts, too, continued into the nineteenth century, though only as shadows of their former selves. From the seventeenth century onwards they had lost most of their judicial functions to the king's courts, and their administrative powers to the justices or to new statutory bodies. Their one remaining role of significance, as regulator of communal husbandry, disappeared with the abolition of common fields, meadows and commons, so that by the 1820s most courts had fallen into disuse or existed only as curious and unimportant survivals. More real was the enduring common bond of interest which permeated the landlord–tenant relationship. A good landlord and a good tenant shared the same objectives of making farming efficient and profitable. With the acceptance of a clear if varying distinction between the capital and function of the landlord and those of the tenant there developed a sense of mutual trust and confidence. The land-lord recognised that the farmer could not prosper unless his farmhouse and barns were adequate to the purpose, his access to market easy, and his land protected from floods and other dangers. The tenant knew that if he stocked the land sufficiently, farmed competently and observed his covenants he had every reason to look forward to undisturbed possession. Furthermore, if times proved difficult the tenant hit by bad seasons or low prices could look to the squire for an abatement of rent, some additional spending on improvements to the farm, or even some help with his normal outgoings, his rates and husbandry expenses. The landlord looked after a good tenant because he wanted to keep his land well tenanted; equally, the tenant performed his part because he valued a good bargain and wanted to continue in occupation.

Security of tenure pertained in these circumstances even when the tenant had no lease and farmed the land by an annual agreement. By the eighteenth century the majority of small tenants were on this apparently insecure form of tenure, but this did not prevent many of them from holding their farms for generation after generation. This was not because small tenants were not easily replaced: in fact it was the bigger farms that landlords found difficulty in tenanting because of the considerable amount of capital required to stock them. In consequence large farms were usually let on long leases. For the annual tenants of small farms the landlord–tenant relationship was a social as well as a business understanding. The landlord saw it as part of his social role to protect his tenants, and his personal reputation and local popularity – which he valued – suffered if he failed in his responsibility. For their part the tenants understood that they were perfectly secure so long as they farmed reasonably, paid their rents, showed the respect to the landlord and his family that was customarily expected, and turned out to vote when required. Of course, it can be said that the relationship was an aristocratic, almost feudal, one. But the age before the nineteenth century was not one of democracy and there was no general belief in equality: it was a relationship which made sense when land-ownership was the principal base of power and wealth, and the small husband-man lived on the brink of poverty, always liable to be pushed over it by any harvest failure or loss of stock that happened to come along.

The traditional paternalism extended beyond the tenants, of course, to embrace the house servants, village craftsmen and the poor. The landlord recognised that his responsibilities extended to the wider rural community and were not limited by the boundaries of his estate. The effectiveness of his role varied, however, with the share of the land that he owned and the nature of the village community. Where the village was dominated by small owner-occupiers and tradesmen, and there was a large element of industrial workers, the land-lord's influence might indeed be slight. Villages of this kind showed a spirit of independence which was often reflected in their politics and their religious nonconformity. Further, some of the larger owners and new arrivals in county society neglected their responsibilities through prolonged absenteeism. As it became more fashionable in the later seventeenth and eighteenth centuries to visit London for the season and travel abroad, and as attendance at Parliament and the court, or army commissions and colonial governorships, took pro-prietors away from home for protracted periods, so absenteeism weakened the old relationship between the squire and the local community.

Another weakening influence was the growing importance in the economy of trade and industry. One of the great advantages resulting from the English landowners' early acquisition of freehold rights over the land was their freedom to exploit it for private industrial and commercial purposes as well as for agriculture: for timber, stone, coal, iron, canal-building and the rest. It was also the landowners, not the Crown, who gained the right to make the best use of commons and wastes. And the initiative and flexibility shown by land-owners in exploiting their rights enabled them to increase their own incomes while tapping unused resources and advancing their local economy. Land-owners worked in harmony with merchants and industrialists in the furthering of their common interests, and this application of landed enterprise and capital to wider ends was one of the factors which made possible the long acceptance by the middle classes of the landowners' political dominance. In the eighteenth century, however, the enterprise of landowners was gradually eclipsed by the widening activities of merchants and industrialists. Already in the Birmingham of 1783, according to the contemporary estimates of William Hutton, three leading citizens could boast of fortunes exceeding £100,000; a further seven Birmingham citizens had over £50,000, while the average wealth of the 115 wealthiest worked out at over £17,000. These figures put the 115 Birmingham citizens on a par with the minor landed gentry – their equivalent was a proprietor of some 800 acres enjoying a rent of some £600 a year. As late as 1850 there were across the whole country still less than 2,000 businessmen whose profits equalled the income of at least £3,000 a year enjoyed by some 2,500 of the large landed proprietors. By 1880 the situation had changed: there were then more than 5,000 businessmen with profits of over £3,000, while in numbers and incomes the very wealthiest businessmen and greatest landowners were broadly comparable [3].

With the successful rivalry of business wealth came certain changes in landed society. Mill argued that the country gentleman of his day had become 'an administrator and a scientific man'; the aristocratic dilettante, connoisseur or collector of former times had become 'the careful and informed manager of landed property' [4]. As the changes which Mill noticed became widespread, the old paternal relationships in the village declined. The growing numbers of the poor and the partial industrialisation of much of the countryside weakened old habits and traditional ideas. Landowners became more practical, more calculating, in their attitudes to their estates and to the communities based on them. Cobbett undoubtedly romanticised the England of his youth as he exaggerated the changes that were evident in the countryside of his maturity, but he was not entirely mistaken in his awareness of a greater commercialism, a disregard of distress, and a harsh callousness in the actions of some landed gentry. Face to face with the misery of underpaid and oppressed labourers, he inveighed against

> the baseness of the English land-owners. . . . It was their duty to stand forward and prevent Power-of-Imprisonment Bills, Six-Acts, Ellenborough's Act, Poaching Transportation Act, New Trespass Act, Sunday Tolls, and the hundred of other things that could be named. On the contrary *they were the cause of them all.* They were the cause of all the taxes and all the debts; and now let them take the consequences!

At Reigate in 1825 he attended a farm auction, an occasion which made him reflect on the change in manners of country gentlemen, their pretensions to high living, and the consequent decay in the old practice of boarding the farm labourers in the farmhouse:

> This, Squire Charington's father used, I dare say, to sit at the head of the oak-table along with his men, say grace to them, and cut up the meat and the pudding. He might take a cup of *strong beer* to himself, when they had none; but that was pretty nearly all the difference in their manner of living. So that *all* lived well. But the '*squire* had many *wine-decanters* and *wine-glasses* and '*a dinner set*,' and a '*breakfast set*,' and '*dessert knives*;' and these evidently imply carryings on and a consumption that must of necessity have greatly robbed the long oak table if it had remained fully tenanted. That long table could not share in the work of the decanters and the dinner set. Therefore, it became almost untenanted; the labourers retreated to hovels, called cottages; and instead of board and lodging, they got money; so little of it as to enable the employer to drink wine; but, then, that he might not reduce them to *quite starvation*, they were enabled to come to him, in the *king's name*, and demand food *as paupers*. . . . Why do not farmers now *feed* and *lodge* their work-people, as they did formerly? Because they cannot keep them *upon so little* as they give them in wages [5].

Professor Perkin has recently argued that the landowners' abdication of their old paternal responsibilities began with the early exploitation of the industrial potentialities of their estates: they 'sold their souls to economic development long before the Industrial Revolution'. The adoption of laissez-faire attitudes towards individual freedom and commercial enterprise, he says, inevitably weakened their social paternalism, and the rise of industrialisation which they encouraged eventually undermined their economic supremacy over the middle classes. Nevertheless, they managed to retain political power, but in doing so neglected the responsibilities that went with it. The turning point came with the Napoleonic Wars and their refusal as justices to set minimum wages under the old Elizabethan code, while at the same time attacking the combinations by which workmen sought to protect their living standards. The highly protective Corn Law of 1815, the new harshness of the Game Laws, and the postwar attack on the Old Poor Law reflected a selfish concern with their own immediate interests at the expense of the other classes in society and fostered a new spirit of antagonism towards the landed interest on the part of the middle and working classes [6].

The basic factor in bringing about this situation, however, was not that landowners had sold their souls to economic exploitation but that the forces of industrialisation had got out of hand. When London was the only really large centre of trade and industry, and much of the country's industrial activity was under the control of the landowners, there was no very serious conflict between industrial growth and the traditional society. The more rapid process of change that set in towards the end of the eighteenth century, however, soon went beyond the limits of estate exploitation. The new upsurge of industrialisation was accompanied by an unprecedented rise of population that doubled the size of some industrial towns within a generation and completely changed the character of many rural communities. Problems developed of a magnitude never before encountered: slumps and concentrated mass unemployment, widespread unrest and violence, and poverty on an entirely new scale. And all these problems were aggravated by the strains of war, the disastrous seasons of the Napoleonic era, and a system of government that while suited well enough to a smaller, more agrarian society proved increasingly inadequate for dealing with the emergence of the newly urbanised masses. Swayed by fears of Jacobinism, pushed in conflicting directions by opposed philosophies of politics and economics, the landowners made but a poor job of steering the country through the uncharted perils of the early nineteenth century. In the face of the strange and apparently insoluble difficulties many resorted to the first principles of the old society they understood: the strict maintenance of law and order and the protection of private property. Their conduct may be interpreted as an abdication of responsibility, but it really reflected the bewildered inadequacy felt by the older agrarian order before the mounting manifestations of the new industrial society.

There was in consequence a division of the ranks. Some landowners adapted themselves to the new conditions by joining the ranks of industrialists, by supporting radical commercial policies and by showing a more businesslike attitude towards the management of their estates; others, like the so-called Tory Radicals, reverted to the old paternalism, and attempted to deal with the evils of the new industry by proposing Factory Bills and suggesting wage-fixing to be carried out by new representative bodies. Meanwhile literary Tories, such as Scott, Wordsworth and Southey, attacked the degradation of the new factory servitude – an attack that was widely extended by other eminent writers of the age, Shelley, Coleridge, Carlyle, Kingsley, the Brontës, Dickens and Disraeli. The transfer of industry from the rural mills and villages of hand-workers to great establishments in the towns had sapped the moral responsibility of the employer for his workpeople, argued Scott: now 'a man may assemble 500 workmen one day and dismiss them the next, without having any further connection with them than to receive a week's work for a week's wages, nor any other solicitude about them than if they were so many shuttles'. Wordsworth saw the ties keeping the different classes in society 'in a vital and harmonious dependence . . . greatly impaired or wholly dissolved. Everything has been put up to market and sold for the highest price it would buy.' In the landowners' own private domain the old relationship between landlord and tenant deteriorated as farming became more market-oriented, more large-scale, and more scientific and capital-intensive. And as the ultimate blow, landownership itself became less profitable. Even in the 'golden age' of the mid-nineteenth century rents failed to rise sufficiently to compensate the landlords for their heavy investment in drainage and buildings, and then there followed the great depression in arable farming and the increased fiscal burdens laid on property in the twentieth century.

Yet despite the loss of political and economic supremacy and the levelling tendencies of an insurgent democracy, the English aristocracy managed to retain a certain eminence even in the new industrial society. Unlike the exclusive noble castes of the continent the English aristocracy was broadly based on inherited wealth and was open to newcomers from all levels of society; hence, as de Tocqueville pointed out, it could never arouse the violent hatreds felt by the middle and lower classes towards the French nobility. The truth was that industrialisation, in demolishing the supremacy of land had set beside it another, greater form of wealth. But it was wealth still, and the attack of the middle classes on the old political power of the landowners stopped short of attacking landed property itself – for from that it might be only a short step to the sharing of all wealth, not merely that represented by land. Tell an English-man that the only sure way to destroy the aristocracy is to change the law of inheritance, exclaimed de Tocqueville, 'and he will draw back at once. I have not yet met one person who did not seem frightened of such an idea'.

> So, too, if you speak to a member of the middle classes; you will find he hates some aristocrats but not the aristocracy. On the contrary he himself is full of aristocratic prejudices. He deeply distrusts the people; he loves noise, territorial possessions, carriages: he lives in the hope of attaining all this by means of the democratic varnish with which he covers himself, and meanwhile gives a livery to his one servant whom he calls a footman, talks of his dealing with the Duke of ——, and his very distant family links with the house of another noble Lord[7].

Even among the English aristocracy, however, there was a strong sense of natural pre-eminence, and sometimes a hint of the idea that their position in society might be divinely ordained. Not a few would have agreed with the sentiments of a sermon preached in 1854 by William Sewell, headmaster of Radley:

> A gentleman, then, and a Christian, whether boy or man, both knows and is thankful that God, instead of making all men equal, has made

them all most unequal. . . . Hereditary rank, nobility of blood, is the very first condition and essence of all our Christian privileges; and woe to the nation, or the man by whom such a principle is disdained, who will honour no one except for his own merits and his own deeds. . . . Noblemen like Christians are to be the salt of the earth.' [8]

The lower orders existed to administer to the needs of gentlemen and perform the menial, laborious and unpleasant tasks of life, a view that was well expressed by a friend of George Lucy of Charlecote, an eighteenth-century country gentleman: he sent Lucy some powders for his health and suggested that 'as you may be fearful, please let any of your servants take a dose first' [9]. Nevertheless, despite their arrogance and conceit the gentry performed a valuable, not to say indispensable, function in English society. By filling the gap between the nobility and the inferior orders of people with a graduated progression of middle ranks and middle levels of wealth, they prevented the emergence of a dangerous fissure between governors and governed, a situation which enabled England to avoid the violent eruptions of the more caste-ridden nations of Europe. Unlike the continental aristocracies, too, the gentry enjoyed no exceptional privileges, and before the law and in matters of taxation they had no special rights or exemptions; their administration of justice and local government, some lapses apart, was reasonably fair and conscientious; they managed their estates with some degree of efficiency and showed a progressive spirit in the development of the country's resources; their links with industry, commerce and the professions made for a span of sympathies and interests that allowed rule by landowners to remain acceptable well into the industrial age; and, not least, their humanity and concern for the community at large kept in being a respect for their status which arose spontaneously, and was not merely a hangover from a feudal past.

Despite the breadth of their economic interests, the English gentry remained essentially land-based, agrarian, most at home in the life of a countryside they loved. Contrary to the ill-informed historical generalisations of sociologists, in England it was not the city that dominated the countryside but the countryside that dominated the city [10]. It was in the mansion-houses of the gentry, not the market towns, that political decisions were taken, economic projects planned, the local community governed, and the cultural life of the age flourished. And the very permanence of the country house itself, its ancient halls studded by darkening ancestral portraits, instilled the sense of continuity and stability that was so strong an element in the squirearchy. In the end the agrarian society they controlled was swamped by the irresistible flood of industrialism. By the later nineteenth century the gentry were economically, socially and politically in retreat. But they survived. As one writer has put it:

They did not understand the new ways of life, but they had unlimited experience of governing. They were not efficient, but, then, many of them worked for nothing! They were not always very industrious, but what they did was all to the good, for they had nothing else to do. In short, tradition gave them an influence over all England, which accepted the notion that they were born to govern; it endowed them with a collective experience, handed on from father to son; it supplied them with an attitude of mastery, an easy self-assurance which in itself gave them an enormous advantage over any competitors [11].

In the twentieth century the gentry have as ever proved adaptable to changed circumstances. The development of a highly commercial, subsidised agriculture, the expansion of modern business and the proliferation of professions, have further diminished their position in society but at the same time have provided them with a new lease of life. They have trimmed their sails to the diverse winds of modern industrial democracy and survived, clinging on to at least some portion of their ancestral homes and estates. The forces of continuity have proved still to be strong, and the modern country gentleman might still like to echo the words written by Sir John Oglander to his son more than three hundred years ago: 'We have kept this spot of ground this five hundred years from father to son, and I pray God thou beest not the last, nor see that scattered which so many have taken care to gain for thee' [12].

Notes and references

Chapter 1   *Who were the gentry?*

1   Quoted by H. A. Lloyd, *The Gentry of South-West Wales 1540–1640*, Univ. of Wales Press, 1968, p. 17.

2   Lawrence Stone, *The Crisis of the Aristocracy*, Oxford U.P., 1965, pp. 71–92, 93–5.

3   R. H. Tawney, 'The rise of the gentry,' *Economic History Review*, xi (1941), 4.

4   J. H. Plumb, *Sir Robert Walpole: the making of a statesman*, Cresset Press, 1956, p. 26.

5   P. Zagorin, *The Court and the Country: the beginning of the English Revolution*, Routledge, 1969, p. 27; Alfred Plummer, *The London Weavers Company 1600–1970*, Routledge, 1972, p. 83.

6   David Mathew, *The Social Structure in Caroline England*, Oxford U.P., 1948, pp. 40–1.

7   P. R. Roberts, 'The Landed Gentry of Merioneth *c*.1660–1832', unpubl. M.A. thesis, University of Wales, 1963.

8   William Lambarde, *Perambulation of Kent*, 1576, p. 10.

9   Alan D. Dyer, *The City of Worcester in the Sixteenth Century*, Leicester U.P., 1973, pp. 186–7; Lawrence Stone, *An Elizabethan: Sir Horatio Palavicino*, Oxford U.P., 1956.

10   Gordon Jackson, *Hull in the Eighteenth Century*, Univ. of Hull Publications, Oxford U.P., 1972, pp. 104–5, 112–15.

11   See Dean Rapp, 'Social mobility in the eighteenth century: the Whitbreads of Bedfordshire, 1720–1815', *Econ. Hist. Rev.*, xxvii (1974), 380–94; R. G. Lang, 'Social origins and social aspirations of Jacobean London merchants', *ibid.*, pp. 28–47.

12   Joyce Godber, *History of Bedfordshire 1066–1888*, Beds. C.C., 1969, p. 143.

13   Derek Wilson, *A Tudor Tapestry*, Heinemann, 1972, p. 10.

14   L. Stone and J. C. F. Stone, 'Country houses and their owners in Hertfordshire, 1540–1879', in W. O. Aydelotte, A. G. Bogue and R. W. Fogel, eds, *The Dimensions of Quantitative Research in History*, Princeton U.P., 1972, p. 59.

15   S. C. Newton, 'The gentry of Derbyshire in the seventeenth century', *Derbys. Arch. Jnl* (1966), p. 3.

16   J. H. Gleason, *The Justice of the Peace in England 1558–1640*, Oxford U.P., 1912, p. 264.

17   D. C. Coleman, ' "The gentry" controversy and the aristocracy in crisis 1558–1641', *History* li (1966), p. 172.

18   See Alan Everitt, *Change in the Provinces: the seventeenth century*, Leicester U.P., 1969, pp. 19, 55.

19   Calais: a reference to the sixty new knights created by the Earl of Essex in his campaign against Calais, 1596.

20   J. T. Cliffe, 'The Yorkshire Gentry on the Eve of the Civil War', unpublished Ph.D. thesis, University of London, 1960, p. 5.

21   F. M. L. Thompson, *English Landed Society in the Nineteenth Century*, Routledge, 1963, p. 113.

22   Daniel Defoe, *A Tour through England and Wales*, Dent, (Everyman's Library), 1928, i, 15.

Chapter 2   *The emergence of the gentry*

1   R. H. Hilton, *A Medieval Society: the West Midlands at the end of the thirteenth century*, Weidenfeld & Nicolson, 1966, pp. 50, 53, 55–6.

2   A. W. B. Simpson, *An Introduction to the History of the Land Law*, Oxford U.P., 1961, p. 48; J. M. W. Bean, *The Decline of English Feudalism 1215–1540*, Manchester U.P., 1968, pp. 29–31, 101, 153.

3   D. M. Stenton, *English Society in the Early Middle Ages*, Penguin, 2nd ed., 1952, pp. 65–7.

4   Hilton, p. 230.

5   Georges Duby, *Rural Economy and Country Life in the Medieval West*, English trans., E. Arnold, 1968, p. 186.

6   Joyce Godber, *History of Bedfordshire, 1066–1886*, Beds. C.C., 1969, p. 84.

7   R. H. Hilton, *The Economic Development of Some Leicestershire Estates in the Fourteenth and Fifteenth Centuries*, Oxford U.P., 1947, p. 15.

8   Duby, p. 331.

9   See F. R. H. Du Boulay, 'Who were farming the English demesnes at the end of the Middle Ages?', *Econ. Hist. Rev.*, 2nd ser. xvii (1964), 443–55; Barbara Harvey, 'The leasing of the Abbot of Westminster's demesnes in the later Middle Ages', *ibid.*, xxii (1969), 20–1.

10   N. Denholm-Young, *The Country Gentry in the Fourteenth Century*, Oxford U.P., 1969, pp. 4–5, 23–4.

11   See W. A. Morris, *The Medieval English Sheriff to 1300*, Manchester U.P., 1927.

12   See R. F. Hunnisett, *The Medieval Coroner*, Cambridge U.P., 1961.

13   May McKisack, *The Fourteenth Century*, Oxford U.P., 1959, p. 189.

14   Godber, p. 79.

15   Denholm-Young, pp. 60, 66–8.

16   A. R. Myers, *England in the Late Middle Ages*, rev. edn, Penguin (Pelican History of England) 1956, pp. 194–6.

17   Hilton, *Medieval Society*, pp. 253–8.

18   T. B. Pugh, in S. B. Chrimes, C. D. Ross and R. A. Griffiths, eds *Fifteenth-Century England*, Manchester U.P., 1972, p. 107.

19   Myers, *op. cit.*, pp. 34–5, 122, 209.

20   Hilton, *Economic Development*, p. 4.

21   A. Hamilton Thompson, 'The English house', in Geoffrey Barraclough,

ed., *Social Life in Early England*, Routledge, 1960, pp. 140, 143, 145, 150–1.
22 L. F. Salzman, *English Life in the Middle Ages*, Oxford U.P., 1926, pp. 94–5.
23 Hamilton Thompson, p. 161.
24 Salzman, pp. 104–7.
25 *Ibid.*, pp. 96–8.
26 A. L. Poole, ed., *Medieval England*, 2 vols, Oxford U.P., i, 625–31.
27 Godber, p. 181.
28 *Ibid.*, pp. 611–13.
29 H. S. Bennett, *Life on the English Manor*, Cambridge U.P., 1960, p. 29.
30 C. G. Coulton, *The Medieval Scene*, Cambridge U.P., 1959, pp. 44–5.
31 Bennett, p. 32.
32 *Ibid.*, pp. 332–3.
33 Salzman, p. 112.
34 Bennett, pp. 329–31.

Chapter 3 *The rise and decline of the gentry*

1 Mathew *The Social Structures in Caroline England*, p. 3.
2 Ruth Hughey, *John Harington of Stepney: Tudor gentleman*, Ohio State U.P., 1972.
3 F. R. H. Du Boulay, 'Who were farming the English demesnes at the end of the Civil War?', *Econ. Hist. Rev.*, 2nd ser. xvii (1964–65), 452–3.
4 W. G. Hoskins, *Old Devon*, David & Charles, 1966, pp. 98–110.
5 See Eric Kerridge, *Agrarian Problems in the Sixteenth Century and After*, Allen & Unwin, 1969, pp. 125, 128.
6 *Ibid.* pp. 37–9.
7 Quoted by Joan Thirsk and J. P. Cooper, eds, *Seventeenth-century Economic Documents*, Oxford U.P., 1972, p. 143.
8 See M. E. Finch, *Five Northamptonshire Families 1540–1640*, Northants. Record Soc., xx, 1956.
9 Sidney Pollard and D. W. Crossley, *The Wealth of Britain 1085–1966*, Batsford, 1968, p. 97.
10 M. D. G. Wanklyn, 'John Weld of Willey 1585–1665', *West Midland Studies*, iii (1970), 88–99.
11 R. B. Smith, 'A Study of Landed Income and Social Structure in the West Riding of Yorkshire, 1535–46', Univ. of Leeds, unpublished Ph.D. thesis, 1962, pp. 143, 175–6.
12 See Alan Simpson, *The Wealth of the Gentry*, Cambridge U.P., 1961.
13 A. R. Maddison, 'Lincolnshire gentry in the sixteenth century', *Associated Architectural Society's Reports and Papers* (1893–94), pp. 205–10; Derek Wilson, *A Tudor Tapestry*, Heinemann, 1972, pp. 62, 67, 151–2.
14 T. H. Swales, 'The redistribution of the monastic lands in Norfolk at the Dissolution', *Norfolk Archaeology*, xxxiv, 1 (1966), 17, 23–33, 38.
15 *Ibid.*, p. 43.
16 J. E. Mousley, 'The fortunes of some gentry families of Elizabethan Sussex', *Econ. Hist. Rev.*, 2nd ser. xi (1958–59), 476–8.
17 A. J. Slavin, *Politics and Profit: a study of Sir Ralph Sadler 1507–1547*,

Cambridge U.P., 1966, p. 186; G. E. Aylmer, *The King's Servants: the civil service of Charles I 1625–1642*, Routledge, 1961, p. 314.

18 *Instructions to a Son* (written in 1660).

19 See Lawrence Stone, *The Causes of the English Revolution 1529–1642*, Routledge, 1972, pp. 84, 92, 95, 116.

20 *The Gentry, 1540–1640*, Supplement No. 1 to *Econ. Hist. Rev.*, 1953.

21 See ch. 1, n. 3.

22 *The Gentry*, p. 43.

23 'The general crisis of the seventeenth century', *Past and Present* xvi (1967), pp. 60–2.

24 J. P. Cooper, 'The Counting of Manors', *Economic History Review* 2nd ser. viii, **3** (1956), 377–85.

25 J. H. Hexter, 'Storm over the Gentry', in *Reappraisals in History* (Longmans, 1961), pp. 143–8.

26 L. Stone, *Social Change and Revolution in England 1540–1640*, Longmans, 1965, pp. 77–8.

27 Stone, *Causes of the English Revolution*, pp. 116–17.

28 Aylmer, p. 246.

29 Martin J. Havran, *Caroline Courtier: the life of Lord Cottington*, Macmillan, 1973.

30 J. T. Cliffe, *The Yorkshire Gentry from the Reformation to the Civil War*, Athlone Press, 1969, p. 360.

31 F. Bamford, ed., *A Royalist's Notebook, the Commonplace Book of Sir John Oglander of Nunwell 1622–1652*, Constable, 1936, p. 75.

32 Perez Zagorin, *The Court and the Country: the beginning of the English Revolution*, Routledge, 1969, pp. 75, 90.

33 See the summary of evidence on rent movements in Joan Thirsk, ed., *The Agrarian History of England and Wales*, Cambridge U.P., 1967, iv, 690–1, where it is remarked that on estates in a variety of areas 'a doubling or trebling of rent receipts in the half century or so preceding the Civil War was by no means exceptional'.

34 Cliffe, ch. 6, 10.

35 Alan Everitt, *Change in the Provinces: the seventeenth century*, Leicester U.P., 1969, pp. 37–8.

36 Stone, *Causes of the English Revolution*, ch. 3; Wallace MacCaffrey, 'England: the Crown and the aristocracy, 1540–1600', *Past and Present* xxx (1965) 54–5, 61–3; see also his *The Shaping of the Elizabethan Regime*, Princeton U.P., 1968.

37 Cliffe, pp. 359–61.

38 See Jerrilyn Green Marston, 'Gentry honor and royalism in early Stuart England', *Journal of British Studies*, xiii (1973), 21–43.

39 Sir Harry Verney, *The Verneys of Claydon*, Maxwell, 1968, pp. 11, 32–3.

40 Zagorin, pp. 342–4; Lloyd, p. 128.

41 B. G. Blackwood, 'the marriages of the Lancashire gentry on the eve of the Civil War', *Geneaologists' Magazine* xvi (1970), 325.

42 Alan Everitt, *The Community of Kent and the Great Rebellion 1640–1660*, Leicester U.P., 1966, pp. 185, 325.

43 Alan Everitt, *Suffolk and the Great Rebellion*, Suffolk Record Soc., iii, 1960; 'Social mobility in early modern England', *Past and Present* xxxiii (1966).

44   H. J. Habakkuk, 'Landowners and the Civil War', *Econ. Hist. Rev.*, 2nd ser. xviii (1965–66), 130–51.

45   Everitt, *Community of Kent*, p. 324.

46   Mary Coate, *Cornwall in the Great Civil War and Interregnum 1642–1660*, Oxford U.P., 1933, p. 233; W. G. Hoskins, in *Devonshire Studies*, ed. Hoskins and H. P. R. Finberg, Cape, 1952, pp. 335–6, 345.

47   Michael Nash, 'Early seventeenth-century schemes to make the Wey navigable 1618–51', *Surrey Archaeological Collections*, lxvi (1969), 37–40.

48   See Christopher Clay, 'Marriage, inheritance, and the rise of large estates in England, 1660–1815', *Econ. Hist. Rev.*, 2nd ser. xxi (1968), 510–15.

49   See Christopher Clay, 'The price of freehold land in the later seventeenth and eighteenth centuries', *Econ. Hist. Rev.*, 2nd ser., xxvii (1974), 173–89; and B. A. Holderness, 'The English land market in the eighteenth century; the case of Lincolnshire', *ibid.*, pp. 559, 574.

50   Christopher Clay, 'Two Families and their Estates: the Grimstons and the Cowpers from *c.* 1650 to *c.* 1815, unpublished Ph.D. thesis, Cambridge, 1966.

51   J. H. Plumb, 'The growth of the electorate in England from 1600 to 1715', *Past and Present* xlv (1969), 112–15; see also W. A. Speck, *Tory and Whig: the struggle in the constituencies, 1701–1715*, Macmillan, 1970.

52   G. S. Holmes and W. A. Speck, *The Divided Society: parties and politics in England 1694–1716*, E. Arnold, 1967, p. 19.

53   Geoffrey Holmes, *British Politics in the Age of Anne*, Macmillan, 1967, pp. 126–7.

54   A. N. Newman, ed., *The Parliamentary Diary of Sir Edward Knatchbull 1722–1730*, Camden Soc., 3rd ser. xciv (1963), pp. vii–ix.

55   H. J. Habakkuk in *The European Nobility in the Eighteenth Century*, ed. A. Goodwin, A. and C. Black, 1953, p. 4.

56   J. Steven Watson, *The Reign of George III 1760–1815*, Oxford U.P., 1960, p. 51n.

57   K. Feiling, *The Second Tory Party 1714–1832*, Macmillan, 1938, pp. 7, 100.

58   Godber, p. 307.

59   Derek Fraser, 'The agitation for parliamentary reform', in *Popular Movements c. 1830–1850*, ed. J. T. Ward, Macmillan, 1970, pp. 50–1.

60   W. O. Aydelotte, 'The business interests of the gentry in the Parliament of 1841–47', in G. Kitson Clark, *The Making of Victorian England*, Methuen, 1962, pp. 293, 296–7.

61   Clark, *The Making of Victorian England*, pp. 209, 247–9.

Chapter 4   *The estates of the gentry*

1   Charles Wilson, *England's Apprenticeship 1603–1763*, Longmans, 1965, pp. 21–2.

2   W. G. Hoskins in Hoskins and Finberg, ed., *Devonshire Studies*, p. 337.

3   D. C. Coleman, *Sir John Banks, Baronet and Businessman*, Oxford U.P., 1963, pp. 47–50.

4   C. W. Chalklin, *Seventeenth-Century Kent*, Longmans, 1965, p. 197.

5   Peter Bowden in Joan Thirsk, ed., *Agrarian History*, iv, 676–9.

6   K. J. Allison, 'Flock management in the sixteenth and seventeenth centuries', *Econ. Hist. Rev.*, 2nd ser. xi (1958–59), 100, 107–9, 111.

7   Alan Everitt in Thirsk, ed., *Agrarian History* iv, 545–6.

8   M. E. Finch, *The Wealth of Five Northamptonshire Families, 1540–1640*, Northants Rec. Soc., 1956; Rosamund Meredith, 'The Eyres of Hassop 1470–1640', *Derbys. Arch. Jnl*, lxxxv (1965), pp. 82–3.

9   *Annals of Agriculture* ii (1783), 135; Audrey M. Taylor, *Gilletts: bankers at Banbury and Oxford*, Oxford U.P., 1964, p. 222; W. Cobbett, *Rural Rides*, Dent, (Everyman's Library), 1912, i, 13–14.

10   G. Eland, ed., *Purefoy Letters, 1735–1753*, Sidgwick and Jackson, 1931, ii, 244.

11   P. Roebuck, 'Absentee landownership in the late seventeenth and early eighteenth centuries: a neglected factor in English agrarian history', *Agric. Hist. Rev.* xxi, 1 (1973), 12–17.

12   Joan Thirsk and J. P. Cooper, eds, *Seventeenth-Century Economic Documents*, Oxford U.P., 1972, p. 82.

13   Eland, i, 30–1.

14   Lincs RO: Hill 22/1/16/49.

15   J. T. Ward, *East Yorkshire Landed Estates in the Nineteenth Century*, East Yorks. Local Hist. Soc., 1967, pp. 10–11.

16   *BPP*, 1881, xvi, 294.

17   See G. E. Mingay, *Enclosure and the Small Farmer in the Age of the Industrial Revolution*, Macmillan (Studies in Economic History), 1968.

18   Glamorgan RO: D/DF 11, ff. 58, 83.

19   For estate management in the eighteenth century see G. E. Mingay, 'The eighteenth-century land steward' in E. L. Jones and G. E. Mingay, eds., *Land, Labour and Population in the Industrial Revolution*, E. Arnold, 1967.

20   Notts RO: DD Sy 56/26.

21   Glamorgan RO: D/DE 426, 428.

22   Bamford, ed., *A Royalist's Notebook*, pp. 231, 237–8.

23   R. W. Ketton-Cremer, *Country Neighbourhood*, Faber, 1951, pp. 47, 205.

24   D. Gardiner, ed., *The Oxinden Letters 1607–1642*, 1933, p. 171.

25   Bamford, p. 14; Joyce Bankes and Eric Kerridge, eds, *The Early Records of the Bankes Family at Winstanley*, Manchester U.P., 1973, p. 8.

26   F.S.A., *Family Records of the Allens of Cresselly*, 1905.

27   C. Radcliffe Cooke, 'John Noble's household and farm accounts', *Trans. Woolhope Naturalists' Field Club*, xxxvi (1959), 200.

28   Eland, i, 158–60, 200.

29   Bamford, p. 241.

30   Chalklin, p. 196.

31   J. Coker, *A Survey of Dorsetshire*, 1732, p. 31.

32   A. L. Rowse, *Tudor Cornwall*, Macmillan, 1957, pp. 216–18.

33   Esther Moir, *The Discovery of Britain: the English tourists 1540–1840*, Routledge, 1964, p. 22.

34   Quoted by D. W. Howell, 'The Landed Gentry of Pembrokeshire in the Eighteenth Century', unpubl. M.A. thesis, Univ. Wales, 1965, p. 116.

35   See Joan Thirsk in *Agrarian History*, iv, 240–53.

36   E. Kerridge, *Agrarian Problems in the Sixteenth Century and After*, Allen & Unwin, 1969, p. 100.

37   G. Dyfnallt Owen, *Elizabethan Wales*, Univ. of Wales P., 1964, pp. 88–9;
      T. Jones Pierce in Thirsk ed., *Agrarian History* iv, 377–81.

38   Frank W. Jessup, *Sir Roger Twysden 1597–1672*, Cresset Press, 1965,
      pp. 123, 129–30.

39   Everitt, *Change in the Provinces*, p. 24.

40   Bamford, pp. 84, 95.

41   W. H. Chaloner, 'The agricultural activities of John Wilkinson, Iron-
      master', *Agric. Hist. Rev.* v, 1, 48–51.

42   Kenneth Hudson, *Patriotism with Profit*, London, Evelyn, 1972, p. 17.

43   Notts RO: DD SR 211/147; Eaton Hall: Grosvenor MSS.

44   Coker, p. 46.

45   J. P. Ferris, 'The gentry of Dorset on the eve of the Civil War', *Genealo-
      gists' Mag.*, xv (1965–68), 111.

46   Hoskins in Hoskins and Finberg, eds, *Devonshire Studies*, p. 411.

47   A. M. Mimardière, 'The Finances of a Warwickshire gentry family 1693–
      1726', *Univ. Birmingham Hist. Jnl*, ix, 2 (1964), 133.

48   Sheffield Central Library: Wentworth Woodhouse MSS. A 230, 235,
      R 174–8.

49   Sussex Arch. Soc., Lewes: Fuller Letter Book.

50   L. A. Clarkson, *The Pre-Industrial Economy in England 1500–1750*, Batsford
      1971, p. 216; Bankes and Kerridge, p. 3; J. T. Ward and R. G. Wilson,
      eds., *Land and Industry: the English landed estate and the Industrial Revolution*,
      David & Charles, 1971, p. 90.

51   C. Roy Hudleston, 'An eighteenth-century squire's possessions', *Trans.
      Cumb. and Westm. Antiq. Arch. Soc.*, n.s. lvii, pp. 130, 133–4; E. Hughes,
      North Country Life in the Eighteenth Century, Oxford U.P., 1965, ii, 162.

52   C. M. L. Bouch and G. P. Jones, *A Short Economic and Social History of the
      Lake Counties 1500–1830*, Manchester U.P., 1961, pp. 131, 217, 258–9,
      271–2; P. Ford, 'Tobacco and coal: a note on the economic history of
      Whitehaven', *Economica* ix (1929), 193–6; A. Young, *Northern Tour*
      (1770), iii, 160–1.

53   Hughes, pp. 163, 170, 179–82, 206, 223–37.

54   A. Young, *Annals of Agriculture*, xvi (1791), 547–65.

55   A. H. Dodd, *Studies in Stuart Wales*, Univ. of Wales P., 1952, pp. 27, 29.

56   H. A. Lloyd, *The Gentry of South-West Wales 1540–1640*, Univ. of Wales
      P., 1968, pp. 81–3.

57   Howell, pp. 146–7, 156, 175–7.

58   Glamorgan RO: D/DL 1 Letter Book 1845–46.

59   Notts RO: Foljambe corres. XI B 83–4.

60   William Albert, *The Turnpike Road System in England 1663–1840*, Cam-
      bridge, U.P., 1972, pp. 102–5.

61   Clarkson, p. 155.

62   J. R. Ward, quoted by F. Crouzet, ed., *Capital Formation in the Industrial
      Revolution*, Methuen, 1972, p. 56.

63   Ward, *East Yorkshire Landed Estates*, p. 7.

64   A. Raistrick and E. Allen, 'The South Yorkshire ironmasters (1690–
      1750)', *Econ. Hist. Rev.* 1st ser. ix (1938–39), 170, 173, 177; A. Young,
      Northern Tour (1770), II, 288–90; III, 51, 53; Harold Perkin, *The Age of
      the Railway*, David & Charles 1970, pp. 126, 221.

65   Lloyd, pp. 86–8.

66 Hoskins in Hoskins and Finberg, eds, *Devonshire Studies*, p. 142.
67 M. Blundell, ed., *Cavalier: Letters of William Blundell to his friends 1620–1698*, Longmans, 1933, p. 119.
68 Dodds, pp. 34–5.
69 Theodore K. Rabb, *Enterprise and Empire: merchant and gentry investment in the expansion of England 1575–1630*, Harvard U.P., 1967, pp. 26–7, 31–3, 42, 51, 81, 87–8, 100.
70 See Richard Grassby, 'English merchant capitalism in the late seventeenth century', *Past and Present*, xlvi (Feb., 1970), pp. 93, 96, 98.

Chapter 5   *The gentry in rural society*

1   Hughes, *North Country Life* I, 34.
2   Bamford, *A Royalist's Notebook*, p. 130; M. Blundell, ed., *Nicholas Blundell's Diary and Letter Book, 1702–28*, Liverpool U.P., 1952, pp. 217–18; J. J. Bagley, ed., *The Great Diurnal of Nicholas Blundell*, Lancs. and Cheshire Rec. Soc., 1968, i, 2–3.
3   Hereford RO: E 31/59.
4   B. G. Blackwood, 'The marriages of the Lancashire gentry on the eve of the Civil War', *Genealogists' Mag.*, xvi (1970), 327–8.
5   J. P. Cooper, ed., *Wentworth Papers 1597–1628*, Camden Society, 4th ser. xii, 1973, p. 20.
6   T. H. Hollingsworth, *The Demography of the British Peerage*, Supplement to *Population Studies* xviii (1965); Christopher Clay, 'Marriage, inheritance, and the rise of large estates in England, 1660–1815', *Econ. Hist. Rev.*, 2nd ser. xxi (1968). But see the conflicting view of the effects of early marriage among the upper ranks in society in the seventeenth century expressed by Lawrence Stone, 'Social mobility in England, 1500–1700', *Past and Present*, xxxiii (1966), 38, 42.
7   See the illuminating discussion by Joan Thirsk, 'Younger sons in the seventeenth century', *History* liv (1969), 358–77.
8   Rowse, *Tudor Cornwall*, pp. 106–7.
9   Esther Moir, 'Benedict Webb, clothier', *Econ. Hist. Rev.*, 2nd ser. x 1957–58), 258.
10 Dyfnallt Owen, pp. 34–5.
11 D. Parsons, ed., *The Diary of Sir Henry Slingsby*, 1836, pp. 51, 63–4.
12 BM Add. MSS. 32,906 ff. 269–70, 35,692 f. 410.
13 R. J. Olney, *Lincolnshire Politics 1832–1885*, Oxford U.P., 1973, p. 35.
14 Joyce Godber, *History of Bedfordshire 1066–1888*, Beds C.C., 1969, p. 400.
15 J. Brierley Watson, 'The Lancashire gentry and public service 1529–1558', *Trans. Lancs. and Cheshire Antiq. Soc.*, lxxiii–lxxiv (1963–64), 47–8.
16 Ketton-Cremer, *Country Neighbourhood*, pp. 96, 112–13.
17 E. Suffolk RO: North MSS. 331.
18 Thirsk, ed., *Agrarian History*, iv, 461.
19 *Oxinden Letters*, pp. 220–1.
20 Bagley, pp. 5, 8.
21 Lincs RO: Hill MSS. 22/2/2/14, 22/1/5.
22 Berks RO: D/Ex 32.
23 Eland, i, 12, 14–15.

24 Notts RO: DD SR 211/24/18.
25 E. Sussex RO: Shiffner MSS. 1549–59.
26 Hughes, i, 72.
27 Bodleian: MS. Top. Kent a. 1.
28 Esther Moir, *The Justice of the Peace*, Penguin, 1969, chs 1, 2; Lloyd, pp. 135–6.
29 J. H. Gleason, *The Justices of the Peace in England 1558–1640*, Oxford U.P., 1969, p. 102; C. M. L. Bouch and G. P. Jones, *The Lake Counties 1500–1830*, Manchester U.P., 1961, pp. 164–5.
30 Rowse, *Tudor Cornwall*, p. 84.
31 A. Hassell Smith, 'Justices at work in Elizabethan Norfolk', *Norfolk Archaeology* xxxiv, 2 (1967), pp. 98, 105, 108–9.
32 W. B. Willcox, *Gloucestershire: a study in local government*, Yale U.P., 1940, pp. 61, 81, 108, 142, 161.
33 Lloyd, pp. 138–9, 142.
34 Willcox, p. 40.
35 E. W. Bovill, *English Country Life 1780–1830*, 2nd edn, Oxford U.P., 1962, p. 76.
36 Thomas Garden Barnes, *Somerset 1625–40: A county's government during the personal rule of Charles I*, Harvard U.P., 1961, pp. 45, 69.
37 Gleason, pp. 48–9; Lloyd, p. 143; Howell, pp. 271–2.
38 Lawrence Stone and Jeanne C. Fawtier Stone, 'Country houses and their owners in Hertfordshire 1540–1879', in Aydelotte, Bogue, and Fogel, eds., *Dimensions of Quantitative Research in History*, p. 84.
39 Moir, pp. 84–5.
40 Beds RO: DD PM 2380.
41 Moir, pp. 85, 107–8; W. Riding RO: DD SY 101/26.
42 Eric J. Evans, 'Some reasons for the growth of English rural anti-clericalism, *c.* 1750—*c.* 1830', *Past and Present*, lxvi (1975), 84–109.
43 See her article in H. P. R. Finberg, ed., *Gloucestershire Studies*, Leicester U.P., 1957, pp. 195–224.
44 Kent RO: U 951 02, 4.
45 L. Radzinowicz, *A History of English Criminal Law and its Administration from 1750*, Stevens and Sons, 4 vols, 1948, i, 92–7.
46 Joyce Marlow, *The Tolpuddle Martyres*, Deutsch, 1972, pp. 55–8.
47 J. L. Hammond and Barbara Hammond, *The Village Labourer 1760–1832*, Guild Books edn., 1948, i, 191.
48 F. M. L. Thompson, *English Landed Society in the Nineteenth Century*, Routledge, 1963, pp. 138–9, 144, 150.
49 Chester Kirby, 'The attack on the English game laws in the forties', *J. Mod. Hist*, iv (1932), 22–5, 29.
50 Moir, *Justice of the Peace*, pp. 127, 141.
51 *Ibid.*, pp. 154–5.
52 *Ibid.*, pp. 161, 183.
53 A. Tindal Hart, *The Man in the Pew*, London, J. Baker, 1966, pp. 54–5.
54 Camden Soc. O.S. 41 (1848).
55 Tindal Hart, *op. cit.*, pp. 189, 192–6; R. C. Richardson, *Puritanism in North-west England*, Manchester U.P., 1972, pp. 123, 158.
56 Dorothy M. Meads, ed., *The Diary of Lady Margaret Hoby 1599–1605*, Routledge, 1930.

57   Alan Everitt, 'Nonconformity in country parishes', in Joan Thirsk, ed., *Land, Church and People: essays presented to Professor H. P. R. Finberg*, Brit. Agric. Hist. Soc., 1970, pp. 178–99.

58   R. G. Wilson 'The Denisons and the Milneses: eighteenth-century merchant landowners', in J. T. Ward and R. G. Wilson, eds., *Land and Industry: the English landed estate and the Industrial Revolution*, David & Charles, 1971, p. 157.

59   Hughes, *North Country Life*, i, 338.

60   J. T. Ward, 'Portrait of a Yorkshire squire: John Fullerton of Thrybergh, 1778–1847', *Yorks. Arch. Jnl*, xl (1960–62), p. 222.

61   Nottingham Univ. Archives: Manvers Ma B 30.

62   M. A. Havinden, *Estate Villages*, Lund Humphries, 1966, p. 87.

63   Hughes, ii, 179–84.

64   *Annals of Agriculture*, xxv (1800), 424.

65   E. Sussex RO: Shiffner MSS. 1370.

66   W. Suffolk RO: E 18/11/455–6.

67   David Owen, *English Philanthropy 1660–1960*, Harvard U.P., 1964, pp. 81–2, 192–3.

68   W. K. Jordan, *The Charities of Rural England 1480–1660*, Allen & Unwin, 1961, pp. 82, 203, 420.

69   Parsons, p. 71.

70   Eland, i, 136–7, 147; ii, 317.

71   Notts RO: DD SY 167/xxxix, xli.

72   F. G. Emmison, *Tudor Food and Pastimes*, Benn, 1964, pp. 27, 34, 38–40, 64, 75.

73   Ferris, p. 116.

74   Anon, *Letter to a Freeholder*, 1732, pp. 33–4.

75   FSA, *Family Records of the Allens of Cresselly*, 1905, p. 29.

76   Surtees Soc. lxxvii (1886), 115–17.

77   Alan Macfarlane, *The Family Life of Ralph Josselin: a seventeenth-century clergyman*, Cambridge U.P., 1970, pp. 150–2.

78   Ward, p. 222.

79   *Blundell's Diary*, p. 138.

80   Eland, ii, 332, 377–8.

81   Notts RO: DD SY 160/xxxviii, 169/xxx.

82   Anthony Hern, *The Seaside Holiday: the history of the English seaside resort*, Cresset Press, 1967, pp. 2–4.

83   Notts RO: DD SY 166/ii, iv, 169/ix.

84   *Maidstone Journal*, 18 Apr. 1848 (I owe this reference to my colleague, Mr J. Whyman).

85   Thirsk and Cooper, eds., *Seventeenth-Century Economic Documents*, pp. 81–2.

86   Tindal Hart, p. 44.

87   Notts RO: DD SR 211/250, 212/81.

88   BM Add. MSS. 35,127 f. 63.

89   Robert W. Malcolmson, *Popular Recreations in English Society*, Cambridge U.P., 1973, pp. 154–5, 169.

90   Stone and Stone, pp. 76, 120–2.

91   A. Hamilton Thompson in G. Barraclough, ed., *Social Life in Early England*, Routledge, 1960, pp. 162–77; Ralph Dutton, *The English Country House*, Batsford, 3rd edn, 1950, pp. 30, 37, 45, 64.

92 Edward Hyams, *Capability Brown and Humphry Repton*, Dent, 1971.
93 Dutton, pp. 54, 71.
94 Macaulay, *History of England*, ch. III.
95 Daniel Defoe, *The Compleat English Gentleman*, 1890 edn, pp. 13, 138–9, 257.
96 A. Young, *A Tour in Ireland*, Dublin, 1780, ii, 113.
97 Eland, ii, 283.
98 G. E. Fussell and K. R. Fussell, *The English Countrywoman A.D. 1500–1900* (Melrose, 1953), repr. New York, Blom, 1971, pp. 56, 83–7; A. S. Turberville, ed., *Johnson's England*, Oxford U.P., 1933, ii, 224–5.
99 Rowse, *Tudor Cornwall*, pp. 421–9; *The Elizabethan Renaissance: II the Cultural Achievement*, Macmillan, 1972, p. 110.
100 Lloyd, pp. 198–9, 204; Dyfnallt Owen, pp. 36–9; David Jenkins, *The Agricultural Community in South-West Wales at the turn of the Twentieth Century*, Univ. of Wales Press, 1971, p. 33.
101 Chalklin, *Seventeenth-Century Kent*, pp. 207–8; D. M. Loades, 'The papers of Geo. Wyatt, Esquire', Camden Soc. 4th ser. v (1968); Felix Hull, 'John Marsham, a forgotten antiquary', *Archaeologia Cantiana*, lxxxiii (1968), 49–52; Dennis Baker, 'A Kentish pioneer in natural history: Robert Plot of Borden, 1640–96', *Trans. Kent Field Club*, iii, 4 (1971), 213: Jessup, *Sir Roger Twysden*, pp, 15, 97, 181–5, 206.
102 Mary A. Welch, 'Francis Willoughby, F.R.S. (1635–1672)', *Jnl Soc. Bibliography Nat. Hist.* vi (1972), 71–85; Godber, pp. 244, 306; Rowse, *Elizabethan Renaissance*, pp. 109, 253.
103 See Turberville, *Johnson's England*, pp. 26, 27; J. Money, 'Taverns, coffee houses and clubs: local politics and popular articulacy in the Birmingham area in the age of the American Revolution', *Hist. Jnl* xiv (1971), pp. 15–47.
104 Bamford, p. 249.
105 Gleason, pp. 85–9; Lloyd, pp. 194–5; Dodd, p. 5.
106 Dyfnallt Owen, p. 209.
107 Joan Simon, *Education and Society in Tudor England*, Cambridge U.P., 1966, pp. 358, 361; Kenneth Charlton, *Education in Renaissance England*, Routledge, 1965, pp. 131, 136–42, 154–6, 166, 168; Hugh Kearney, *Scholars and Gentlemen: universities and society in pre-industrial Britain 1500–1700*, Faber, 1970, pp. 21–4, 126, 160–1.
108 Archibald Campbell, *Instructions to a Son*, 1743 edn, p. 74.
109 Wilfred R. Prest, *The Inns of Court under Elizabeth I and the Early Stuarts*, Longman, 1972, pp. 21–8, 31, 36–42.
110 Wilfred Prest, 'Legal education of the gentry at the Inns of Court 1560–1640', *Past and Present* xxxviii (1967), 35, 37, 39; Charlton, pp. 171–2, 177–84, 186–7, 192–5; Barnes, p. 32.
111 Prest, *Inns of Court*, pp. 44–6, 151–3.
112 Charlton, pp. 289–95.
113 Quoted by Charlton, p. 210.
114 Blundell, ed., *Cavalier*, p. 177; Parsons, p. 54.
115 Simon, pp. 354, 363, 368.
116 *Ibid.*, pp. 395, 402.
117 Lawrence Stone, 'Literacy and education in England 1640–1900', *Past and Present* xlii (1969), 71–3.
118 Jenkins, p. 35.

Chapter 6 *The closing phase*

1   R. J. Olney, *Lincolnshire Politics 1832–1885*, Oxford U.P., 1973, pp. 231–2.
2   T. J. Raybould, *The Economic Emergence of the Black Country*, David & Charles, 1973, pp. 70–5.
3   J. T. Ward and R. G. Wilson, eds, *Land and Industry: the landed estate and the Industrial Revolution*, David & Charles, 1971, pp. 90–1, 100–1.
4   W. O. Aydelotte, 'The business interests of the gentry in the Parliament of 1841–47', in G. Kitson Clark, ed., *The Making of Victorian England*, Methuen, 1962, pp. 293, 296–7.
5   F. M. L. Thompson, *English Landed Society in the Nineteenth Century*, Routledge, 1963, pp. 130, 267.
6   *Ibid.*, p. 266.
7   Ward and Wilson, p. 91.
8   Thompson, pp. 246–52.
9   J. T. Coppock in H. C. Darby, ed., *A New Historical Geography of England*, Cambridge U.P., 1973, pp. 625–7.
10 H. Rider Haggard, *The Days of my Life* (1926), ii, 136–7, 140, 151–2.
11 Thompson, pp. 319–20.
12 *Ibid.*, pp. 293–4.
13 *Ibid.*, pp. 302, 307.
14 *Ibid.*, pp. 322–3.
15 *Ibid.*, pp. 332, 335–7.
16 *Ibid.*, p. 334.
17 *Ibid.*, p. 277.
18 Eric Richards, *The Leviathan of Wealth*, Routledge, 1973, p. 284.
19 See J. A. Perkins, 'Tenure, tenant right and agricultural progress in Lindsey, 1780–1850', *Agric. Hist. Rev.* XXIII, 1 (1975), 3–11.
20 Olney, pp. 40–8.
21 Haggard, I p. 19.
22 Kenneth Hudson, *Patriotism with Profit*, London, Evelyn, 1972, pp. 15, 35, 46–7, 98.
23 E. W. Bovill, *English Country Life 1780–1830*, Oxford U.P., p. 115.
24 Thompson, pp. 132–3.
25 See Bovill, ch. ix.
26 Thompson, p. 122.
27 Bovill, pp. 124–6.
28 Christopher Sykes, *Four Studies in Loyalty*, Collins, 1946, pp. 12–14; E. Wingfield-Stratford, *The Squire and his Relations*, Cassell, 1956, p. 253.
29 E. D. Cuming, ed., *Squire Osbaldeston: his autobiography*, Lane, 1926, pp. vii–viii, 3, 312.
30 *Ibid.*, pp. 3, 10, 278, 281, 301, 312.
31 Wingfield-Stratford, pp. 344–9.
32 Bovill, p. 65.
33 *Ibid.*, pp. 177–8.
34 *Ibid.*, p. 187.
35 *Ibid.*, pp. 184–5.
36 Wingfield-Stratford, p. 189; Bovill, p. 219.
37 Bovill, pp. 201–7.
38 See Anthony Trollope, *Hunting Sketches* (1865).

39 Notts RO: Foljambe correspondence XI B; R. S. Surtees, *Hillingdon Hall* (1845), ch. 14.
40 Bovill, pp. 225–9.
41 *Ibid.*, pp. 227, 230.
42 F. E. Green, *The Tyranny of the Countryside*, 1913, pp. 178–80.
43 See Alan Rogers, ed., *Stability and Change: some aspects of North and South Rauceby in the nineteenth century*, Nottingham U.P., 1970, pp. 20, 76–8.
44 J. S. Hurt, 'Landowners, farmers, and clergy and the financing of rural education before 1870', *J. Ed. Admin. Hist.* i, 1 (1968), 6–12.
45 W. J. Reader, *Life in Victorian England*, Batsford, 1964, pp. 26–8, 44.
46 Thompson, p. 342.
47 J. D. Chambers and G. E. Mingay, *The Agricultural Revolution 1750–1880*, Batsford, 1966, p. 208.
48 Thompson, pp. 271–2.
49 *Ibid.*, pp. 22, 272–4, 280.
50 *Ibid.*, p. 345.

Chapter 7 *Conclusion*

1 Glos RO: D 340a C22 (1715).
2 F. E. Green, *The Tyranny of the Countryside*, 1913, p. 141; B. Seebohm Rowntree and May Kendall, *How the Labourer Lives*, 1913, pp. 319–21.
3 Asa Briggs, *The Age of Improvement*, Longmans, p. 64; Harold Perkin, *The Age of the Railway*, David & Charles, 1970, p. 196.
4 Quoted by Moir, *The Justice of the Peace*, p. 103.
5 W. Cobbett, *Rural Rides*, Dent, (Everyman's Library), 1912, i, 249, 266–7; ii, 71.
6 Harold Perkin, *The Origins of Modern English Society 1780–1880*, Routledge, 1969, pp. 184–5. 187–8.
7 J. P. Mayer, *Alexis de Tocqueville: Journeys to England and Ireland*, Faber, 1958, pp. 67, 70–1.
8 Quoted by W. L. Guttsman, *The English Ruling Class*, Weidenfeld & Nicolson, 1969.
9 A. Fairfax-Lucy, *Charlecote and the Lucys*, Oxford U.P., 1958, p. 233n.
10 For this curiously unhistorical view see Gideon Sjoberg, 'The rural-urban dimension in pre-industrial, transitional and industrial societies', in R. E. L. Faris, ed., *Handbook of Modern Sociology*, Rand McNally, 1964, pp. 138–9.
11 Chester Kirby, *The English Country Gentleman* (n.d.), p. 211.
12 Bamford, *A Royalist's Notebook*, p. 251.

Index